CNUT
ENGLAND'S
VIKING KING

M. K. Lawson teaches History at St Paul's School in Barnes, London and is an acknowledged authority on Anglo-Saxon England. His other books include the widely acclaimed *The Battle of Hastings 1066,* also published by Tempus.

Acclaim for *The Battle of Hastings 1066*

One of the *BBC History Magazine* Books of the Year 2003

'Deeply considered and provocative'
Professor John Hudson, BBC History Magazine

'Blows away many fundamental assumptions about the battle of Hastings... an exciting and indispensable read'
Professor David Bates, Director of the Institute of Historical Research

'M.K. Lawson knows more about the Battle of Hastings than most who have lived since the twelfth century; this is the book that he owed to history and he has paid his debt with aplomb... the result of Lawson's painstaking investigation is an involved portrayal of a long, desperately contested engagement'
The Times Literary Supplement

'Extensively illustrated, thoroughly documented, and clearly written, this must remain the definitive book on this famous battle'
The Journal of Military History

CNUT
ENGLAND'S
VIKING KING

M.K. LAWSON

TEMPUS

Cover picture: *Cnut*, British Library (BL MS Stowe 944 f6r)

This edition first published 2004

Tempus Publishing Limited
The Mill, Brimscombe Port,
Stroud, Gloucestershire, GL5 2QG
www.tempus-publishing.com

British Library Cataloguing in Publication Data.
A catalogue record for this book is available from the British Library.

ISBN 0 7524 2964 7

Typesetting and origination by Tempus Publishing Limited
Printed in Great Britain

CONTENTS

LIST OF
GENEALOGICAL TABLES

PREFACE TO
THE SECOND EDITION

My book on King Cnut, which first appeared in 1993 as *Cnut: the Danes in England in the Early Eleventh Century*, is here republished under a different title. I have little reason to believe that the intervening eleven years have left it in need of extensive revision, and hence have made few alterations to the main text. However, I have reworked some of the footnotes and revised the bibliography, thus taking account of a certain amount of significant secondary work and of new editions of a number of the primary sources.

Chessington, Surrey.
April 2004

REFERENCES
AND ABBREVIATIONS

For events between 1017 and 1035 I have not provided references either to the *Anglo-Saxon Chronicle* or to John of Worcester's chronicle. Nor, on spelling, have I sought consistency: personal names are given in an English form, modern if still in use (Alfred, Edward), eleventh-century if not (Æthelred, Cnut), with a distinction between Scandinavian Haralds and English Harolds, and a degree of anglicisation of the names of the Scandinavian skaldic poets (Ottar the Black rather than Óttarr svarti and Hallvard Hareksblesi rather than Hallvarðr Háreksblesi). Scandinavian place names have their native spelling, except where it would have seemed pedantic not to use their familiar English form (Denmark, Norway, Sweden, Jutland). The poems of the Scandinavian skalds are listed in detail in the Primary Sources section of the Select Bibliography under author (or title if anonymous), and have only rarely been included in the notes. The following abbreviations appear in the notes and in the Select Bibliography.

ASC	*Anglo-Saxon Chronicle*, ed. Plummer.
ASE	*Anglo-Saxon England*.
ASP	*Anglo-Saxon Prose*, ed. Swanton.
BAR	*British Archaeological Reports*.
BL	British Library.
BNJ	*British Numismatic Journal*.
Chron. Ab.	*Chronicon Monasterii de Abingdon*, ed. Stevenson.
Chron. Eve.	*Chronicon Abbatiæ de Evesham*, ed. Macray.
Chron. Rams.	*Chronicon Abbatiæ Rameseiensis*, ed. Macray.
Commentationes	*Commentationes de nummis saeculorum IX-XI in Suecia repertis*.
DB	Domesday Book.
EHD	*English Historical Documents c.500–1042*, ed. Whitelock.

EHR	*English Historical Review.*
Encomium	*Encomium Emmae Reginae*, ed. Campbell.
END	*English and Norse Documents*, ed. Ashdown.
FNC	Freeman, *The History of the Norman Conquest.*
Gesetze	*Die Gesetze der Angelsachsen*, ed. Liebermann.
GP	William of Malmesbury, *De Gestis Pontificum*, ed. Hamilton.
GR	William of Malmesbury, *Gesta Regum Anglorum*, ed. Mynors, Thomson and Winterbottom.
Hemming	Hemming, *Chartularium Ecclesiae Wigorniensis*, ed. Hearne.
Henry, *Historia*	Henry of Huntingdon, *Historia Anglorum*, ed. Greenway.
Jónsson	*Den norsk-islandske Skjaldedigtning*, ed. Jónsson.
JW	John of Worcester, *Chronicle*, ed. Darlington and McGurk.
Kennedy	'Cnut's law code of 1018', ed. Kennedy.
KHL	*Kulturhistorisk Leksikon for nordisk middelalder.*
Kock	*Den norsk-isländska Skaldediktningen*, ed. E.A. Kock.
Lib. El.	*Liber Eliensis*, ed. Blake.
Robertson, *Charters*	*Anglo-Saxon Charters*, ed. Robertson.
RS	Rolls Series.
S (followed by a number)	The designation of an Anglo-Saxon charter as listed in *Anglo-Saxon Charters: an annotated list and bibliography*, ed. Sawyer.
SBVS	*Saga-Book of the Viking Society for Northern Research.*
SEHD	*Select English Historical Documents*, ed. Harmer.
Thietmar, *Chronicon*	Thietmar of Merseburg, *Chronicon*, ed. Holtzmann.
TRHS	*Transactions of the Royal Historical Society.*
VCH	*Victoria County History.*
Wills	*Anglo-Saxon Wills*, ed. Whitelock.
WJ	William of Jumièges, *Gesta Normannorum Ducum*, ed. van Houts.
WM *Glaston*	William of Malmesbury, *De Antiquitate Glastonie Ecclesie*, ed. Scott.
Writs	*Anglo-Saxon Writs*, ed. Harmer.

INTRODUCTION

The conquests of England by King Swegen Forkbeard of Denmark in 1013 and his son Cnut in 1016 were events natural to a long-established order; the Anglo-Saxons had always lived to a greater or lesser extent within a Scandinavian world. They migrated to Britain in the fifth and sixth centuries not only from what is now northern Germany, but also from Jutland in modern Denmark.[1] In a famous passage, the eighth-century Northumbrian historian Bede records a tradition that the people of Kent and the Isle of Wight were descended from the Jutes, and says that some of the West Saxons adjacent to Wight were called Jutes in his own day. Modern analysis of the pottery evidence suggests the possibility of influence from Norway and Sweden too.[2] This would not be surprising. In 1939 a magnificent seventh-century ship burial was discovered at Sutton Hoo in Suffolk. It included a helmet and shield which have their closest known parallels in burials in eastern Sweden, and which probably either originated there or were made in England by Swedish craftsmen.[3] If the grave was that of a king, as is often supposed, these men may have worked for an East Anglian dynasty which had Swedish origins. Nor were the partly Scandinavian roots of the English people, together with their more general Germanic background, forgotten in later years. The perhaps eighth-century epic *Beowulf*, the longest and most celebrated of all surviving Anglo-Saxon poems, presents us with a story set in the Denmark and southern Scandinavia of two to three hundred years earlier, and without a single reference to Britain.[4]

[1] Myres, *The English Settlements*, pp.46–47, 115–16. The Jutes may also have occupied East Holstein.
[2] Myres, *A Corpus of Anglo-Saxon Pottery*, i. 114–16.
[3] Evans, *The Sutton Hoo Ship Burial*, pp.113–17.
[4] The date of *Beowulf* is uncertain; some scholars now assign it to the tenth century. Kiernan, *Beowulf and the Beowulf Manuscript*, argues that it is from Cnut's reign, but this view has not won much support.

Similarly, the possibly slightly older *Widsith* is a catalogue of chiefly Germanic tribes and heroes, which shows particular interest in the Danish kings Hrothgar and Hrothwulf, and in Offa the Angle, who was claimed as an ancestor by the great eighth-century English king Offa of Mercia.[5] Not only was the past remembered: in some way it still mattered.

Continued interest in Scandinavia may well have been stimulated by a degree of continued contact, for it seems unlikely that the period between the migrations and the beginning of the Viking Age (around 800) saw no intercourse whatever. There was maybe some trade, although few hints of it have yet come to light apart from fragments of vessels of blue glass made in Kent and found in Norway; the early eighth-century English missionary Willibrord was at least interested enough in the Danes to attempt their conversion. Even so, links with northern Europe were certainly much increased by the Viking attacks of the ninth century.

A period of raiding was followed by one of settlement. The kings of Northumbria, Mercia and East Anglia were overthrown. Under one of its most remarkable rulers, Alfred (871–99), the West Saxon dynasty alone survived, and by a narrow margin. Alfred's successors were able to assert their authority over the areas subjugated and settled by the invaders, and his grandson Æthelstan (925–39) was the first king to rule all England, but this process was not without its reverses. Edmund (939–46), Æthelstan's brother, lost control of Northumbria and part of Mercia for a time to Olaf Guthfrithsson, Scandinavian king of Dublin, and although they were eventually recovered, Northumbria became independent again early in the reign of Eadred (946–55). Not until 954, with the expulsion of the Norwegian Eric Bloodaxe, did it finally come under southern rule. Together with the Danelaw – the name historians use to denote the part of eastern England occupied by the invaders – its loyalty to Alfred's descendants was probably long in doubt, for whatever the actual density of the ninth-century settlements, these areas seem to have been thought of as distinctively Danish. To this we shall return.

The impact of the Scandinavian arrival was not confined to politics: it may also have given a considerable boost to the English economy and the growth of urban settlement. This is a difficult matter, because little is known about many English towns before the Vikings came, and comparisons between one period and another are rendered dangerous by our inability to

---

[5] For the text of *Widsith* and its significance, see *The Earliest English Poems*, ed. Alexander, pp. 34–35, 38–42; on the Mercian royal genealogy, Dumville, 'Kingship, Genealogies and Regnal Lists', p. 93.

quantify economic activity in the way sometimes possible for the later Middle Ages. Nevertheless, it is arguable that the Scandinavians contributed considerably to the substantial growth of Norwich in the late Saxon period, and that its pottery industry, along with that of Thetford and Stamford, owed its inception to them.[6]

Even towns which lay well away from their settlements in England may have benefited from their commercial operations. Thus, contacts between western England and Norse trading centres in Ireland, especially Dublin, were probably responsible for the prosperity at different times in the tenth century of Chester and Exeter, and for the emergence of Bristol as a port in the early eleventh, with the slave trade as one of its main concerns.[7] Archaeology has suggested a certain amount about the histories and trading contacts of York and Lincoln from the ninth century onwards. In addition to acting as markets and manufacturing centres for their surrounding areas, they had contacts, doubtless often commercial, with foreign lands, including Scandinavia. As well as Byzantine silk, an inhabitant of Lincoln could have handled pottery from the Low Countries, the Rhineland, the Baltic, Syria and even China, while a pot used for a cremation burial in the Swedish town of Birka in the tenth century may have come from Lincoln.[8]

Citizens of York were likewise familiar with Rhineland pottery, which would originally have contained wine, and with Byzantine silk. They also ground corn using quernstones from the Niedermendig area of Germany, and sharpened their knives with hones made from schist quarried in the Eidsborg region of Norway. Soapstone bowls, too, may have arrived in York from Norway, perhaps together with the amber which is washed up on the shores of the Baltic and was used extensively by York jewellers.[9] The city was visited by merchants from all sides, but especially those of the Danish people, according to Brihtferth of Ramsey's *Life* of Archbishop Oswald (d.992), written in around 1000.[10]

A common Germanic background must often have rendered Anglo-Scandinavian fusion easy. It is unlikely that the two peoples differed greatly in either social custom or law. Similarities between their administrative

---

[6] On Norwich and Thetford, see Campbell, 'Norwich', pp.5–6; on Stamford, Mahany and Roffe, 'Stamford: the Development of an Anglo-Scandinavian Borough', pp.197–99.

[7] Maddicott, 'Trade, industry and the wealth of King Alfred', pp.27–31.

[8] Roesdahl *et al.*, *The Vikings in England*, pp.101–02, 105.

[9] Roesdahl *et al.*, *The Vikings in England*, pp.126, 137; Hall, *The Viking Dig*, pp.85–91. The bowls may alternatively be from the Shetlands.

[10] *Vita Oswaldi*, ed. Raine, i. 454. The evidence for pre-Conquest Anglo-Scandinavian trade is surveyed in Sawyer, 'Anglo-Scandinavian trade in the Viking Age and after'.

systems have been attributed both to their shared Germanic roots and to direct borrowing in the Viking Age. Such matters can quickly become a complex web. A.G. Kristensen, for example, has argued that the Vikings organised their conquests in the Danelaw on a *centena* principle (i.e. one based on hundreds) originally borrowed by the Franks from late-Roman military practice, but that in doing so they may have been influenced by a hundred organisation already existing in English districts when they arrived.[11] Equally, while Helen Cam thought that tenth-century English kings borrowed their system of levying a fleet from the Scandinavians, Inge Skovgaard-Petersen has suggested that the Danes got the inspiration for their military system from the English.[12]

Influence and counter-influence in a Germanic setting, and with a result which was often neither purely English nor purely Scandinavian, was frequent. It was presumably as a result of the basic similarity of the two languages that the English spoken in some of the areas settled by the Danes became for a time a hybrid dialect, and that the language as a whole received a large influx of Scandinavian vocabulary and was altered syntactically and grammatically.[13] Along with this went a substantial Scandinavianisation of place-names, in some areas extending even to the names of fields and minor geographical features.[14] There was also a fusion of art and folklore. Large numbers of stone crosses were produced in northern England in the tenth and eleventh centuries, in an English tradition, but with Scandinavian as well as English ornamental features. The stories of Sigurd and of Wayland the Smith occasionally appear in this context, and the popularity of the latter, who was known to the English before the Vikings came, demonstrates how contact was facilitated by a shared Germanic past.[15] Moreover, recent history was soon providing a common folklore of its own. A.P. Smyth has suggested that the story of Ragnar Hairy-Breeks, a celebrated Viking leader of the ninth century, was popular in the Danelaw, and that it was connected with the cult of St Edmund, the king of East Anglia killed by the invaders in 869.[16]

---

[11] Kristensen, 'Danelaw institutions and Danish society in the Viking Age'.

[12] Cam, *Liberties & Communities in Medieval England*, p.94; Skovgaard-Petersen *et al.*, *Danmarks Historie* i., p.196.

[13] Jespersen, *Growth and Structure of the English Language*, pp.60–77.

[14] Cameron, 'The Minor Names and Field-Names of the Holland division of Lincolnshire', pp.81–88.

[15] On the sculpture generally, Bailey, *Viking Age Sculpture in Northern England*, espec. pp.103–25 on Wayland and Sigurd; the former appears in the Anglo-Saxon poem *Deor*, and is probably one of the figures shown on the eighth-century Franks Casket, made in Northumbria and now in the British Museum.

[16] Smyth, *Scandinavian Kings in the British Isles 850–880*, pp.54–67.

It is interesting that in the 980s, when the storm-clouds of invasion were beginning to gather again, the monks of the Fenland abbey of Ramsey asked their guest, the continental scholar Abbo of Fleury, to write a Latin account of Edmund's martyrdom, and that this was soon afterwards adapted into English by Ælfric, one of the leading native writers of the day. There is other evidence that a new wave of Viking attacks may have increased interest in the Scandinavian aspect of English history. The now-destroyed manuscript of the biography of King Alfred written by his friend Bishop Asser was made about the year 1000,[17] and so were the surviving copies of the poems *Beowulf* and *Widsith*, with their northern associations.[18] Clearly, the churchmen who produced these texts were interested in history and military affairs, an interest they shared with the Anglo-Saxon aristocracy into which they had often been born, and whose mentality was in all likelihood that of a warrior world to an extent which the surviving sources often tend to conceal. However, the famous poem on Æthelstan's great victory over a coalition of his enemies at *Brunanburh* in 937, which exults in the slaughter of foes whose corpses will serve as a feast for scavengers, is indicative,[19] and similar in outlook to the work of Icelandic poets in praise of Scandinavian leaders of the period. It is therefore hardly surprising that Æthelred II (978–1016), who enrolled northern warlords and their followers in his military forces, is said to have patronised the Icelandic skald (court poet) Gunnlaug Serpent's Tongue, who created what was probably a martial piece in praise of him;[20] this may mean that the king and other Anglo-Saxons could understand the Old Norse in which the verses were composed.

In an apparent attempt to make their lordship more attractive to Scandinavians settled in England, Æthelred's forebears had about a century earlier incorporated into their genealogy the Danes Scyld and Scef, also claimed as ancestors by the dynasty to which Cnut belonged, and by employing a Scandinavian poet Æthelred was following the sort of example set by his father Edgar, who according to a verse in the *Anglo-Saxon Chronicle* was too fond of bad foreign customs and of inviting foreigners to enter the country.[21] The description of some of the practices he introduced

---

[17] Ker, *Catalogue*, p.221.
[18] Ker, *Catalogue*, pp.281, 153.
[19] *ASC*, i. 106–10.
[20] Only the refrain survives, but the fact that it refers to the army's attitude to Æthelred makes it likely that the poem dealt with his military exploits. See the Select Bibliography under Gunnlaug.
[21] *ASC*, i. 114–15.

as *hæðen* (heathen) suggests that these foreigners were Scandinavians, like the *pagani* who according to Asser had earlier entered the service of Alfred and been enriched by his liberality.

Conversely, it was maybe not unusual for Englishmen to visit Scandinavia and its courts. The *Sigefridus Norwegensis episcopus*, who appears in a list of monks from Glastonbury Abbey, may have been a tenth-century English missionary to Norway,[22] while King Harald Bluetooth of Denmark possibly brought men from northern England to design the highly decorated great rune stone, which includes a crucifixion scene, at Jelling in Jutland.[23] His son Swegen Forkbeard was the first Danish monarch to issue coins bearing his own name. They also carried that of Godwin, the English moneyer who produced them, and their design imitated the silver pennies of Æthelred II's *Crux* type. It was common for Scandinavian mints to copy English coins, and even to acquire some of the English dies used to strike them. Such dies, and the odd English moneyer too, also found their way to Dublin, whose earliest pennies, again modelled on English prototypes, were made for its king, Sihtric Silkbeard, in the late tenth century. The York moneyer Colgrim, on the other hand, seems to have struck coins of Æthelred's *Helmet* issue, current just after 1000, with a die manufactured by a Dublin die-cutter.[24] When Cnut had dies naming him *REX DÆNOR* (king of Danes) made probably in Lincoln in around 1015,[25] he was showing an appreciation of the advanced English monetary system shared by many Scandinavians.

Furthermore, their poetry reveals that they too were interested in the past, and aware that the history which they had in common with the English was a link between the two peoples. The contemporary skald Sighvat describes the English as 'Ælle's kin' in a verse on the battle of Ringmere fought in 1010 and his *Knútsdrápa*, a poem in praise of Cnut, begins with a stanza referring to the Viking Ivar's responsibility for Ælle's death. These allusions are to the king of Northumbria killed in York in 867, and, together with Ottar the Black's description of the English as 'noble descendants' of Edmund of East Anglia in his poem lauding Cnut, imply that the raiders who finally triumphed in 1016 were conscious of their place in a tradition of English conquest. Hardly any poetry on Cnut's father, Swegen

---

[22] Sawyer, 'Anglo-Scandinavian trade', p.304.

[23] *Danmarks Runeindskrifter*, ed. Jacobsen and Moltke, i. col. 78. German rather than English influence on the stone has also been suggested, see Moltke in Nielsen, 'Jelling Problems', 186–87, and the article 'Ottonsk kunst', *KHL*, xiii, cols. 60–61. However, Bailey, *Viking Age Scuplture*, pp.139–40, thinks that an English piece found beneath York Minster supplies at least part of the background for the designs on the Danish monument.

[24] Blackburn, 'Hiberno-Norse coins', pp.13–15.

[25] Below, p.88.

Forkbeard, survives, but a single verse by Thorleif Rauthfeldarson has him bloodying swords in England with God's help. He was almost certainly proud of his exploits in this country, and conceivably named his son after a Cnut who struck coins in York and Mercia in the 890s.[26] When this son finally took the English throne in 1016, it was an event which frequent contact with the Danes had long anticipated, which the partly Scandinavianised population of Northumbria and the Danelaw may not have greatly resented, and which the new king himself doubtless saw as the culmination of the victories of his countrymen a century and a half previously.

[26] Galster, 'Cnvt Rex = Gorm den Gamle's fader'.

I

DENMARK, ENGLAND AND THE CONQUEST OF 1016

D anish kings emerge from a period of obscurity in the middle of the tenth century, when a dynasty based on Jelling in Jutland, and represented by Gorm the Old and his son Harald Bluetooth, seems to have extended its authority over the whole country, which then included the province of Skåne in modern Sweden. Harald was probably also recognised for a time as ruler of part of Norway. He accepted Christianity when the missionary Poppo proved the efficacy of the Christian god by undergoing the ordeal of carrying hot iron,[1] and may have entered into a subordinate relationship with the German emperor Otto I. However, he rebelled after Otto's death in 973, and the following year was defeated at the Danevirke, a Danish defensive rampart in southern Jutland connected to the east with the important town of Hedeby. The Germans then built a defensive fortress (*urbs*) in the border area, which in 983 was captured and burnt by the Danes,[2] an action almost certainly connected with the great Slav rising which followed the death of the emperor Otto II. The Slavs on Germany's eastern frontier were obvious allies for the Jelling dynasty, and Harald had probably taken as his wife the daughter of Mistivoj, of the tribe of the Abodrites.[3] A little later he was wounded in battle during a dispute with his son Swegen, and fled to the Slavs, among whom he died.[4]

This is almost all that can be gleaned from broadly contemporary written sources about the Danish monarchy between about 950 and the accession

---

[1] Widukind, *Rerum Gestarum Saxonicarum Libri Tres*, iii. 65, ed. Hirsch, pp.140–41.
[2] Thietmar, *Chronicon*, ii. 6, 24, pp.102–05, 128–29.
[3] She is named as Tufa on the rune stone she raised in memory of her mother at Sønder Vissing, *Danmarks Runeindskrifter*, ed. Jacobsen and Moltke, i. cols. 93–94; illustrated Roesdahl, *Viking Age Denmark*, p.204. Adam, *Gesta*, ii. 28, p.88, calls her Gunnhild, which if not a reference to another wife must mean that she took a Danish name.
[4] *Encomium*, i. 1, p.8; Adam, *Gesta*, ii. 27, p.87.

in around 989 of Swegen Forkbeard, who conquered England in 1013 and whose son Cnut ruled it for nineteen[5] years. The evidence is meagre, comprising stones in Denmark bearing inscriptions in the runic alphabet, the German chroniclers Widukind of Corvey, Thietmar of Merseburg and Adam of Bremen, and the work known as the *Encomium Emmae*, written in praise of Cnut's queen, Emma, in St Omer in the early 1040s. Of the two famous rune stones which stand outside the church at Jelling, the smaller states that 'King Gorm made these memorials to Thyre his wife, Denmark's ornament'; the larger that 'King Harald commanded these memorials made to Gorm his father and Thyre his mother. That Harald who won for himself all Denmark and Norway and made the Danes Christian'.[6] In the last sixty years, however, this scanty material has been substantially augmented by archaeology.

The site at Jelling now consists of two turf mounds, and between them stand a stone church and the rune stones, the larger of which weighs nearly ten tons. The diameter of the north mound is about seventy yards and that of its southern fellow some eighty-four yards. The former is a burial mound, containing in its centre a timber chamber which proved upon examination in 1820–21 to be empty of the body originally placed there. This was to be expected, as there were also signs that after the construction of the mound someone had dug down and entered the chamber through its roof, but it was not until the late 1970s that excavations in the church revealed their likely motives.

Beneath the present stone building were found traces of three earlier structures, all of timber, and all interpreted as churches. Concurrent with the building of the earliest, a timber grave chamber was constructed beneath its floor to receive the decomposed remains of a middle-aged man. This is plausibly believed to be Gorm, Harald's father, originally interred in pagan fashion in the north mound, and later moved to the church built by his Christian son. The purpose of the south mound, which excavation has shown not to be burial, is unclear, but dendrochronology, a method which dates timber according to the pattern of its tree-rings, indicates that it was built between about 960 and about 970. As the north mound contained wood felled no earlier than 958, not more than twenty or thirty years at the most seem likely to have separated the construction of the mounds and the

---

[5] Cnut was born *c*.990–1000, see below, p.160.
[6] *Danmarks Runeindskrifter*, ed. Jacobsen and Moltke, i. cols. 78–79; illustrated Lund, 'The Danish Perspective', p.135; see also Roesdahl, *Viking Age Denmark*, pp.171–72.

earliest church, and the positioning of the larger of the two rune stones exactly between the mounds. All this work, in fact, was evidently carried out by Harald Bluetooth.[7]

It was almost certainly Harald too who reconstructed and extended the Danevirke, a linear earthwork dating originally from about 737 which protected Jutland's southern frontier. Excavation has provided dendrochro-nological dates of about 951–61 and 968 for part of the. small section known as the Double Wall, which lies at the junction of the central section and the rampart which connects with Hedeby to the east. Although the excavators have warned that these dates are only a broad indication of that of the com-plex and segmented line which is this phase of the Danevirke as a whole, they nevertheless believe that in a period of danger from Germany Harald rebuilt the central section, and was also responsible for the first phases of the flanking lines to east and west. The result, stretching west from Hedeby, whose semicircular defences also seem to have been renewed at this time, was a rampart over eight miles long, about thirteen yards wide, and nearly ten feet high, not counting the wooden palisade with which it was presum-ably crowned.[8]

A large bridge near Ravning, about six miles from Jelling, was seemingly also built by Harald, perhaps for a military purpose. This too was a major piece of engineering, some half a mile long and eighteen feet wide, and making use of an estimated 4,000 oak trees.[9] Dendrochronology suggests construction in about 979, very close to the date now assigned to the most famous of all the revelations of Danish archaeology, the four camps of Fyrkat and Aggersborg in Jutland, Nonnebakken on the island of Fyn, and Trelleborg on Zealand. Discovered and excavated in the last sixty years, they have often been described. All were circular and closely similar in plan, although differing slightly in dimensions and details. Aggersborg, the largest, contained forty-eight houses, arranged in blocks of four grouped in threes in each of the quadrants formed by two internal roads intersecting at right angles. The others had only one such group in each quadrant, although Trelleborg also had fifteen houses outside the circular rampart but within an outer defence work. The ramparts themselves were of earth, but were timber-faced and had an internal wooden framework to give additional

[7] Krogh, 'The Royal Viking Age Monuments'; Roesdahl, *Viking Age Denmark*, pp.171–76; Hvass, 'Jelling from Iron Age to Viking Age', p.149; Lund, '"Denemearc", "tanmarkar but" and "tanmaurk ala"', pp.162–63.

[8] Andersen *et al.*, *Danevirke*, i. 91; Roesdahl, *Viking Age Denmark*, pp.141–45.

[9] Ramskou, 'Vikingebroen'; Roesdahl, *Viking Age Denmark*, pp.47–48.

strength. All were pierced by four gates which gave access to the internal roads.[10] The geometrical plan of these structures, and the accuracy of their laying-out, caused astonishment upon their discovery, but otherwise the more that has emerged about them the more difficult in some ways they have become to understand. An early interpretation saw them as barracks for troops used by Swegen Forkbeard to conquer England, with each house containing a ship's crew. However, wood from Trelleborg now implies a construction date of about 980, and if the other camps are of the same period this would seem to be too early for a connection with Danish raids on England, which are not known to have begun until a decade later (but see pages 29–30). Furthermore, it is now clear that some of the houses were used as workshops not dwellings, and that others were occupied by women and children as well as men. Also, habitation only seems to have lasted for a short time, and Aggersborg may never have been finished. Perhaps these camps still have surprises in store. Certainly the recent discovery of what is believed to be a fifth example, at Trelleborg in Skåne, may add significantly to our knowledge. Initial excavations indicate that it was related in some way to the others, but had no buildings within the rampart.[11] At present, the most plausible interpretation is probably that these forts were centres of royal power intended to enable Harald to control the areas which the Jelling rune stone suggests he had won for himself. The fact that none are so far known in the vicinity of Jelling itself seems to support this idea. But from the current point of view, their significance is no less important than their purpose. The argument that structures of such scale and uniformity must be the work of the Danish monarchy is difficult to resist, and so they have to be added to the features at Jelling, the renewal of the Danevirke, and the bridge at Ravning, as evidence of a burst of building activity under Harald Bluetooth all the more remarkable because it was quite without parallel in the history of the Danish monarchy in the Viking Age. Clearly, Harald was a highly efficient organiser of labour and materials: the felling and transportation of the large quantities of timber used in the camps and at Ravning, for example, must have been major operations in themselves.

Moreover, this raises other questions about Cnut's predecessors, questions without definite answers, but worth airing nonetheless, because they are

[10] Roesdahl, *Viking Age Denmark*, pp. 147–55; Roesdahl, 'The Danish Geometrical Viking Fortresses'. Nonnebakken now lies beneath modern Odense, and minor excavations have not revealed major structures, so it did not certainly have the same internal arrangements as the other three.
[11] I am grateful to Professor P.H. Sawyer for sending me information on this excavation.

relevant not only to the issue of how Swegen conquered England but also that of whether Cnut was already familiar with administrative institutions of an English type when he became its king. This is a matter upon which no contemporary written evidence survives, and has been much disputed. The large unit known as the *syssel*, a subdivision of the country broadly similar to the English shire, is in Jutland believed to be pre-Christian, although its function is something of an open question, as it is now best known in connection with later ecclesiastical organisation.[12] Maybe more interesting is whether a smaller unit, the *herred*, dates from the Viking period. Some historians remain sceptical about this, while others are convinced that it does, and that an early form of military organisation was based upon the *herred* system;[13] that it appears in southern Norway and Västergötland in Sweden too has led to the contention that it was introduced there in Viking times; perhaps by Swegen or Cnut.[14] Certainly the obligation to perform military service for the king existed in Skåne in 1085, for it is mentioned (as *expeditio*) in St Cnut's donation to a church in Lund in that year, the only surviving Danish royal charter from before 1100.[15] There is also the question of whether a national ship levy, the *leding*, goes back to the Viking period. Again, this is uncertain, although some recent opinion has been favourable to the idea.[16] In fact, if the problem is set within the context of an evidently powerful late tenth-century Danish monarchy, it is difficult to believe that Harald Bluetooth or his son could not have introduced a naval system had they wished, and when the concern about the country's southern land defences is remembered, along with the importance that must also have been attached to protection from sea-borne attack, it might seem more likely than not that they did wish. Also, the way in which the *Encomium Emmae* describes the assembly of the forces with which Swegen invaded England in 1013 certainly suggests that both men and ships were raised on the country,[17] while the Norman William of Jumièges, writing probably in the late 1050s, has Swegen both commanding his countrymen to take part in the expedition and sending messengers to other kingdoms to attract men eager for loot.[18]

[12] *KHL*, xvii, cols. 649–50.
[13] *KHL*, vi. cols. 488–90.
[14] The attribution to Swegen or Cnut is that of Skovgaard-Petersen *et al.*, *Danmarks Historie*, p.196.
[15] *Diplomatarium Danicum*, ed. Weibull, ii. 43–50.
[16] Skovgaard-Petersen *et al.*, *Danmarks Historie*, pp.196–97.
[17] *Encomium*, i. 3, pp.10–12.
[18] WJ, v. 7, ed. van Houts, ii. 16–19; see also Lund, 'The armies of Swein Forkbeard and Cnut'.

Both may be guessing, although the Encomiast is reasonably well informed on the campaigns late in Æthelred II's reign, and William's report of mixed methods need not be far wrong, even if it is a guess; the armies which troubled England over the long period between about 985 and 1016 do often seem to have comprised the warbands of a number of men, are unlikely to have been organised and commanded solely by Danish kings, did not consist entirely of Danes, and frequently appear to have been motivated mainly by a desire for booty. Three leaders are mentioned in the treaty which Æthelred made with one group probably in 994 – Justin, Guthmund, and Olaf (Tryggvason), who shortly afterwards became king of Norway.[19] Another, Tosti, although, absent from contemporary documentary sources, appears on a Swedish rune stone as having secured tribute for his followers,[20] while John of Worcester, writing in around 1100, says that a force which appeared in 1009 was led by Thorkell, and was almost immediately joined by a second group under Hemming and Eglaf.[21] Olaf Haraldsson (St Olaf), also a future king of Norway, is known to have been present too.[22] The army with which Cnut eventually conquered England in 1016 also included a number of these largely independent warlords. Thorkell was there, having in the interval been in English service, and so was the Norwegian Earl Eric of Lade, and, if we can trust Thietmar of Merseburg, one Thorgut. These men and their followers were mainly attracted by the prospect of plunder and tribute, and expeditions to England were probably popular throughout Scandinavia, as rune stones from the province of Uppland in Sweden tend to confirm. Ulf, commemorated at Yttergärde, served with Tosti, Thorketil (almost certainly Thorkell) and Cnut, and received payments from all three. Alli, from Väsby, also 'took Cnut's geld in England', while Ulfric, mentioned on a stone at Lingsberg, was paid two gelds, although we are not told by whom. Bjor, from Galteland in southern Norway, was less fortunate. He went with Cnut to England, but died there.[23] Given the certainty that freebooters were among the raiding armies, it is clearly possible that the contingents contributed by Swegen and Cnut were wholly or partly comprised of such men too, rather than exclusively of Danish levies. We do not know.

---

[19] *Gesetze*, i. 220–24; *EHD*, pp.437–39; Keynes, 'The Historical Context of the Battle of Maldon', pp.103–07. Sawyer, 'Ethelred II, Olaf Tryggvason and the conversion of Norway', p.305, doubts the extent of Olaf's authority and suggests that it would be more accurate to call him a king in Norway.
[20] Jansson, *Swedish Vikings in England*, p.12.
[21] JW, ii. 462–63.
[22] See Alistair Campbell's comments, *Encomium*, pp.76–77.
[23] Wessen, *Historiska Runinskrifter*, pp.10–11; Jansson, *Swedish Vikings in England*; Lund, 'The armies of Swein Forkbeard and Cnut', pp.117–18.

In fact, for all its interest and importance, the nature of Danish govern-ment, and the extent to which it provided the forces which conquered England, must be left ill defined. Cnut may have been familiar with institu-tions of an English type. At the least, Swegen's victories are likely to have owed something not only to his doubtless considerable abilities as a com-mander, but also to an administration capable of utilising resources effectively and controlling the country in his absence. Harald's building works imply the existence of a system for organising labour, and it would be surprising if his achievements bore no relation to those of his son and grandson. Much is uncertain, but the triumphs of Swegen and Cnut are not, and the ability to organise men and materials suggested by works such as the Trelleborg camps would have been vital in orchestrating campaigns against the English, who had considerable administrative resources of their own.

THE CONQUEST OF 1016: I

Their country can seldom have been free from the threat of sea-borne attack in the tenth and eleventh centuries, when piracy and coastal harrying were seemingly endemic. The will of King Eadred (946–55) left £1,600 so that his people could redeem themselves from famine or a heathen army, Cnut defeated thirty ships of pirates early in his reign,[24] and Domesday Book says that under Edward the Confessor (1042–66) the hidage (broadly, tax) assessment of Fareham in Hampshire was reduced 'on account of the Vikings, because it is on the sea'.[25] Times were troubled, and England a rich source of plunder. Nor can it be assumed that all its invaders came directly from Scandinavia. Professor Dolley argued that raids on western England in the 980s were partly the responsibility of Scandinavians who had settled in Ireland, and that Æthelred's expedition into Cumberland in 1000, and the activities of his fleet in the Irish Sea, were in all likelihood the result of provocation in that area.[26] As we shall see, there seems to have been provo-cation from Normandy too.

Much of our most detailed source on the raids around 980–1016 was written early in Cnut's reign and survives in three of the sets of annals (now denoted C, D and E) known collectively as the *Anglo-Saxon Chronicle* (see Chapter 2). Its author, who may have written most of every entry between

---

[24] Below, p.86.
[25] DB, i. 40c.
[26] Dolley, 'An Introduction to the Coinage of Æthelraed II', p.119; also Keynes, 'The Historical Context of the Battle of Maldon', pp.85–86.

991 and 1016, has a distinctive and somewhat dramatic style, and knew a great deal. Even so, his work has its limitations. It seems at times to dwell excessively and inaccurately on the ineffectiveness of the English resistance (see below), and is likely for the 990s at least to be at best a partial record. The original entries for 995 and 996 may have been lost,[27] and it says nothing of the hostile relations which probably existed with Normandy for a time,[28] and only hints at the troubles in the Irish Sea mentioned above. Also, one of the sums said to have been paid to the enemy in either 991 (£10, 000) or 994 (£16,000) may be wrong, as a surviving treaty which almost certainly belongs to one of these years (and most likely to 994) gives a figure of £22,000.[29] Furthermore, although the chronicler was well informed, and has something to offer on events in Mercia and Northumbria, he seems to have known most, or perhaps merely wished to say most, about what happened in southern England and East Anglia. Therefore, despite the extent of his knowledge, the further we recede from the date at which he wrote, and the geographical area on which he is most forthcoming, the less it is possible to be confident that important events were not omitted from his work. Even the detailed entries on 1015 and 1016 can be supplemented by the *Encomium Emmae*, Thietmar of Merseburg, Icelandic poetry, and later English sources.[30]

The *Chronicle* C text puts the first attacks on Æthelred's England under 980, when Thanet and Cheshire were harried, and Southampton ravaged and most of its citizens killed or captured. Further coastal assaults followed, apparently initially of a fairly intermittent kind, with raids on Devon and Cornwall in 981, Dorset in 982, and Watchet (Somerset) in 988. Goda, a Devonshire thegn, was evidently killed in a fierce battle resisting the latter attack, and 991 saw the defeat of an army under Ealdorman Brihtnoth of Essex at Maldon, and the first known payment of tribute – £10,000.[31] No harrying is recorded for 992, although a victory over part of the English navy is, and in 993 there were raids around the mouth of the Humber, and Bamburgh on the Northumbrian coast was sacked. 994 saw the most serious campaign so far, with Swegen of Denmark and Olaf Tryggvason assaulting London unsuccessfully and then apparently plundering inland, as

---

[27] Lawson, '"Those stories look true": levels of taxation in the reigns of Aethelred II and Cnut', 393, n. 1.

[28] Campbell, *Essays in Anglo-Saxon History*, pp. 198–201.

[29] See above, n. 19.

[30] Below, pp. 77–79.

[31] The reliability, and in particular the magnitude, of the *Chronicle* tribute figures has been doubted; see below, pp. 173–74.

they are said to have obtained horses and ridden far and wide, before being bought off with £16,000. Subsequent years saw further visitations on coastal shires, extending from Somerset in the west to Kent and Essex in the east, and a tribute of £24,000 was paid in 1002, but the situation seems to have worsened between 1003 and 1006, when an army led by Swegen burnt Exeter, Wilton, Norwich, Thetford and Wallingford. This force, unlike its predecessors, captured sizeable towns, and in reaching Wilton and Wallingford penetrated a considerable distance inland. It was finally given £36,000 to leave the country in 1007, and the following year, when Æthelred ordered the construction of a fleet, seems to have been peaceful. Unfortunately, in 1009 a particularly large force of Scandinavians appeared. Active for three years, they too penetrated into the heart of England; capturing Oxford late in 1009, Thetford, Cambridge and Northampton in 1010, and Canterbury in 1011. Among the captives from the latter was Archbishop Ælfheah, who refused to be ransomed and was murdered at Greenwich in April 1012, shortly before his killers received a tribute of £48,000. It is clear from the *Chronicle* account that the English were by now in considerable disarray and incapable of offering serious resistance, so it is hardly surprising that when Swegen arrived with his son Cnut and a further army in 1013 the whole nation submitted to him, and Æthelred went into exile with his brother-in-law, Duke Richard II of Normandy.

This exile might have been permanent had Swegen not died in February 1014. Æthelred was invited back, and wasted little time in expelling Cnut and his army from their Lincolnshire base. Before returning to Denmark, he touched at Sandwich to put ashore hostages given to his father, having first cut off their hands, ears and noses.

But in September 1015 he appeared off Sandwich again, to initiate fourteen months of campaigning, largely against Æthelred's son Edmund Ironside, and of an intensity not seen since the days of Alfred the Great. Wessex, long ruled by the dynasty to which both Alfred and Æthelred belonged, submitted to Cnut late in 1015, as it had to his father two years earlier. He was also joined by Ealdorman Eadric of Mercia and forty Scandinavian ships probably under Thorkell, who had entered Æthelred's service in 1012. Early in 1016 Cnut crossed the Thames into Mercia and harried Warwickshire. Edmund's early attempts at opposition seem to have come to nothing. The chronicler says that when the men summoned for military service appeared they soon disbanded because the king and the citizens of London were not present. A further summons assembled another army, which this time was joined by the king, but when they all met 'it came to nothing as so often before', and Æthelred returned to London on hearing that some intended to betray him. Edmund then went north to join Earl Uhtred of Northumbria, and together they harried in Staffordshire, Shropshire and Cheshire, possibly because these areas were identified with Cnut's ally Eadric of Mercia.[32] Cnut countered by occupying Northumbria, whereupon Uhtred submitted and was executed. London remained unsub-dued, and elected Edmund as king when Æthelred died on 23 April.

At this point the Danes evidently divided, some besieging London while others fought Edmund, who seems by now to have succeeded in raising forces in Wessex. The battles of Penselwood and Sherston were apparently inconclusive, although hard fought in the case of the latter, but Edmund was able to relieve London, driving the enemy away and defeating them after crossing the Thames at Brentford. He then returned to Wessex to raise more men, whereupon there was another unsuccessful assault on the city, which ended with the Scandinavians being pursued into Kent, where Ealdorman Eadric went over to Edmund; Cnut used his fleet to cross the Thames estuary to Essex, and proceeded from there to ravage Mercia. He seems to have been retiring to his ships again when Edmund overtook him at the hill called *Assandun* (probably Ashdon in north-west or Ashingdon in south-east Essex). Here, on 18 October 1016, he defeated the English in a struggle in which the chronicler says that all their best men fell. This is likely to have been followed by another battle near the Forest of Dean, for Edmund had an alliance with some of the Welsh,[33] but by now both sides were doubtless exhausted, and winter was approaching. Also, Edmund may already have been suffering from the illness, or possibly wound, of which he was soon to die.

However that may be, peace was made, Cnut taking Mercia and probably Northumbria, and Edmund Wessex.[34] They also agreed that the Scandinavian army would be given tribute, and it at last occupied London, thus gaining in peace what it had never gained in war. On 30 November Edmund died, Cnut had little difficulty persuading the English to ignore the claims of his relatives, and the country was reunited under his rule. In 1018 the English paid the very large sum of £82,500, and came to an agreement with the Danes at Oxford which may have marked the formal end of hostilities; the same year part of Cnut's fleet sailed to Denmark. The conquest was complete.

[32] JW, ii. 482–83, says that it was because they had refused to fight the Danes.
[33] Below, pp.77–79.
[34] See *FNC*, i. 690–92.

THE DANISH MONARCHY AND THE CONQUEST

After 1013 the Scandinavian forces were obviously led by Danish kings. This is unlikely to have always been so, but assessing the precise extent and purpose of their involvement in England at this time entails the use of some difficult source material. Adam of Bremen's history of the archbishopric of Hamburg-Bremen, which claimed ecclesiastical primacy over Scandinavia, was written in the 1070s. Adam had spoken to the Danish king Swegen Estrithsson, Cnut's nephew, and cannot be dismissed out of hand, although nor can he be regarded as infallible. He reports that Harald (Bluetooth) established his authority over both the English (*Angli*) and the Norwegians, having sent an army to England under his son Hiring, who subdued the island but was at length betrayed and killed by the Northumbrians. Swegen is also said to have invaded England later to avenge his brother.[35] Adam is known to be broadly correct in stating that Harald exercised some kind of power in Norway, but obviously errs in having Hiring rule all England. Moreover, his tale might be a wild distortion of the fate of the Norwegian Eric Bloodaxe, whose father was called Harald, and who was killed just after being expelled from his Northumbrian kingdom in 954.

Nevertheless, the story merits further consideration, as other evidence can be connected with it. The poem on the battle fought in 991 at Maldon, where an army led by Ealdorman Brihtnoth of Essex was defeated by Scandinavian raiders, says that the native forces included a Northumbrian hostage, Æscferth.[36] If Hiring did invade England, he perhaps occupied the north, like Swegen in 1013 and Harald of Norway in 1066, and was betrayed and killed by the Northumbrians when Æthelred's forces appeared on the scene. They may then have been required to give hostages as a guarantee of future good behaviour. Another reflection of this could be the twelfth-century belief in the abbey of Ely, where Brihtnoth was buried, that he had been earl of Northumbria.[37] Conceivably connected too is the possibility that Æthelred took as a consort the daughter of a Northumbrian earl, Thored,[38] maybe to mollify such of the northerners as had supported him. Finally, there is the primarily southern distribution of his *Second Hand* coin type of *c*.985–*c*.991. Only one penny of this issue has survived from the York

35 Adam, *Gesta*, ii. 25, 51, pp.83–84, 112.
36 *The Battle of Maldon*, lines 265–67, ed. Scragg, p.65.
37 *Lib. El.*, ii. 62, p.134.
38 See Keynes, *The Diplomas of King Æthelred 'The Unready'*, p.187, n.18.

mint, and none from Lincoln, suggesting that very few of the dies used to strike it ever reached the north; the reason could have been some sort of political crisis.[39]

This body of evidence is not strong, for Adam was capable of error and there may have been other reasons why the Maldon army had a Northumbrian hostage (even assuming that the poem is reliable) and Æthelred a Northumbrian wife, quite unconnected with the absence of *Second Hand* dies from northern mints. But that English sources are silent about Hiring and trouble in the north in the 980s is not particularly significant: there is much silence in the early history of Northumbria.

Danish interest in conquering England, if indulged by Harald at all, must have lapsed during the fatal quarrel with his son Swegen. This may have been quickly followed by the capture and ransom of the latter, by Northmen if we believe Thietmar of Merseburg, by Slavs according to Adam.[40] Once free of these troubles he wasted little time in turning his attention to England. The *Anglo-Saxon Chronicle* first refers to his presence under 994, but this may not have been his first visit. Æthelred's confirmation of the will of Æthelric of Bocking, which is from no later than 999, says that there was a plan to receive Swegen in Essex when he first came there with a fleet, and that Æthelred was told of Æthelric's involvement in it many years before he died.[41] Although conceivably not before 994, this was probably earlier, for the greatest possible length of time that could have elapsed between 994 and Æthelric's death is five years – assuming that he died in the last year that the will could have been confirmed – and whether even this justifies the description 'many years' seems questionable. Also, the way we are told that the plan was connected with Swegen's first visit to Essex suggests that he had been there again since this occasion and the drawing up of the confirmation. His harrying of Essex in 994 could well have been this second occasion, and if so the first may have been the Maldon campaign in 991.

Whatever the truth of this, in 994 he and Olaf Tryggvason, possibly also his ally in 991, made an unsuccessful attack on London, and then ravaged Essex, Kent, Sussex and Hampshire before taking winter quarters in

---

[39] On *Second Hand*, which has been much discussed by numismatists, see Stewart, 'Coinage and recoinage after Edgar's reform', pp.471–74. Blackburn, 'Æthelred's Coinage and the Payment of Tribute', p.160, comments that 'the mints of Lincoln and York may have been closed for some years, hinting at some economic or political crisis in Northumbria and north Mercia'.

[40] Thietmar, *Chronicon*, vii. 26, pp.442–43; Adam, *Gesta*, ii. 29, p.91.

[41] S 939; *Wills*, pp.44–47; *EHD*, pp.579–80.

Southampton and receiving a payment of £16,000.⁴² It therefore looks as
though Swegen wintered in England, and in the following spring perhaps
went plundering in the Irish Sea, for one of the versions of the Welsh
chronicle known as the *Annales Cambriæ* records the harrying of the Isle of
Man by a 'Swegen son of Harald' in a year which is likely to be 995.⁴³

His history in the next few years is obscure. According to Adam, he was at
some time expelled from Denmark by King Eric of Sweden, unsuccessfully
sought help in Norway and England, and was eventually welcomed by a *rex
Scothorum*, with whom he lived in exile for fourteen years until Eric's death.
He then returned to marry Eric's widow, but was again expelled by his step-
son, the new Swedish king, Olaf, who later, for his mother's sake, restored
him to his kingdom.⁴⁴ Adam later added that Eric was allied with Boleslav
of Poland, having married his sister or daughter, and that the Danes were
attacked by Slavs and Swedes.⁴⁵

This tale about Swegen's Slavonic wife may fit with Thietmar's statement
that he had Cnut and his brother Harald by a sister of Boleslav whom he
later abandoned, which may in turn tie in with the Encomiast's story that
after their father's death Cnut and Harald brought their mother back from
among the Slavs.⁴⁶ It therefore seems fairly certain that Swegen did have a
Slavonic consort, probably for political reasons.

Whether he was expelled by Eric of Sweden is another matter. Lauritz
Weibull suggested that Adam drew inspiration from the biblical story of the
capture of Manasseh, pagan king of Judah, by the Assyrians, and thought it a

⁴² The *Chronicle* is clear that Swegen and Olaf operated together thus far, although the former is not
named in the treaty II Æthelred, which seems to have been concluded with Olaf at about this time,
Keynes, 'The Historical Context', pp.103–04.
⁴³ Public Record Office, Exchequer, Miscellaneous Books, Series 1 (E.164), vol. 1. Breviate of
Domesday Book, verso of sixth fly leaf; printed *Annales Cambriæ*, ed. Williams ab Ithel, p.20. *Swein
filius Haraldi* may have been related to the Harald and the *Gothrit filius Haraldi* who appear in the same
source in the 980s, so the identification with Swegen Forkbeard is far from certain.
⁴⁴ Adam, *Gesta*, ii. 30–34, 39, pp.91–95, 99–100. The *rex Scothorum* possibly ruled in Ireland: see Adam's
equation of *rex Scothorum* and *rex Hiberniae* in his account (p.196) of the battle of Stamford Bridge in
1066. Swegen's history in these years is also discussed by Sawyer, 'Cnut's Scandinavian empire',
pp.14–16.
⁴⁵ Adam, *Gesta*, scholium 24, p.95; for Adam's authorship, see Schmeidler's comments, pp.xli–xlii. Two
rune stones from just outside Hedeby may also be relevant to Swegen's difficulties. One says that it
was set up by King Swegen for his soldier Skarde, who had journeyed west but found death at
Hedeby, the other that it was raised by Thorulf, a soldier of Swegen, for his companion Eric, who
found death when drengs besieged Hedeby. On the assumption that both Swegens are identifiable
with Swegen Forkbeard, and that Skarde had participated in his campaigns in Britain, it is conceivable
that he returned home to find enemies in possession of Hedeby, which he then besieged. The stones
have, however, also been connected with fighting around the town in the early 980s, and in the time
of Cnut's nephew Swegen Estrithsson seventy years later; see *Danmarks Runeindskrifter*, ed. Jacobsen
and Moltke, i. cols. 5–10; illustrated Lund, 'The Danish Perspective', pp.127–28.
⁴⁶ Thietmar, *Chronicon*, vii. 39, pp.446–47; *Encomium*, ii. 2, p.18.

distortion of Swegen's expeditions to the British Isles.[47] Even so, a verse attributed to the contemporary poet Stefnir Thorgilsson, which refers to a man with
a crooked nose who betrayed Swegen out of his land,[48] indicates that there
may be something in the exile story after all. This is the kind of matter upon
which historians will forever disagree, but it may be that Swegen did have his
position in Denmark threatened by Swedes and Slavs at some time in the 990s.
His union with Boleslav's sister may have both removed any danger from the
Poles and secured their assistance against other tribes, and he subsequently
turned his attention, in alliance with Olaf of Sweden and the Norwegian Earl
Eric of Lade, to the destruction of Olaf Tryggvason, king of Norway.

This he accomplished at the sea-battle of Svold, on 9 September 999.[49]
Olaf was killed, and Swegen and Earl Eric subsequently controlled Norway
together. In 1003 Swegen appears in England again, not returning home
until 1005. The wording of the *Chronicle* implies that the same force
returned in mid-1006, and Swegen may have accompanied it and remained
until the payment of tribute in 1007; the twelfth-century chronicler Henry
of Huntingdon associates him with the ravaging at this time.[50]

This brings us to the raiders of 1009–12. In the late eleventh century,
Osbern, the precentor of Christ Church Canterbury, wrote both a life of
St Ælfheah, the archbishop killed by the Scandinavians in 1012, and an
account of the removal of his relics from London to Canterbury in 1023.
As proof of his sanctity, the latter describes various miracles after the saint's
death, one of which concerns the Danish leaders who were among his
murderers. They put to sea in an attempt to escape the martyr's wrath, and
were shipwrecked, with 160 of their vessels sinking and another sixty-five
being driven to distant and unknown regions, where their occupants were
slaughtered.[51] Now Osbern's account of the circumstances surrounding
Ælfheah's martyrdom contains some spectacular blunders,[52] and if this
account of a shipwreck stood alone it would be worthless, because saints'
lives frequently contain miracles about distress at sea. Nevertheless,
according to a version of the *Annales Cambriæ*, Swegen the father of Cnut
was shipwrecked in a year which was almost certainly 1012.[53] The annal

[47] Weibull, *Nordisk historia*, i. 306–07.
[48] See the Select Bibliography under Stefnir, and Fidjestøl, *Det norrøne Fyrstediktet*, p.24.
[49] On the date I follow Einarsdóttir, *Studier*, p.118.
[50] Henry, *Historia*, vi. 3, pp.342–43.
[51] Osbern, *Translatio Sancti Ælfegi*, ed. Rumble, pp.296–99.
[52] See *FNC*, i. 658–62.
[53] As note xxx above; printed *Annales Cambriæ*, ed. Williams ab Ithel, p.22; noted by Steenstrup,
     Normannerne, iii. 265.

concerned cannot in its present form be strictly contemporary, for nobody would have identified Swegen by referring to him as Cnut's father at this date, but this is not an adequate reason for rejecting its information. There is a coincidence with Osbern's story, and it may be that Swegen was present in England when tribute was paid in 1012, and then set off for the Irish Sea (thus repeating the possible pattern of 994–95) only to be shipwrecked, perhaps off the Welsh coast. It is not inconceivable that his son Cnut was with him. Other evidence may support Swegen's connection with the army of 1009–12. Among those responsible for Ælfheah's death, if Osbern can be relied on, was Hakon, son of Earl Eric of Lade, and called *dux* by the Canterbury writer because he was later an earl under Cnut. With him may have been his father. Two verses in Thord Kolbeinsson's poem *Eiríksdrápa* describe Earl Eric as fighting west of London and at the battle of Ringmere. They were assumed by the Icelandic author of the mid-thirteenth-century *Knytlinga Saga*, the only source in which they appear, to refer to Cnut's conquest of 1015–16, but this is likely to be an error, for attacks were made on London in 1009 too, and Ringmere was certainly fought in 1010.[54] If Earl Eric was in England at this time, it may increase the likelihood that Swegen was also, for the two had collaborated in the defeat of Olaf Tryggvason, and Eric later fought for Cnut and was given the earldom of Northumbria.

What is evident, apart from the fact that Swegen on any reckoning spent much time in England between about 990 and his death in 1014, is that our knowledge of his activities is patchy, and that English sources may omit important matters. We owe much to the *Annales Cambriæ*, for example, and would gladly know more of whatever lay behind the Norman chronicler William of Jumièges's statement that shortly before his conquest of England Swegen visited Rouen and agreed with Duke Richard II that booty taken by the Danes was to be sold through the Normans, who would provide a refuge where wounded men could recuperate.[55] This may have been Swegen's response to the attempts by Æthelred to get Norman help reported by Henry of Huntingdon under 1009.[56] When the thought of conquering England first entered his mind is unknown. It is unfortunate that the confirmation of Æthelric of Bocking's will, with its reference to a

---

[54] For the possibility that the verse on Ringmere is not genuine, below, p.75; for the name Ringmere, JW, ii. 464–65.

[55] WJ, v. 7, ed. van Houts, ii. 16–19.

[56] Henry, *Historia*, vi. 5, pp.344–45; see Campbell, *Essays*, p.200.

plan to receive him in Essex perhaps as early as 991, gives no further details. The plan may have envisaged no more than provisioning the Danish fleet when it was already on the scene.[57]

If, alternatively, it originated before Swegen's arrival, it could have been concerned with some kind of political submission. But perhaps he was long content for the profitable plundering of England to continue indefinitely. His absence from Denmark must have been easy to justify. It had no national coinage and possibly no taxation system. England had both (see below), and Swegen forced it to disgorge large amounts of coin and precious metal, while also taking plunder and gaining a reputation as a successful commander which must have both drawn further contingents to his banners and strengthened his position in Scandinavia. Also, his experience of the frequently inept English resistance doubtless caused him to guess that it would eventually weaken to the point where he would be accepted as king. By 1013, when his arrival in the Danelaw implies a change of tactic consequent upon a change of purpose, this had happened. Why?

THE ENGLISH

At first glance, late Anglo-Saxon political history portrays a state riven by internal discord and highly vulnerable to external enemies: only fifty years after the Danish conquest it was subjugated again by the Normans. The notion of a country united under Alfred's West Saxon successors gained ground but slowly in the tenth century. Northumbria's last Scandinavian king, Eric Bloodaxe, was not expelled until 954, and only three years later Eadwig's brother Edgar formed it and Mercia into a separate kingdom, a division terminated by Eadwig's early death in 959. It was revived in the exceptional circumstances of late 1016, and perhaps also envisaged in 1035, during the succession dispute which followed Cnut's death, when Mercians were ranged against West Saxons.[58] But no blows were struck then, or in the similar crises of 1051 and 1052, when Edward the Confessor first secured the expulsion and then accepted the return of the powerful Godwin family. The idea of fighting against men of their own race was hateful to them, says the *Chronicle* C text under 1052, because there were few but Englishmen on each side. In 1065 the Northumbrians were in a less conciliatory mood

[57] As Mr E. Christiansen has suggested to me.
[58] *ASC* E says that in 1035 it was agreed that Emma and Harthacnut's housecarls (troops) were to hold all Wessex for him. Had he appeared immediately it seems likely that he would have taken Wessex and Harold Harefoot the midlands and north.

when they expelled their earl, Tostig Godwinsson, marched south with men from the Danelaw, and demanded Morcar, brother of Earl Edwin of Mercia, as his replacement. This was a shrewd move, which brought Edwin in on their side, and the demand was conceded. More remarkable, as it now seems, while awaiting the king's decision at Northampton they ravaged the surrounding countryside, and are said to have eventually returned home with hundreds of captives and much livestock. Early in 1066 they were reluctant to accept Harold Godwinsson as their new king, and he and Bishop Wulfstan II of Worcester had to visit York to conciliate them, where-upon the Northumbrians overcame their reluctance to be associated with southern softness[59] – an attitude not uncommon in the north even today. There is little doubt, as these events hint, that the loyalty of the Danelaw and Northumbria to southern kings could be suspect. Edgar thanked the Danes for their support and allowed them to live under such laws as they might choose, and it must be significant that Swegen landed in Lincolnshire when he made his bid for the kingship in 1013, and that in 1066 King Harald of Norway made for York, where he had hopes that the citizens would assist him in his endeavours.

Yet if narrative sources can imply that late Anglo-Saxon government was ineffective, other evidence indicates beyond reasonable doubt that it was not. The most important is Domesday Book, the great survey compiled for William the Conqueror in 1086. The administrative system that Domesday reveals is English. The country was divided into shires, themselves com-posed of units known as hundreds (or wapentakes in some areas). At regular shire and hundred meetings royal orders were implemented and local affairs, including the administration of justice, transacted. Most estates were assessed in numbers of hides (roughly 70,000 to 80,000 in all), units used in the allocation of public burdens which might be military, as in 1008, when every 300 hides[60] provided a ship and every eight a helmet and byrnie (mail-coat) for the navy, or financial, with each hide taxed at a particular rate. In the early twelfth century it was two shillings; a century earlier it must often have been considerably more.

To run this system the king had not only his ealdormen (later, earls) but also reeves, some of them in charge of shires, who looked after royal estates and aspects of the judicial system, and sometimes led armies. Indeed, it has been convincingly argued that there was an extensive network of minor

[59] William of Malmesbury, *Vita Wulfstani*, i. 16, ed. Darlington, p.22.
[60] *ASC* C and E, i. 138, say every 310 hides, but see *Writs*, pp.266–67.

officials, not all necessarily employed in the king's service full-time, but all involved in some way, and to their own financial advantage.[61] Such men operated in the Danelaw and Northumbria just as in Wessex. Domesday mentions the activities of the reeve of West Derby hundred, between Ribble and Mersey, and the riding divisions of Yorkshire and Lincolnshire may all have had reeves of their own.[62] However lukewarm the feelings of the citizens of York towards their southern overlord, his officers were there to be obeyed. Domesday shows that they provided Edward the Confessor with a revenue of £53 a year and the three works of the king – probably the maintenance of fortresses and bridges, and service in the army.[63]

Close examination of Domesday and associated documents suggests that late Anglo-Saxon government kept extensive written records.[64] Recent work on the silver coinage has revealed a complex system of which even Domesday contains little trace. After about 973 all the pennies struck at numerous mints throughout the country (including York) bore the king's name and portrait, and were produced from iron dies distributed by the government so that all looked alike. They also carried the names of mint and moneyer, which made those responsible for sub-standard specimens easier to trace. At intervals, initially of roughly six or seven years, but more frequently after 1035, a new design was issued. The previous type may then have become invalid, and coin users presumably had to replace it with the new one, a troublesome process, as the volume of some types ran into millions of coins. The main purpose of this elaborate system was almost certainly profit for the king. Thus it may be that the exchange of old pennies for new was at a rate favourable to king and moneyers – for example, for every six old coins handed in, only five new ones might be issued. Certainly the king made a profit out of supplying the new dies which a different type necessitated: the moneyers at Worcester each paid £1 for them.[65] This coinage system is discussed in more detail in Chapter 5. Recently described as 'surely the most sophisticated and complex western coinage of the early Middle Ages',[66] it looks like the product of an administrative system regularly able to ensure that its will was done.

Nor is this likely to have been a novel feature of the tenth and eleventh centuries, whose rulers were building on traditions of public authority

[61] Campbell, *The Anglo-Saxon State*, pp.201–25.
[62] Campbell, *The Anglo-Saxon State*, pp.210–11; DB, i. 269c–270b.
[63] DB, i. 298b.
[64] Harvey, 'Domesday Book and its predecessors'.
[65] DB, i. 172a.
[66] Stewart, 'Coinage and recoinage after Edgar's reform', p.481.

already old. Their most remarkable expression is the earthwork which an eighth-century king of Mercia constructed on his western frontier. Offa's Dyke, covering lines some 150 miles long, although at points perhaps relying on rivers rather than ramparts for defence, is a work which reveals a tremendous ability to organise labour: the Danish Danevirke is child's play compared with it. Yet if Mercian royal government was unable to fend off Viking invasion a century later – a warning of weaknesses to be discussed shortly – that of the West Saxons was. King Alfred's successes may well have owed a great deal to his predecessors, but in the construction of his network of defensive fortresses we see an ability to command similar to Offa's, and perpetuated by his son Edward the Elder and grandson Æthelstan, who conquered all England for the West Saxon dynasty. Of course, the capacity of societies with little technology but plentiful manpower to erect impressive structures can be widely illustrated. Stonehenge is an obvious example from this country, the remarkable road network and buildings of the Inca empire, which possessed neither writing nor the wheel, one from elsewhere.

Nevertheless, that we are often surprised by works such as Offa's Dyke and Alfred's fortress system indicates a poor understanding of the world which produced them. One factor to be remembered here is that the bounds of political action could be surprisingly wide. For example, one of the techniques of persuasion available to late Anglo-Saxon kings was that of harrying.[67] 1041 saw a pretty example.[68] The people of Worcestershire, displeased by royal taxation, rioted and killed two of the collectors, who had attempted to hide in a church tower. King Harthacnut, Cnut's son, thereupon despatched an army with instructions to burn Worcester itself, devastate the entire shire, and kill all the men. These orders were partly implemented. Worcester was burnt, and the shire ravaged, but few people killed: they had fled in all directions. After four days peace was restored, the royal anger appeased, and the ravagers returned home loaded with booty. That Harthacnut was a Dane is less relevant to this than one might think. Not only is the avenging army said to have included all the English earls, including Leofric of Mercia, within whose territory Worcestershire lay, but other English kings acted similarly. Edgar ravaged the Isle of Thanet in 969, and Æthelred the estates of the bishopric of Rochester in 986, while it was Earl Godwin's refusal to obey Edward the Confessor's order to attack Dover which precipitated the crisis of 1051. When Bishop Asser says that Alfred

[67] Pointed out by Campbell, *Essays*, p. 169.
[68] Described by JW, ii. 532–33.

severely chastised those who disobeyed his orders, he may be referring to action of a similar sort. It is a reminder that his achievements, and those of others, were partly based on the threat of large-scale violence.

Extensive as the network of government may have been, kings delegated much power to the handful of men holding the office of ealdorman (or earl), who often came from families rich in land. For example, the will of Wulfric Spott, brother of Ælfhelm, an ealdorman of Northumbria under Æthelred, has survived, and shows that he possessed estates in Staffordshire, Derbyshire, Shropshire, Leicestershire, Nottinghamshire, Warwickshire, Gloucestershire, Lincolnshire and Yorkshire.[69] How many held land on this kind of scale is unknown. Professor Sawyer has argued that many of the small pre-Conquest landowners who appear from Domesday Book to be independent were in fact tenants of lords not named, and thus that lordship may have been more extensive than has sometimes been realised.[70] However that may be, there certainly were great men, who wielded considerable political power. Probably neither kings nor anyone else could have imagined society without them. Carefully used, they were an instrument which enhanced and profited from royal authority. Earls often took a share of the fines levied in the courts, and gained from their role in the royal exploitation of towns; Edward the Confessor received £10 a year from Worcester, Earl Edwin of Mercia £8.[71] A strong ruler used not only a complex administrative system inherited from his predecessors, but also an ability to keep a significant number of his chief men moderately well rewarded, or charmed, or cowed. Otherwise their existence might be a source of danger, for they had followings of their own which were likely to support them against the king in a political crisis.

But this is not to say that the great were the only people who mattered politically; and they could not always rely on their followers. A major cause of Godwin's banishment in 1051 was almost certainly the unwillingness of his men to fight the king when the time came. The network of shires and hundreds brought royal government to all landowners of any substance, and must have acted as some kind of counter-weight to the influence of local lords and feelings of local separatism. It must also have provided opportunities for men to meet regularly to discuss politics, and such discussions, and the attitude of those in the shires in times of crisis, may often have centred

[69] S 1536; *Wills*, pp.46–51; translated *EHD*, pp.586–89.
[70] Sawyer, '1066–1086: A Tenurial Revolution?'; Fleming, *Kings and Lords in Conquest England*, is an important study of the late Anglo-Saxon aristocracy.
[71] DB, i. 172a.

on how far they thought the king and his officials were living up to what was expected of them.

Kings, for all their power, had duties to their people. They are known largely from the writings of churchmen. By the late tenth century the coronation service included a royal promise to provide peace for the nation, to forbid wrongdoing, and to guarantee just judgements, all matters referred to elsewhere in the service too. By the early eleventh century Archbishop Wulfstan of York was outlining the king's duty in his *Institutes of Polity*.[72] It included, not surprisingly, the protection of the Church and promotion of Christianity, and the suppression of evildoers. Wulfstan also repeatedly stressed the importance of justice. One of the eight virtues of a well-ruled kingdom was just judgement, one of the seven things befitting a righteous king the provision of just judgement for friend and stranger alike. The views of laymen are not likely to have differed significantly, at least on the importance of peace and justice. The former was desirable for obvious reasons, the latter scarcely less so. Much has been said above about what the king demanded of his people: justice was among the things they demanded of him. The shire and hundred meetings did not simply serve the royal will. They also enforced the law and judged local disputes, especially over land, the principal source of wealth. Surviving records show that land disputes were common, and mattered. Widespread dissatisfaction over the quality of justice might eventually be to the king's loss, although rulers may often have been able to manipulate the legal system to their advantage with relative impunity. Indeed, the fact that serious crime was often punished by confiscation of all the malefactor's possessions must have been a sore temptation, and doubtless tended to prejudice kings towards verdicts of guilty. Similarly, royal officials profited from their duties, and there was inevitably corruption. The shire and hundred meetings may have been able to exercise some kind of control over this, although a king who allowed himself and his servants too much leeway would have been difficult to oppose directly. Nevertheless, he was also building up a store of resentment which might be inconvenient in a crisis.

Crisis was most likely in certain circumstances. Failure to deal with external attack was one, strife within the royal family another. The accession of a child-king was also a dangerous time, especially if he, or indeed a mature monarch, was dominated by one group at the expense of others. Some of the forces from which a strong ruler forged powerful government

[72] See the Select Bibliography.

were then likely to contribute to disorder. Moreover, the frequent mention of the king in this context highlights the greatest single weakness of this political system, as of most others in the Middle Ages. For all its elaboration, it depended heavily on the capacity of one individual, and if he was incapable trouble of some sort was likely. This the subjects of King Æthelred II doubtless knew all too well.

THE CONQUEST OF 1016: 2

An attempt to explain what went wrong in Æthelred's reign must begin with the sources. The *Anglo-Saxon Chronicle* is the most important, but needs to be treated with care. Its author dispensed with the laconic and often uninformative methods adopted by many medieval annalists, writing at length and in a distinctive style not unlike that of homilists of the period, and with the same purpose – heightened effect. Among the devices he used were puns. A play on words involving the verb *feran* (to go) and the noun *fyrd* (army) occurs several times. Thus, when in 1010 the English should have been engaging the enemy, *ferde seo fyrde ham* – the army went home.[73] It is evident from this and other comments, several describing treachery, that he often thought little of the English resistance, and on at least one occasion he did it injustice, saying under 1001 that an immense levy from Somerset and Devon met the raiders at Pinhoe but fled immediately battle was joined, whereas an independent entry in the A text reports that the English fought with such forces as they could gather, which gives a rather different impression. It seems that the main annalist's fondness for tales of woe in this case led him to distort the facts, or that he was misled by sources which did so. All the same, characterising him is not easy. He records stout English resistance too, and while his work was undoubtedly intended to be dramatic, it is difficult to discern any purpose beyond that. This should increase faith in its general reliability. Unfortunately, it deals mainly with the fighting, and says little about internal politics or the king, although what it does say is very interesting. Also useful are land charters, law codes, some the work of Archbishop Wulfstan of York, and Wulfstan's other writings, together with those of the scholar Ælfric, monk of Cerne in Dorset and from 1005 abbot of Eynsham. The final picture, as so often, is incomplete. Æthelred can be known little better than Cnut or most other early medieval kings. He was

---

[73] For the chronicler's style, see Clark, 'The narrative mode of *The Anglo-Saxon Chronicle* before the Conquest', pp.224–30.

important for all that, because his reign does much to reveal the strengths and weaknesses of the late Anglo-Saxon state, and because the political situation which Cnut inherited late in 1016 was partly his creation.

Some features of the *Chronicle* account of the fighting need emphasis. One is that there seem to have been many years when there was little or no nationally-coordinated resistance. At Maldon in 991 it was the local Essex levy which was defeated, as were the northerners in 993, the men of Kent in 999, those of Hampshire and of Devon and Somerset in 1001, of Wiltshire and Hampshire in 1003, of East Anglia in 1004, and of East Anglia and Cambridgeshire in 1010. Similarly, the treaty which Æthelred made with Olaf Tryggvason shows that different localities were also sometimes allowed to buy peace for themselves separately. All this would be understandable, of course, if these local forces had merely been dealing with minor coastal raiding, and one cannot always be sure that their enemies were very numerous. The deaths of only eighty-one men of Hampshire at the battle of *Æthelingadene* in 1001 does not suggest fighting on a large scale, and it is noticeable that the same raiders shortly afterwards attacked Exeter and were repulsed. But elsewhere this argument will not work. The host led by Swegen and Olaf in 994 comprised ninety-four ships, was strong enough to assault London, and threatened to attack Canterbury.[74] In 1003 and 1004 Swegen penetrated inland and captured towns, as did the raiders of 1006 and of 1009–12. Whatever their size, these armies were being more than a minor nuisance, and in any case the frequent defeats of local levies imply that they were often outnumbered or outclassed or both. Why did they not receive greater support? Why could not Æthelred have brought the enemy to battle with a national army at his back, as Alfred did many times, as Æthelstan did to gain his great victory at *Brunanburh* in 937, as King Harold Godwinsson did in 1066, and, most significantly of all, as Æthelred's own son did in 1016?

Obviously, there were alternatives. One was paying the enemy to go away, an expedient which Æthelred adopted on several occasions, and which was also used by Alfred and envisaged by Eadred. On occasion it worked. The payment made to Olaf Tryggvason in 994, for example, seems to have been part of a deal in which Olaf agreed to be confirmed (with Æthelred standing sponsor), and promised that he would never return to England. This may have been a conscious effort on Æthelred's part to divide

---

[74] This is known from S 882; translated *EHD*, pp. 569–70.

Olaf from Swegen,[75] with the intention that he should then conquer Norway (as he did) and be a thorn in Swegen's flesh (as he was, until Swegen defeated and killed him). Similarly, the payment of 1007 gained two years' respite, but then the enemy returned apparently in greater numbers. This is not surprising, and is unlikely to have surprised contemporaries, or in 1008 Æthelred would hardly have issued orders for the raising of a fleet. Of course, some may in the early years have argued plausibly that the payments would rid England of the raiders for good, for it need not have been evident in the 990s that the problem would intensify as it did. Nevertheless, the policy of buying off the enemy was a long-term failure, and as time passed was surely increasingly viewed as such.

Yet Æthelred was not always militarily inactive, reluctant to see himself in a military light, or unwilling to make military preparations. Nor, as the successful defence of some towns, especially London, demonstrates, did such preparations invariably fail. When the raiders left England for Normandy in 1000 the king led an army which harried Cumberland, and his fleet operated in the Irish Sea. At some time he may also have sent an expedition against Normandy which was defeated,[76] and his *Helmet* coin type, perhaps current from 1003 to 1009, depicts him in armour; according to the surviving verse on him by the Icelandic poet Gunnlaug Serpent's Tongue, the army feared Æthelred no less than God, and Professor Brooks has shown that he increased the military burdens on his people by requiring more of his soldiers to wear helmets and byrnies.[77]

As the will of Archbishop Ælfric of Canterbury (d. 1005) bequeaths to the king a ship together with sixty helmets and byrnies this must have happened at a fairly early date.[78] Certainly, the fleet raised in 1009 was not the first. The *Chronicle* refers to fleets in 992, 999 and 1000: that of 992 was defeated, those of 999 and 1009 never saw action. Æthelred did organise resistance, then, but apparently only sporadically, and with little discernible effect. Why?

Firstly, it should be remembered that raising well-equipped military forces may sometimes have been no less expensive than paying the enemy to go away. In 992 the navy was seemingly formed from vessels already in

---

[75] As argued by Andersson, 'The Viking Policy of Ethelred the Unready'. See also Sawyer, 'Ethelred II, Olaf Tryggvason, and the conversion of Norway'.
[76] WJ, v. 4, ed. van Houts, ii. 10–15; see Campbell, *Essays*, pp. 199–200.
[77] Brooks, 'Arms, Status and Warfare in Late-Saxon England'; Brooks, 'Weapons and Armour', pp. 216–17.
[78] S 1488; *Wills*, pp. 52–55; translated *EHD*, pp. 589–90.

existence, but in 1008 the *Chronicle* says that they were built. This was doubtless a windfall for shipwrights, if expensive for others. The cost of warships is
unknown, but something can be done with the byrnies which every eight
hides were ordered to provide in the same year. A national assessment of
about 70,000 to 80,000 hides should have produced something like 9,000 to
10,000 of them, and if this figure seems high, it might be remembered that
Thietmar of Merseburg heard that there were 24,000 byrnies in London in
1016.[79] The cost of such an item in eleventh-century England is not known,
but in Normandy in the 1040s it could be £7.[80] Thus, the byrnies of 1008
might alone have been worth over £50,000 – a greater sum than any hitherto paid to the raiders. Archbishop Ælfric's bequest to the king of a ship and
sixty helmets and byrnies was a gift indeed, and when he gave a ship each to
the men of Kent and Wiltshire he was perhaps being no less generous than in
forgiving the people of Middlesex and Surrey the money which he had paid
on their behalf, possibly as tribute. Of course, these statistics are crude, but
they strongly suggest a world in which war may often have seemed prohibi-
tively expensive, especially once it came to be realised that Æthelred's
military operations tended to be unsuccessful.

   The decision to fight or pay cannot therefore have been easy, not least
because the Mercians and Northumbrians, who apparently saw considerably less of the enemy than the south and east,[81] may often have been
disinclined to do either. Even in Wessex and East Anglia the ravaged territories were not always particularly extensive at any one time, and much of the
population may have reckoned that they had a good chance of escaping.
Also, the raids may frequently, and especially at first, have appeared to pose
little threat to Æthelred's position as king, and so his circumstances were
arguably not comparable with those faced by Alfred, Edmund Ironside and
Harold Godwinsson. Discretion may have tended to appear the better part
of valour, and certainly better than defeat and its resultant loss of prestige.
Ultimately, of course, Æthelred's inactivity did cost him his throne, but the
point at which this could reasonably have been foreseen may have been
little clearer to contemporaries than it is today. Furthermore, the collection
of the payments may itself have provided some with opportunities for profit
which they were loth to abandon, and which prejudiced them against
fighting. Unfortunately, little is known about how Æthelred raised tributes:

---

[79] Thietmar, *Chronicon*, vii. 40, pp.446–47.
[80] *Receuil des actes*, ed. Fauroux, No. 113, p.275. I owe this reference to James Campbell.
[81] For what follows, see further Lawson, 'The collection of Danegeld and Heregeld in the reigns of
   Æthelred II and Cnut'.

the charter S 943 of 1006x11 shows that he sometimes sold land for the purpose, but as the national council (the *witan*) usually participated in the decision to pay, the main burden almost certainly fell on the people. In Cnut's reign those unable to meet their taxes were liable to forfeit their estates to whoever could provide the money due on them. If this was a practice inherited from his predecessor, it may be that those of Æthelred's followers well able to afford the levies could also acquire fairly cheaply the estates of those who were not.[82]

Of his ealdormen, a certain amount is known about Eadric of Mercia who according to the late eleventh-century Worcester monk Hemming was nicknamed Streona – the Acquisitor. The *Chronicle* says that in 1009 an opportunity to fall on the enemy was let slip on account of Eadric, 'as it always was'. This statement needs treating with care, as it was written after 1016, by an annalist rather free with allegations of treachery, who was aware of Eadric's defection to Cnut in 1015. If, nevertheless, it is accurate, and Eadric was known as someone unwilling to oppose the Scandinavians, one can speculate that it was because he profited from the raising of tribute by acquiring the lands of defaulters. This might throw light on his uncomplimentary nickname too, and on how, as the charter S 933 of 1014 reveals, 'the attacks and plunderings of the evil Danes' gave him possession of a Dorset estate of the church of Sherborne, which he eventually sold for a great price in gold and silver to a friend of the monks, who returned it to them. Correct or not, this hypothesis does at least hint at the complexities which could have been involved when Æthelred's counsellors sat down to decide whether to pay or fight, and offers one of a range of reasons why individual self-interest may have resulted in less fighting than might have been expected.

Explaining why the national forces which were raised did little good is not easy. They apparently brought the enemy to battle only in 992, when part of the fleet was defeated, and 1014, which saw Æthelred drive Cnut out of Lincolnshire after taking the Scandinavians unprepared. This seems to have been the only time that the English king led his men to victory: had the negotiations which preceded his return from exile the same year included a stipulation by those who complained about his previous behaviour (see below) that henceforth there should be more determination in dealing with the enemy? We do not know, for this is an area where the

[82] Lawson, 'The collection of Danegeld and Heregeld', 724–31; and below, pp.174–79.

chronicler is at his most unhelpful. In 999 he speaks of delay in getting the fleet into action, and suggests that delay occurred on other occasions, but without explaining why. Similarly, the English levies attempting to cope with the raiders of 1009–12 are criticised for never being in the right place, but again without further explanation. Moreover, the failure of national forces to intercept the enemy is especially remarkable when one remembers that local ones often had no problem. It is true that the early coastal attacks may have been difficult to counter because of uncertainty about where they would occur, and that interception at sea depended on the availability of reliable intelligence. In 992 it was the ships of London and East Anglia alone which met the Scandinavians and were defeated, and this implies that the fleet may have been dispersed around the coast. Yet this argument will not work with the later forces which struck deep inland. They were running a great risk of being intercepted and possibly destroyed, unless they knew what we are bound to suspect: that the English leadership was incompetent, and perhaps divided.

Æthelred gained his throne in difficult circumstances. The death of his father Edgar was followed by a dispute between the magnates over whether Æthelred, still a child, or his older half-brother Edward, should succeed. The latter prevailed, but on 18 March 978 was assassinated by his rival's followers at Corfe in Dorset. Later tradition accused Ælfthryth, Æthelred's mother, of plotting the murder. She may have done: it is surprising, and must have struck contemporaries as highly suspicious, that vengeance was not taken on the murderers. The most interesting aspect of the affair, however, is the very swift growth of the cult of St Edward, something which his assassins may have foreseen, if Archbishop Wulfstan is correct in saying that they burnt the corpse, presumably in an attempt to destroy remains which might become relics.[83] Even so, in 979 a body was moved from Wareham to the nunnery at Shaftesbury, and in 1001 transferred again from the churchyard to inside the abbey. It is extremely difficult to believe that this cult did not have political overtones. Edward's supporters are hardly likely to have welcomed his death. Making him into a saint must have been highly embarrassing for the opposition, and some of the satisfaction derived thereby is hinted at in a probably contemporary poem in the *Chronicle*. Those who would not bow to him in life, it says, now go down on their knees to his bones. Æthelred's own interest in the cult seems to have been considerable, and can be interpreted as an

---

[83] Wulfstan, *Sermo Lupi*, ed. Whitelock, pp. 56–57.

attempt to disarm the opposition, to dissociate himself from the murder, and to enhance the prestige of kingship.[84]

It is impossible to prove that the rivalries thus engendered endured, or that the king subsequently failed to impose himself on his major followers, favouring some individuals at the expense of others, and allowing his officials to get out of hand, all at the expense of national unity. Nevertheless, this, or something similar, is very likely to be what happened. In the 980s he had followers who took church lands, some of which he returned a decade later, blaming previous actions on bad influence during his youth.[85] Maybe he was a tool for any strong hand, including that of Eadric Streona, who became ealdorman of Mercia in 1007 after what Professor Keynes has described as a palace revolution.[86] In 1006 the *Chronicle* says that 'Wulfgeat was deprived of all his property, and Wulfheah and Ufegeat were blinded, and Ealdorman Ælfhelm was slain'. These men were related. Ælfhelm, ealdorman of Northumbria, was from a Mercian family, and Wulfheah and Ufegeat were probably his sons, while Wulfgeat may have been their associate. The fall of Ælfhelm's party coincided with the rise of Eadric's. Keynes has shown that he and his brothers, six of them according to John of Worcester, appear in the witness lists of royal charters for some time before 1006; but it was in 1007 that Eadric received his ealdormanry, and John says that it was Eadric who had Ælfhelm murdered and the king who blinded his sons. This certainly looks like 'the exposed tip of an iceberg of intrigue',[87] in which the king connived at the removal of Ælfhelm and his associates to please Eadric, who was thereafter a major influence on the reign.[88] He does not seem to have been one universally approved, for a man known as the Acquisitor, and who may have acquired the estates of tax defaulters, probably had enemies, and Keynes has suggested that the retirement from court of the king's uncle Ordulf and the prominent West Saxon

[84] Keynes, *Diplomas*, pp.163–74; Rollason, 'The cults of murdered royal saints in Anglo-Saxon England', pp.17–19; Ridyard, *The Royal Saints of Anglo-Saxon England*, pp.155–68; Rollason, *Saints and Relics in Anglo-Saxon England*, pp.142–44. I do not share Professor Keynes's belief that Æthelred and his mother had nothing to do with the crime and that contemporaries did not associate them with it. Considering the circumstances in which Edward was killed, the latter, in particular, seems extremely unlikely.

[85] Keynes, *Diplomas*, pp.176–93. Keynes thinks that Æthelred genuinely reformed in the 980s; but that he may have been more generous to some churchmen does not prove that he was less partisan, or, indeed, more virtuous. One ecclesiastic, Bishop Wulfgar of Ramsbury, had participated in the 'wrongdoings' (p.177). Cnut promises to rectify injustice committed through the intemperance of youth in the Letter of 1027.

[86] What follows is drawn entirely from Keynes's important work on the charter witness lists, *Diplomas*, pp.209–14.

[87] Keynes, *Diplomas*, p.213.

[88] Keynes, *Diplomas*, pp.213–14.

Æthelmær occurred because they could not countenance his growing influence.[89] We meet Æthelmær again in 1013, leading the West Saxon submission to Swegen.

Aristocratic rivalries might go a long way to explain the ineffectiveness of English armies, as one of the chronicler's few detailed descriptions of internal affairs indicates. In 1009 Æthelred assembled a fleet off Sandwich, and Eadric's brother Brihtric made an accusation to him against a nobleman of Sussex, Wulfnoth. The latter fled, taking twenty ships with him, and harried along the south coast. Brihtric pursued him with eighty vessels, which were driven ashore by a storm, and then burnt by Wulfnoth. Whether the original charge against him was justified is unknown, but the incident cost the English 100 ships, and the remainder returned to London shortly before the arrival of a fresh force of raiders; in the chronicler's words, the effort of the whole nation came to nothing. Similar divisions among the nobility, and the confusion into which it seems to have thrown the English leaders, might well explain why national armies were raised infrequently and achieved little, especially if there was dispute over the best policy to adopt, for reasons of the sort outlined above.

The fall of Wulfgeat in 1006 is also interesting from an other angle. John of Worcester says that Æthelred had esteemed him greatly, and that he was deprived of his property for unjust judgements and proud deeds, while charter evidence speaks of most serious crime and treachery, leading to the loss of all that he had unjustly acquired.[90] These references to injustice are of considerable value. Again, and again in his work, Archbishop Wulfstan condemns injustice and urges justice. There are several such comments in the sermon which he preached to a national council apparently in 1008, and which became the law codes V and VI Æthelred.[91] His *Institutes of Polity* also repeatedly refers to the need for justice, saying that of the reeves since Edgar's death more have been robbers than righteous men, and his *Sermo Lupi* (Sermon of the Wolf); probably written in 1014, complains of many injustices (*unrihta*) and shameful laws.[92] Ælfric wrote on much the same lines. His *Homily for the Sunday after Ascension Day*, which may date from

[89] Keynes, *Diplomas*, p.213.

[90] S 918 from 1008, and S 934 from 1015; JW, ii. 456–57; Keynes, *Diplomas*, pp.210–11. It is not certain that the Wulfgeat referred to in these charters is the same man, see Keynes, 'Crime and Punishment in the Reign of King Æthelred the Unready', p.80, n. 90.

[91] V Æthelred 1.1, 23–25; VI Æthelred 8, 28.1, 28.2, 40, 49, 50; *Gesetze*, i. 236, 242, 250, 254, 256, 258; V Æthelred is translated *EHD*, pp.442–46; see below, pp.60–63.

[92] Wulfstan, *The Institutes of Polity*, ed. Jost, p.81. This may have been written in Cnut's reign, but the comment on reeves clearly applies to Æthelred's too. Wulfstan, *Sermo Lupi*, ed. Whitelock, pp.54, 59.

soon after 1000, says that a king should protect his people against an attacking army and rule with love and justice, and on the advice of his
counsellors.[93] Ælfric seems to have been much influenced by the contemporary continental churchman Abbo of Fleury, who had spent two years
at Ramsey in the 980s, for he translated into English not only his *Passio* of
St Edmund of East Anglia, but also the treatise *De duodecim abusivis sæculi*,
written in seventh-century Ireland, and used by Abbo in his *Collectio
canonum*, addressed to the French monarchs Hugh Capet and Robert the
Pious. The ninth of the twelve abuses of the age was an unjust king. It is true
that Wulfstan and Ælfric were preachers, intent on demonstrating that disas-
ters are the wages of sin, and that their work may contain a degree of
exaggeration. Nevertheless, their statements suggest that injustice on a considerable scale was a feature of Æthelred's reign, and this is confirmed by a
passage of crucial importance in the *Anglo-Saxon Chronicle*.

In describing the negotiations for Æthelred's return from exile in 1014,
this says that the king was informed that no lord was dearer to them than
their native lord, if he would govern them more justly (*rihtlicor*) than before,
and that he then promised to remedy the things that they all hated. This is
not one of the chronicler's purple passages, but seems to be a sober report of
the negotiations,[94] and it matters a great deal. It does much to explain
Wulfstan's preoccupation with injustice, and coincides with what we are
told of Wulfgeat and can suspect of Eadric the Acquisitor. The great twelfth-
century historian William of Malmesbury says that Æthelred deprived his
people of their possessions without proper reason, and as the late Anglo-
Saxon legal system is known to have confiscated property for a wide range
of misdemeanours it would certainly have been open to abuse of this sort.
Moreover, this may be why Æthelred's charters sometimes take care to
describe the legitimacy of the way the King had acquired the land being
granted away.[95] How far he promoted injustice personally, or simply tolerated it excessively in his followers, is unknown. One of Wulfstan's legal texts
says that the king has stopped one kind of injustice and hopes that he will

---

[93] Ælfric, *Homilies*, ed. Pope, i. 380–81, lines 46–63. See also Pope's valuable comments (372–75),
including the judgement that Ælfric's remarks 'throughout this passage seem to be directed to the
needs of his time as he sees them'.

[94] F.E. Harmer, *Writs*, pp.516, 541–42, deduced from the chronicler's phraseology that he had, or knew
of, a writ sent from Normandy during the negotiations.

[95] *GR*, ii. 165, ed. Mynors *et al.*, ii. 276–77. I owe this reference to Kirby, *The Making of Early England*,
p.116, whose comments on Æthelred seem to me the most perceptive of relatively recent years. On
William of Malmesbury, see below, pp.72–73, and on the charters, Keynes, *Diplomas*, pp.95–98, and
Keynes, 'Crime and Punishment', pp.76–81.

do more.[96] It may have been a vain hope. Although a degree of corruption was inevitable, it seems in Æthelred's reign to have gone so far beyond what many of his subjects considered acceptable that it was their main preoccupation when they considered having him back. Nor was it the only way in which he was inadequate as a Christian ruler.

He also failed to protect his people: if anything is clear it is that, and it cannot have increased his popularity. The policy of buying off the raiders may often have seemed sensible, and it should not be assumed that he was always criticised for it, even by those who provided the money. Yet there must have been a point at which it had clearly failed as a general expedient, and some may always have considered it shameful.

The chronicler does not seem to have been among them, although he does say that in 1006 the king and his councillors thought offering tribute distasteful. Other writers are more forthright. Wulfstan's *Sermo Lupi* (Sermon of the Wolf) refers to English powerlessness against the enemy as shameful; Ælfric to the heathen army holding them to scorn and of days when English kings had been strong and theirs the only fleet around.[97] This was hardly a comparison to Æthelred's advantage, and must have occurred to many, who would doubtless have further agreed with Ælfric that a just war was one 'against the cruel seamen or against other nations who desire to destroy our homeland'.[98] Another of his works is a piece on the defence of the kingdom, known today (from its first word) as *Wyrdwriteras*, which has only survived in part. It begins by showing that some of the most successful rulers delegated their military responsibilities to effective generals, to lighten their burdens, avoid depriving their people of leadership through sudden death, and gain time for other business, and then moves to the theme that the kingdom's well-being depends on God. *Wyrdwriteras* may have been produced in response to attacks on Æthelred for not leading his troops personally, and although Ælfric seems (in the extant portion, at least) to defend this policy, there could be implied criticism of the king's choice of commanders who were often less successful than those in the examples

[96] This is the version of V Æthelred in Corpus Christi College Cambridge, MS 201, which also says that the king frequently commanded the stopping of injustice; *Gesetze*, i. 244–45.
[97] Wulfstan, *Sermo Lupi*, ed. Whitelock, p.60; Ælfric, *Homily on the Prayer of Moses* and *Life of St Swithin*, ed. Skeat, pp.294–95, 468–69; translated *EHD*, p.927. On the first of the Ælfric texts, apparently datable to c.995, see Godden, 'Apocalypse and Invasion', pp.133–37, who notes that Ælfric also says that the people of King David were destroyed by God because of the king's own sin, and wonders whether there is 'a suggestion that the Viking attacks relate to the specific sins of Ethelred or Edgar'.
[98] See Cross, 'The ethic of war in Old English', pp.272–73, whose translation I have used. Godden, 'Ælfric's Saints' Lives and the Problem of Miracles', 95, says that this is the most explicit statement about the just war in Old English.

cited.[99] It is worth remembering that one of Ælfric's patrons, and the founder of his abbeys of Cerne and Eynsham, was the nobleman Æthelmær who may have retired from court rather than face the growing influence of Eadric Streona.

It is hardly surprising that there are signs of disenchantment with Æthelred's government. Open opposition is strongly implied by his offer in 1014 to forgive all the things that had been said against him. There is also his nickname *Unræd*, a sarcastic play on his name, which thus became 'Noble Counsel, No Counsel'. Although it only appears in the sources in around 1200 this may not be significant, for the chronicler does not refer to Eadric as Streona or to Edmund as Ironside, but there is eleventh-century evidence for both names. That one of Æthelred's chief ministers received an uncomplimentary name increases the likelihood that the king did so too, and there is possibly a reference to it in the chronicler's sarcastic or despairing comment on Edmund's reconciliation with Eadric in 1016, 'there was never worse *unræd* counselled than that'; J.C. Pope has commented that it is hard not to detect in Ælfric's statement in *Wyrdwriteras* that *we sceolon secan æt Gode sylfum urne ræd mid anrædum mode* (we should seek our counsel from God himself with unanimous spirit) 'an allusion to the *unræd* so unhappily associated with Ethelred'.[100] A passage in Wulfstan's *Institutes of Polity* is also relevant: 'Through an unwise king, the people will be made wretched not once but very often, because of his misdirection (*misræd*). Through the king's wisdom the people will become prosperous and successful and victorious.'[101] Ælfric wrote similarly.[102] It is almost impossible to believe that they did not have contemporary events in mind, and as Æthelred was certainly not victorious, the implication is that he was unwise. Some of his opponents evidently went beyond words. He also offered in 1014 to forgive

---

[99] Ælfric, *Homilies*, ed. Pope, ii. 725–33. Pope suggests that the tract belongs to the period of Ælfric's abbacy, that is 1005 or later; see also Keynes, *Diplomas*, pp.206–08. In 1016 the *Chronicle* records that English levies gathered by Edmund dispersed because the king and the citizens of London were not with them; this seems less likely to reflect a desire for Æthelred's leadership than the need for an excuse to go home.

[100] Ælfric, *Homilies*, ed. Pope, ii. 727.

[101] Wulfstan, *The Institutes of Polity*, ed. Jost, p.47.

[102] *The Homilies of the Anglo-Saxon Church*, ed. Thorpe, ii. 318–20. Ann Williams' suggestion (*Æthelred the Unready*, p.124, n.74) that such passages in the works of Ælfric and Wulfstan 'are simply general aphorisms on the theme of kingship' is difficult to credit given the way in which many of the comments seem clearly to refer to contemporary conditions; see now Clayton, 'Of Mice and Men', 17–22, who argues convincingly that in a homily for the feast of a Confessor written in around 1007 Ælfric sought to 'censure obliquely some of his more powerful contemporaries'; Godden, 'Apocalypse and Invasion', stresses the extent to which both Ælfric and Wulfstan were concerned with contemporary ills, and suggests that the latter's *Sermo Lupi* was (p.156) 'an intensely topical text, repeatedly revised in the space of a year or two, in response to the developing political situation'.

all the things that had been done against him, providing that the English returned to their allegiance without treachery. The existence of treachery finds confirmation elsewhere. Whatever the nature of the plan to receive Swegen in Essex in around 991 it was certainly treacherous; suspicion of treachery led Æthelred to order the killing of Danes in England in 1002, and in his sermon of 1008 Wulfstan warns that plotting against the king is punishable by death. In 1016 Æthelred left his levies because he was informed that betrayal was afoot. A king not universally popular, who owed his throne to assassination, must have been sensitive on such an issue, and maybe sometimes nervous of joining large assemblies of armed men.

Mention of treachery is a reminder that the fighting saw no clear division between Danes and English. The Anglo-Scandinavian background outlined in the Introduction fuses here with Æthelred's inability to keep the loyalty of all his subjects and use of Scandinavians as soldiers. Among them were Pallig, who joined the enemy in 1001, and, later in the reign, Olaf Haraldsson and Thorkell. Conversely, some influential Englishmen fought for the Danes. Eadric was one, along with a considerable number of his Mercian subordinates, but there were doubtless others. Cnut at an early stage took as his consort Ælfgifu of Northampton, daughter of the ealdorman Ælfhelm murdered in 1006. This is very likely to signify an alliance with her family, and nothing illustrates better how discontent among the English provided political opportunities for the Scandinavians. It is significant, too, that one of Cnut's major English supporters after 1016 was Godwin, who may have been a son of the Wulfnoth accused by Eadric's brother in 1009. [103]

Æthelred must have had his friends, few kings had not; but as a king he was a failure. Apart from the alienation of some of his followers, the loyalty of many others was so tried that by 1013 they submitted to Swegen with little resistance. By then southern and eastern England had been extensively ravaged, and £137,000 paid in attempts to rid it of the enemy. Yet, well organised and commanded as that enemy may have been, they were not invincible, as Edmund Ironside showed in 1016. That his own son could achieve a measure of success so late in the day is the greatest single indication of Æthelred's incapacity, and hints at the resilience of English government. Edmund was able to raise effective armies, and as late as 1012 Æthelred had levied a tribute of £48,000 and instituted a new tax, the *heregeld* (army-payment), to reward Scandinavians in his service. His coinage

[103] *FNC*, i. 701–11; Raraty, 'Earl Godwine of Wessex', pp.4–6.

system seems to have been in good order for most of the reign,[104] although its development and exploitation for the king's benefit may have been another cause of popular unrest. Æthelred's henchmen were perhaps able to stifle or ignore discontent for much of the time, but even so it had its price. The resultant political disunity, probably exacerbated by quarrels over the best methods to adopt against the Scandinavians, and coupled with the king's apparent inability to provide the necessary leadership, made it impossible to assemble successful armies. Such forces are seldom the product of the ill-feeling which can be generated by a powerful but badly led and manned administrative system. It was the thoroughness of English government which to some extent caused its defeat. At no period are the strengths and weaknesses of the late Anglo-Saxon state as obvious as in the reign of Æthelred *Unræd*. Late in 1016, Cnut succeeded to a kingdom not only politically divided, and therefore containing important men eager to serve him, but exhausted and ready for peace. Yet it was also wealthy and powerfully organised, a strong weapon given a strong hand. This was the fruit of victory.

[104]Dolley, 'An Introduction to the Coinage of Æthelred II'.

2

THE SOURCES

The reign of Cnut has tended to attract relatively little attention from historians largely because of the scarcity of the sources. Yet, few as they are, it is necessary to establish what they can and cannot be expected to reveal. This chapter discusses all the important written material, including the *Anglo-Saxon Chronicle*, the *Encomium Emmae*, the laws, the charters, the poetry of the Icelandic skalds, and (more briefly) the difficult but occasionally very useful works produced within a century and a half of Cnut's death. The coinage evidence is no less significant, but its nature will become sufficiently apparent when we examine what it has to offer in Chapter 5.[1]

THE *Anglo-Saxon Chronicle*

The sets of annals known collectively as the *Anglo-Saxon Chronicle* are major texts for pre-Conquest history, and it is particularly unfortunate that their entries for Cnut's reign are both uninformative and (after 1023) increasingly sparse. All the same, three of them provide the best available narrative and chronology, and their reliability must be examined in some detail. The one usually denoted C (B ends in 977 and A is of little use for this period) survives in British Library (BL) MS Cotton Tiberius B i, which contains Alfred's translation of Orosius's *Histories against the Pagans*, and three further items also in Old English: a metrical calendar, some gnomic verses, and the *Chronicle*. The Orosius is in four hands dated by N.R. Ker to the early eleventh century. A fifth, mid-century, scribe wrote the calendar, the verses and the *Chronicle* entries down to 490, and a sixth the annals probably to the end of 1048; those to 1044 seem to have been written at one time, while

[1] Below, pp.179–84.

changes in the appearance of the script suggest that subsequent entries were made year by year. In other words, C is a contemporary chronicle in the 1040s, when, as comments on local monastic affairs show, it was fairly clearly in Abingdon Abbey. D, which now forms part of British Library (BL) MS Cotton Tiberius B iv, and is usually thought to have been produced in either Worcester or York, may date from little if at all before 1100. The annals for Cnut's reign are contained in quire 9 (1016–51), and Ker thought that the scribe responsible for this also wrote the entries for 1071–79. If so, it would seem to be a replacement, dating from no earlier than the 1070s or 1080s, for material which had been lost. E is more straightforward: Bodleian MS Laud 636 ends in 1154, but was written by a single hand to 1131, in Peterborough, as local material indicates.[2]

The history of these texts is considerably more complex than this bare recital might imply. Theoretically, for example, none of the entries in E need be older than the twelfth century. However, sets of annals were over the years repeatedly copied, added to, and recopied, and E was demonstrably derived from earlier manuscripts which no longer survive, but whose entries were mostly unchanged by later scribes. One, as Charles Plummer showed, was probably in the abbey of St Augustine's Canterbury in the mid-eleventh century, and it fathered not only the immediate precursor of E, but also F, a Canterbury version of the *Chronicle* in English and Latin which ends damaged in 1058. Furthermore, this St Augustine's manuscript was also connected in some way with C and D, and C and D with each other, for the eleventh-century entries contain much material common to two of the texts, or all three. Plummer argued that D was partly derived from a predecessor of the St Augustine's chronicle, and that this was itself descended from an Abingdon manuscript which also lies behind C.[3]

He thus explained the presence in E of various entries on abbots of Abingdon which are also in C. Possibly an Abingdon version of the *Chronicle* was taken to Canterbury in 1044 when its abbot, Siward, replaced Archbishop Eadsige, who had resigned because of ill health,[4] or was subsequently sent there at Siward's request. Siward himself fell ill, and returned to Abingdon in 1048; and it may be significant that at about this point close

[2] Ker, *Catalogue of Manuscripts containing Anglo-Saxon*, pp.251–55, 424–26. Dumville, 'Some aspects of annalistic writing', 34, suggests limits of 1080x1130 for the compilation of D. Thorpe's edition of the *Chronicle* is the only one to give all the versions in parallel columns; for a translation see Appendix 1.
[3] *ASC*, ii. xlviii–lii, lx–lxvi. Dumville, 'Some aspects', 49, thinks that the compiler of F worked in the archives of Christ Church Canterbury between about 1090 and about 1130.
[4] A point made by Dumville, 'Some aspects', 28–29.

resemblances between C and E cease. Of course, if this is correct the chronicle presumably reached St Augustine's by way of the Cathedral, Christ
Church. It contained an account of Æthelred's reign and entries on Cnut
which are common to all three texts. The latter extended at least as far as
1022, and maybe to 1028, when all record Cnut's journey to Norway in
similar words, or even to 1030 or 1034, which give the deaths of King Olaf
of Norway and Bishop Æthelric of Dorchester. But this was only the beginning of the process which resulted in the C, D and E of today.

The second scribe of C wrote initially down to 1044, the year of Siward's
appointment to Canterbury, and what he wrote differed slightly from the
chronicle taken there. Either the C scribe or one of his predecessors added
to the 1017 entry that the Ætheling Eadwig was afterwards killed, and
(perhaps inadvertently) omitted from it the expulsion of Eadwig king of
the ceorls, which appears under 1020; the information in 1030 that Olaf
'was afterwards holy' (i.e. regarded as a saint) must also have been included
at a fairly late stage in C's composition. Moreover, under 1020 the death of
Archbishop Lyfing is given first, although it occurred on 12 June, after
Cnut's return to England and the Easter meeting at Cirencester. E places it
after these events, and so is here more likely to preserve the original form of
the annal. The dislocation in C may be because its scribe entered Lyfing's
death under 1020 from another record, and only after this turned to the
entry in the main Cnut chronicle, from which he then omitted it. Further
indications of the use of other material in C are the addition to the 1030
annal of the death of Earl Hakon, and the 1023 entry on Cnut's reconciliation with Thorkell; but maybe this stood in the common original and a
precursor of D and E left it out.

The E text, despite surviving in a manuscript eighty years younger than
that of C, may sometimes preserve better readings. Not only does it apparently have the oldest version of the entry for 1020 (see above), but under
1018 it has the death of an Abingdon abbot which is not in C.[5] Other material now in D and E was probably only added after the Abingdon chronicle
reached Canterbury. D is of considerable interest here. It seems to err in
moving the death of Archbishop Lyfing to 1019 (C and E together speak
strongly for 1020), but D adds that his other name was Ælfstan and that he
was very firm in counsel whether in matters of church or state. Under 1021
D alone has the death of Bishop Ælfgar of Elmham, a former monk of

---

[5] Plummer, *ASC*, ii. lxv, judged this a mistake by E, but see Knowles *et al.*, *The Heads of Religious Houses*, p.24, and Dumville, 'Some aspects of annalistic writing', 27–28.

Christ Church Canterbury, and under 1022 it has together with E a fulsome entry on Archbishop Æthelnoth's journey to Rome. However, only D gives 7 October as the date of his consecration by the Pope, and in 1023 D alone gives a lengthy, detailed and enthusiastic account of the translation of the relics of St Ælfheah from London to Canterbury; it also adds material to E's entry on Æthelnoth's death in 1038. It looks as though there lies behind D a chronicle which received additions in Christ Church Canterbury, and at least one of those additions, on Æthelnoth's journey to Rome, was possibly present in a version which reached St Augustine's, where it was copied in a slightly modified form into the predecessor of E. St Augustine's may also have received the 1023 entry in D, but abbreviated it to the single sentence which E now contains. They did not have Ælfheah's relics, and no doubt lacked Christ Church's enthusiasm for them.[6]

Other material common to D and E may also have been added to the Cnut entries in Canterbury in the 1040s or 1050s, perhaps from existing annals. This includes the comment under 1028 that Cnut drove Olaf from Norway and took that country, the entry on his return to England in 1029, and that on Olaf's death at the hands of his countrymen in 1030. The 1031 annal on Cnut's visits to Rome and Scotland could have been inserted at this time too. E alone names the Scottish kings involved, but this information was present in its Canterbury precursor, as it appears in F. The latter also has E's 1025 entry on the battle of Holy River, its 1032 annal on the appearance of wildfire and death of Bishop Ælfsige of Winchester, and its 1033 material on the death of the bishop of Wells. Entries peculiar to D are those for 1026 on Archbishop Ælfric of York's visit to Rome, and 1033 on the death of Leofsige of Worcester and succession of Brihtheah. Possibly these entered an ancestor of D only when it reached York or Worcester. The same may be true of its addition to the 1018 entry that the meeting between Danes and English at Oxford agreed to observe Edgar's law, which was probably taken from chapter 13 of the Letter of 1019–20, now preserved only in a York manuscript, although there may have been a Worcester copy too. Another entry peculiar to D, the death of King Malcolm II of Scotland placed under 1034, was almost certainly inserted with other information on Scottish history at a late stage in its composition.[7]

---

[6] The date of the Christ Church insertions in D is unclear. All those common to E could be derived from it (although it is doubtful whether a St Augustine's chronicler would have composed the entry on Æthelnoth's journey to Rome in 1022), and may be post-Conquest. But that they concern only 1019–38, and that D is thereafter silent on Christ Church affairs, implies an earlier origin.

[7] See *ASC*, ii. lxxviii.

Although the *Chronicle* for Cnut's reign is evidently something of a patchwork, much of it may be from an early date. C, D and E all use a detailed account of the fighting under Æthelred apparently composed between 1016 and 1023. The entries from 1017 onwards are much briefer, lack the Æthelred chronicler's distinctive style, and are perhaps the work of different authors. Most of each one down to 1022 may in its oldest form be practically contemporary with the events described; C adds to the 1017 entry that the exiled ætheling Eadwig was afterwards killed, which could imply that the original was written before this happened; but it should be noted that the final sentence of the same annal, on Cnut's marriage to Emma before 1 August, comes after the notice of Eadric of Mercia's execution, which John of Worcester says happened at Christmas; if so, the sentence on the marriage looks like a relatively late addition. At the worst, the entries for 1017–22 were not compiled later than the 1040s, when C becomes a contemporary chronicle. The annals in C after 1022 also originated no later than this, and may be earlier, while those common to D and E, as we have seen, were possibly written in Canterbury under the Confessor. Much of this material may have been copied from older sets of annals, and some conceivably derived from the brief comments sometimes made against individual years in the Tables which told churchmen the date of Easter. It has already been suggested that comment in C under 1020, 1023 and 1030 was added from other sources, and E's entry on Archbishop Wulfstan's death in 1023 could have come from an Easter Table entry, although the additions made by D and E to 1022, and by D alone to 1023, seem too extensive to be from such a source. Finally, it must be stressed that while many of the entries are arguably early, this is not to say that all have been correctly dated. Mistakes were easily made: the C scribe, for example, originally omitted the year number for 1029 and had to squeeze it in. It would therefore be foolhardy to argue that those who entered the battle of Holy River under 1025 and Cnut's visits to Rome and Scotland under 1031 were necessarily correct.

THE *Encomium Emmae Reginae*

It was evidently during the reign of Harthacnut (1040–42) that a St Omer churchman wrote the untitled Latin work now known as the *Encomium Emmae*. He says that he worked at Emma's request to produce a record of the deeds which touched upon the honour of her and hers, and the oldest surviving manuscript, which is very close to the author's original, may be

CNUT

the copy she received: it contains a miniature which shows an ecclesiastic presenting a book to a woman while two figures, presumably her sons Harthacnut and Edward, look on.[8] The Encomiast was a competent Latinist, familiar with works by Lucan, Sallust, Virgil and possibly other classical authors, and well able to meet Emma's wishes. It may be that she commissioned the piece under the influence of the Norman history written for her brother Duke Richard II by Dudo of St Quentin,[9] while some have thought it political propaganda intended to influence events after Cnut's death.[10] However that may be, it is primarily a work of praise, and this is important in judging its reliability. Emma, committed to the cause of her son Harthacnut in the succession dispute of 1035–40 and exiled for a time to Flanders as a result, seemingly wished to forget her previous marriage to Æthelred. The Encomiast accordingly omits it, and begins with the history of Swegen Forkbeard and the Danish conquest of England. He is not badly informed here, perhaps because participants had accompanied Emma to Flanders, and his account generally complements and sometimes extends that of the *Anglo-Saxon Chronicle*. Nevertheless, it may at points be untrustworthy. The story of how Cnut's brother Harald became king of Denmark after Swegen's death and refused either to divide it or to help Cnut re-conquer England does not square with Thietmar of Merseburg's statement that he was in England in 1016: were there aspects of Cnut's relationship with Harald upon which the Encomiast, if he knew of them, did not wish to dwell? Similarly, it is hardly surprising that he speaks in glowing and not always accurate terms of Cnut's reign itself. The way in which royal messengers allegedly searched far and wide for a suitable bride ignores the likelihood that the union with Emma was motivated purely by political considerations, while the statement that they sent other sons to Normandy to be educated is a misleading reference to the exile of Emma's offspring by Æthelred. The insistence that Cnut intended Harthacnut to succeed to his entire kingdom may also be suspect, given the succession dispute which followed his death. On other aspects of the reign, which is treated very

[8] For a facsimile, Roesdahl *et al.*, *The Vikings in England*, p.156; Backhouse *et al.*, *The Golden Age of Anglo-Saxon Art*, p.144. For commentaries on the *Encomium*, see those of Alistair Campbell in *Encomium* and of Professor Keynes in his introduction to the 1998 reprint of Campbell's edition; also, Gransden, *Historical Writing in England c.550 to c.1307*, pp.56–60. Keynes suggests that it may be the work of a Flemish monk working in Emma's service in England.
[9] See *Encomium*, pp.xxii, xxxiv–v.
[10] For example, Körner, *The Battle of Hastings, England, and Europe*, pp.47–74; M.W. Campbell, 'Queen Emma and Ælfgifu of Northampton'; John, 'The *Encomium Emmae Reginae*: a riddle and a solution'; Keynes, 'Introduction to the 1998 Reprint', espec. pp.lxvi–lxxi, but see my review, *EHR*, cxiv (1999), 1283–84.

briefly, the *Encomium* is of little value. Cnut is said to have defended the weak, exalted justice and suppressed injustice, and been a great friend of churchmen and a generous benefactor of churches. Indeed, the Encomiast claims to have witnessed his lavish gifts to the churches of St Omer on his way to Rome.[11] He then deals with Cnut's death, the grief of his subjects, and the quarrel over the succession. Although his statements about Cnut's piety find ample confirmation elsewhere (see Chapter 4), it is difficult to avoid the impression that this account of Cnut is simply a stock description of a good Christian king, intended to reflect as much credit upon Emma as possible. Other churchmen, too, had ideas about the duties of Christian rulers, and may have been less convinced than the Encomiast that Cnut lived up to them.

CNUT'S LAWS

Law codes are a major source for the Anglo-Saxon period, and those which Archbishop Wulfstan of York wrote for Æthelred and Cnut are among the most extensive. Shot through with sermonising, piety, and concern for good government, they are ostensibly valuable sources on the law-giving activities of these kings, who appear in a very favourable light. Unfortunately, an examination of the circumstances in which they were produced gives a much less favourable impression.[12]

Churchmen had long admonished monarchs on their duties to God and people, and some kings had made church aims their own. The great Frankish king and emperor Charlemagne (d.814) convoked synods and gave their decisions the force of law by issuing them as royal capitularies. Churchmen also joined laymen in his national councils, which legislated on church reform as well as secular affairs, and were particularly concerned about the establishment of peace. The later Ottonian rulers of Germany behaved similarly. In 1004 Henry II ordered a halt in his campaign in Italy so that no Christian blood would be shed at Easter. In 1005 he held a synod at Dortmund which issued a decree on the keeping of fasts, and in 1006 he prohibited illegal marriages and the selling of Christians to the heathen. But in circumstances where rulers failed to provide the peace thought essential

---

[11] Gransden, *Historical Writing*, p.58, suggests that this is fictional.
[12] For what follows, see Lawson, 'Archbishop Wulfstan and the homiletic element in the Laws of Æthelred II and Cnut'. There is a detailed treatment of the legislation of this period in Wormald, *The Making of English Law*, espec. pp.330–66, 449–65.

to a Christian society, ecclesiastics sometimes took matters into their own hands. There developed in tenth-century France, where kings and territorial princes were often ineffective, a movement characterised by councils in which enthusiastic assemblies of laymen were harangued by bishops about oppression of churches, public disorder, and the necessity for peace. Peace became the popular cry. Without it, said Bishop Guy of Le Puy in 994, no one will see the Lord.

English churchmen, who must have been aware of these activities, were sometimes also familiar with the conditions which gave rise to them. Peace was somewhat lacking under Æthelred II, and when his ecclesiastics too sought rectification they acted in an English as well as a continental tradition. In England too, kings and laymen had been admonished about their lives and duties, and the church often sought royal authority for the measures it put forward. The *Constitutions* of Archbishop Oda of Canterbury (941–58), apparently intended for recitation, told King Edmund to obey his bishops, and insisted that he rule justly. They also lectured bishops, priests, clerics, monks and laymen. Occasionally such provisions seem to have been promoted as royal law. R.R. Darlington stressed that the ecclesiastical content of several tenth-century law codes suggests that they originated as the canons of synods. Æthelstan's first code, for example, and his Ordinance on Charities, both say that they were framed on the advice of Archbishop Wulfhelm of Canterbury and other bishops, and the text known as I Edmund appears from its prologue to be a set of decisions taken purely by the ecclesiastical wing of the *witan* (royal council); they may eventually have been issued as a royal decree, but that I Edmund in its surviving form is something other than this is implied by the fifth chapter, which exhorts the king to put churches in order. As Edmund is unlikely to have issued law in which he exhorted himself, these provisions may be no more than a programme laid before the full *witan*, and perhaps preached to it. National councils were an obvious forum in which churchmen could attempt to secure lay assent to their wishes, and this can seldom have seemed more desirable than in the years around 1000.

Æthelred's failure to protect his people and rule them justly, and the resultant dissatisfaction of Abbot Ælfric, Archbishop Wulfstan and presumably other ecclesiastics, were discussed in Chapter 1. Wulfstan, as primate of York, doubtless had more political influence than most, and clearly did his best to rectify social conditions worsened by enemy harrying, heavy taxation, the severe famine of 1005, and maladministration. His most relevant texts here are those on the national council held at Enham in Hampshire probably in 1008.[13] Two of them, known as V and VI Æthelred, are in Old English; a third (VI Æthelred Lat.) is in Latin, and contains important information on the procedure adopted at Enham which is absent from the others. The meeting is said to have assembled at Pentecost (16 May), at the instigation of the archbishops Ælfheah and Wulfstan. The bishops apparently began with a meeting of their own in which they established a pact of peace and concord. Then, having assembled the people, and by the king's order, they preached about believing in one God and spurning pagan superstitions. The rest of the Latin text, which deals with both religious and secular matters, including the preparation of a fleet, seems also to be what they preached, and it ends by stating that these were the statutes issued by King Æthelred which the nobles promised to observe. In fact, all Wulfstan's Enham material, including the Old English V and VI Æthelred, seems to be a record of his preaching, agreed by those present, and later publicised as the decrees of the meeting. This is also implied by VI Æthelred itself, where the opening chapter announces itself as 'the first ordinance of the bishops', but the introduction used thereafter is 'and the decision of the *witan* is'.

Moreover, these texts fit well into the English and European context described above. Carolingian influence on Wulfstan's thought seems to have been marked, and doubtless increased his desire for a more peaceful society, but his aims and methods were so common that identifying his precise source on particular matters is difficult. His prohibition of the sale of Christians to the heathen, for example, was drawn from an English source, although he may have known of Henry II's identical measure in Germany in 1006. Equally, while the procedure which produced the Enham texts may have been similar to those responsible for some of Æthelstan's codes and I Edmund, the promulgation of archiepiscopal admonitions as royal decrees is also reminiscent of those issued by Henry II after the synod of Dortmund in 1005. Furthermore, the interest shown by V and VI Æthelred in protecting the weak, suppressing disorder and improving the church was characteristic not only of Carolingian material, but of the contemporary continental peace movement too. When secular affairs are mentioned, such as the prohibition of plots against the king's life, they are always such as to promote public order.

This may in fact may have been the prime interest of most of those gathered at Enham, who seem to have been attending something very like a

[13] Fully discussed by Patrick Wormald in 'Æthelred the Lawmaker' and *The Making of English Law*, pp.331–35.

French peace meeting. Not long afterwards, Æthelred introduced his short-
lived *Agnus Dei* penny,[14] which replaced the royal portrait with a depiction
of the Lamb of God, and bore on its reverse a dove. Interest in the Lamb is
known to have been considerable at this period, when the third invocation
addressed to it in the Mass was changed from 'have mercy upon us' to 'give
us peace'. Hence, if the introduction of the *Agnus Dei* penny was decided at
Enham, or intended to reflect events there, it would look more like a continental peace meeting than ever; and in this context, it is very unlikely to be
coincidence that the name Enham apparently means 'the place where lambs
are bred'. The choice of the village as the meeting's location may have owed
much to the symbolic value of its name, and to the fact that there are quite
likely to have been lambs in the surrounding fields at the time, as there still
are in May. Maybe they provided Wulfstan, who used as his pseudonym the
name *Lupus*, the Wolf, with ready sources of illustration. That the Dove of
the Holy Spirit also appears on the penny is appropriate. It is found with
the *Agnus Dei* elsewhere, and also had an association with the Enham meeting held at Pentecost.

The foregoing both explains why Wulfstan's legal texts have such a
homiletic tone, and raises considerable doubts whether they were really the
means by which Æthelred's government implemented its decisions. The
fleet of 1008–09 is interesting here. Wulfstan simply says that warships ought
to be made ready every year after Easter. The vagueness of this is understandable if it was simply intended to encourage the raising of a fleet before
the meeting discussed it, and the archbishop later inserted with his own
hand into a version of this chapter the words 'if it is decided upon'. The
instructions eventually issued, as the *Anglo-Saxon Chronicle* says, were that
every 310 (probably rightly 300) hides were to produce a ship and every
eight hides a helmet and byrnie. So when Wulfstan's texts mention secular
affairs it should be remembered that they may not fully reflect the decisions
of the meeting which heard them preached. Nor are they likely to reveal
aspects of royal administration of which churchmen disapproved. If they
make Æthelred's activities appear considerably rosier to us than they did to
contemporaries, this at least does something to explain how the king in

---

[14] See Dolley and Talvio, 'The Twelfth of the Agnus Dei pennies of Æthelraed II'; Dolley and Talvio, 'A
Thirteenth *Agnus Dei* Penny of Æthelraed II'; Leimus, 'A fourteenth *Agnus Dei* penny of Æthelred
II'; Moesgaard and Tornbjerg, 'A Sixteenth *Agnus Dei* Penny of Æthelred II', and especially Dolley,
'The nummular brooch from Sulgrave'. Only sixteen specimens of the type are currently known.
Stewart, 'Coinage and recoinage after Edgar's reform', p.477, comments that 'there is much to be said
for the explanation that *Agnus Dei* was a type of limited issue for a special purpose'.

whose name these high-sounding utterances were issued could be charged by his subjects in 1014 with hateful practices and injustice.

The Enham material has been discussed at such length because it suggests much about contemporary conditions, and is essential to an understanding of the documents which Wulfstan wrote under Cnut, some of whose actions must have been disapproved. The irregularity of his semi-bigamous relationship with Ælfgifu of Northampton (see Chapter 4) and levy of £82,500 in 1018 did not fulfil the Christian king's duty to tax his people lightly and set them a good example, and in the early years of the reign many churchmen doubtless feared the worst. Indeed, Bethurum Loomis[15] argued that Wulfstan's disillusion with Æthelred, and perhaps with Cnut too, can be traced in his work, stressing that he modified his views on royal sanctity, seems not to have wished to rely on the king's ability to keep public order, and eventually stated that bishops should direct all affairs, both lay and ecclesiastical. Such attitudes she plausibly connected with the difficult circumstances in which he lived, and which required that his work should continue under Cnut, as it had under Æthelred.

Professor Whitelock showed that a set of provisions contained in Corpus Christi College Cambridge MS 201 was drawn up by Wulfstan after the meeting at Oxford in 1018.[16] It says that it is the counsel of the *witan* determined upon as soon as Cnut and his witan established peace and friendship between Danes and English, and that one of the first things the *witan* decided was that they would zealously observe Edgar's law and 'investigate further at leisure what was necessary for the nation, as best they could'. This implies that, as at Enham, churchmen laid a programme of reform (that of the Corpus manuscript) before the laymen, who maybe promised to observe it. A.G. Kennedy, its most recent editor, has noted that 'apart from chs 25–27 there is nothing that amounts to much more than injunctions that justice should be done and that every man should do his duty.'[17] The emphasis on Edgar's law is understandable, as Wulfstan evidently considered it the most favourable to the church and the most conducive to righteous rule. It could well be significant that Cnut is not himself said to have had any connection with the document, and it may reveal little of the real business of the Oxford meeting.

[15] Bethurum Loomis, '*Regnum* and *sacerdotium* in the early eleventh century'.
[16] Whitelock, 'Wulfstan and the Laws of Cnut', 433–44.
[17] Kennedy, p.67. Chapters 25–27 specify the fines payable by perpetrators of injustice.

The promised deliberations probably resulted in the texts known as I and
II Cnut, compiled by Wulfstan[18] and given royal approval one Christmas at
Winchester. I Cnut is solely concerned with religion, and owes much to the
1018 text (which had itself drawn heavily on VI Æthelred), to VIII Æthelred
(a Wulfstan document from 1014), to some of Edgar's provisions, and to various Wulfstan homilies. Largely concerned with the protection of church
and clergy, correct religious observance by ecclesiastics and laymen, and the
rendering of church dues, it ends with exhortation: possibly it too was
preached to king and court before it received the royal assent. II Cnut is
more complex. It contains religious admonition despite announcing itself
as a secular ordinance, and many chapters are about the promotion of
Christianity and the welfare of the church, while some of the secular material reflects the ecclesiastical desire for justice, public order and the
protection of the weak. It is also partly a conscious codification of existing
law. Chapter 12, for example, is a list of crimes in Wessex for which the fines
are payable to the king, while Chapter 18 states how often borough and
shire courts should meet. This is from one of Edgar's codes, and many other
provisions either owe something to earlier edicts or are drawn directly from
them. A number are not known to be from previous material, and Wulfstan
may have taken them from records of Cnut's administration. However, some
or all may equally be from earlier texts which have not survived.

Given the archbishop's motives, it is likely that II Cnut often presents a
somewhat optimistic view of events. Chapter 79, for example, gives undisputed possession of their land to all those who have defended it (i.e.
discharged public burdens upon it) before the shire court. This is pretty certainly a reference, among other things, to taxation, which is known[19] to have
resulted in the confiscation of defaulters' estates. Wulfstan was not interested
in recording this, presumably because as he thought that a king should levy
only light taxes he disapproved of the procedure. But he was concerned to
prevent the system becoming a greater burden than ever through malprac-
tice of the sort which the Worcester monk Hemming reports when he says
that estates were sometimes taken even when the money due had been paid
on time. Clearly, such aspects of Cnut's rule as Wulfstan found displeasing
are unlikely to be directly represented in his work, and some chapters are
accordingly very difficult to interpret. II Cnut 30, for example, is drawn

[18] Whitelock, 'Wulfstan and the Laws of Cnut', 444–52; Whitelock, 'Wulfstan's Authorship of Cnut's
Laws'.
[19] Below, pp. 174–79.

mainly from I Æthelred 1, but changes its death penalty to mutilation, which inflicts no injury on the soul. One can be confident that this is Wulfstan's own opinion, and the chapter, if one of Cnut's actual measures, might be an important indication of the archbishop's influence on him. Alternatively, the change may have been made by Wulfstan himself, in much the same way that in his different records of the Enham meeting he omitted from VI Æthelred death penalties contained in V Æthelred.

Assessing the extent of Cnut's association with these texts is therefore no simple matter. That the similar material produced under Æthelred may reflect badly, rather than well, upon his administration is a conclusion that could be applied to Cnut too. Certainly II Cnut 54.1, which forbids the keeping of a woman in addition to a wife, sits ill with the king's own relationship with Ælfgifu of Northampton, and suggests that he occasionally turned a deaf ear to Wulfstan's entreaties; but this does not necessarily mean that he lacked interest in the archbishop's work. On the contrary, law-giving was an important part of Christian kingship, and there are consequently good reasons for thinking that some aspects of Wulfstan's activities would have been welcome to him, for he was certainly concerned to appear the Christian king (see Chapter 4). If it is thus hardly surprising that he gave I and II Cnut his backing at a Christmas court at Winchester, it is also impossible to prove that his regime otherwise paid them much heed. Cnut's laws, which initially look such promising sources, are in reality something of a quicksand in which their compiler and his motives can never be forgotten.

THE LETTERS OF 1019–20 AND 1027

Letters apparently written on Cnut's behalf in 1019–20 and 1027 need consideration too. The first is preserved in the York Gospels, a contemporary manuscript annotated in Wulfstan's hand. After a greeting Cnut announces that he will be a gracious lord and will support the rights of the church and just secular law. Other chapters deal with church rights, just judgements and fair penalties, the adherence to Edgar's law promised at Oxford, non-interference with nuns, Sunday observance, and the keeping of fasts and festivals. There also seems to be a stress on the function of bishops which fits with Bethurum Loomis's view of Wulfstan's attitude to them late in his life. The secular part of the Letter deals with Cnut's visit to Denmark and the suppression of danger to the English. No doubt this was the real point of the missive, but it is rather vaguely expressed and makes one wonder whether the author really had much idea what had happened. The Amen at the end implies that it was in its extant form intended to be preached, as does its survival, along with three of Wulfstan's homiletic tracts, in a gospel book. It was perhaps originally an oral message from Cnut, committed to writing by an ecclesiastic for circulation to the shire courts, and then redrafted into its present state by Wulfstan. It may be significant, as Professor Keynes has suggested, that the chapters which bear most signs of his influence come at the end, and that their subject matter is closely related to that of the tracts entered before the Letter.[20] The Letter of 1027 survives in Latin (presumably translated from Anglo-Saxon) in John of Worcester's chronicle. Well informed on Cnut's doings, and a valuable source on his dealings with the Pope and the German emperor in Rome[21] and his Scandinavian wars, it is similar to Wulfstan's material in ordering intolerance of injustice and prompt payment of church dues, but cannot be his as he died in 1023. It could have been written by its bearer, given by John as Abbot Lyfing of Tavistock, who eventually became bishop of Worcester, for this would further explain how John had a copy. Lyfing was later a pluralist with no good reputation, but it is worth noting the *Chronicle* D text's description of him as 'the eloquent bishop': like Wulfstan, he may have been a notable preacher. Certainly the Letter of 1027 is a reminder that the sentiments found in the works of Wulfstan and Ælfric may have been shared by other churchmen whose writings (if they ever existed) have not survived. When the author of the *Life* of Edward the Confessor says that he trusted the cause of God to his bishops, and ordered secular judges to act fairly, so that honesty could have royal support and evil its just condemnation,[22] this may be an indication that someone did for Edward what Wulfstan had done for Æthelred and Cnut.

THE CHARTERS AND WRITS

Surviving charters and writs are important. The former, generally in Latin, are normally grants of land or privileges by kings and others, while writs, also in royal and private usage, were addressed to named individuals in the vernacular. In the eleventh century the type now denoted the writ-charter was often employed to inform shire courts of royal transfers of lands and privileges, and this may partly explain a decline in the numbers of surviving charters. By the reign of Edward the Confessor royal writs were

[20] Keynes, 'The Additions in Old English', pp.92–96. The letters are printed, *Gesetze*, i. 273–77.
[21] Upon which it receives a certain amount of confirmation from an Italian document, below, p.185.
[22] *The Life of King Edward*, ed. Barlow, pp.18–19.

authenticated by having a two-sided seal attached. Charters bore no authentication: even the crosses and so-called 'signatures' of the witnesses were written by the scribe responsible for the rest of the text. Kings sometimes instructed or allowed churchmen to draft and write these documents,[23] and Cnut apparently often did so. An examination of his surviving charters and writs suggests that many originated in major churches, which recorded grants not only to themselves but also to local laymen. The possibility that some were produced in a royal secretariat cannot be totally excluded, although the evidence for the existence of such an office under Cnut is far from compelling.[24]

This material has various uses. Obviously it records when and to whom the king was giving what, and so provides evidence on royal possessions and patronage, although some texts specify that the grantee purchased the item concerned, and this may sometimes have occurred even when not stated. Important land transactions probably often took place at meetings, and charter witness lists are valuable evidence on the king's major followers, and, if enough survive, the careers of bishops, abbots, ealdormen and thegns can to some extent be reconstructed from them. Charters also occasionally describe the circumstances and nature of the transaction concerned. It is their evidence, for example, which shows Æthelred alienating and restoring church estates, while Cnut's request in 1035 for daily prayers and masses for his soul in his donation (S 975) to the monastic community at Sherborne implies awareness of his approaching death. Forgeries can on occasion be no less informative: the texts probably fabricated in Canterbury in Cnut's reign hint strongly at the problems the church was facing.[25]

It is a pity that the utility of Cnut's charters is limited by their scarcity: only thirty-six have survived.[26] Even adding the eight writs,[27] his reign is the least well-represented of any between those of Æthelstan and Edward the Confessor,[28] and seven of the documents we have are fairly definitely later

---

[23] *Writs*, pp.39–40; Keynes, *The Diplomas of King Æthelred 'The Unready'*, pp.81–83; Chaplais, 'The Royal Anglo-Saxon "Chancery" of the Tenth Century Revisited', p.45.

[24] See Appendix III. One of Cnut's charters, S 950 from 1018, is translated in Appendix IV, and all are listed in Appendix IV.

[25] Below, pp.119–20.

[26] S 949–984; another two, S 1642 and 1643 (which mainly summarises S 981), exist incomplete in records from Christ Church Canterbury, while two more appear to have been lost – the foundation charter of Buckfast Abbey, Finberg, *'Supplement to "The Early Charters of Devon and Cornwall"'*, pp.29–30, and an alleged confirmation of the possessions of Ely, *Lib. El.* ii. 85, p.154.

[27] S 985–992; edited in *Writs*.

[28] Hill, *An Atlas of Anglo-Saxon England*, p.26. I exclude that of Edward the Martyr.

forgeries, while nearly half the rest are suspect.[29] Furthermore, only nine, a very low number, are to laymen, and the first to a donee with a Scandinavian name is from 1019. Hence, these documents offer little on the important and possibly substantial grants of lands to Scandinavians immediately after Cnut's accession, probably because the majority were never recorded in this form, and little more on his lay patronage at other times. A further limitation, true of charter material generally, is that they deal primarily with southern England, because most survived in the archives of the great southern churches.

Other warnings need sounding too. Witness lists, for example, although doubtless often accurate records of those present at a transaction, are not always what they seem. Some exhibit a suspicious symmetry: S 960, from 1023, is witnessed by six bishops (including Æthelnoth of Canterbury), six abbots, six earls and six *ministri*. The scribe of S 961, extant on its original single sheet of parchment, was equally concerned about the aesthetics of his product, and as an archbishop and four bishops are balanced by five abbots, and three earls by three priests, the list seems to have been curtailed so that the different orders match. Three other apparent originals are similar. S 963 has eight bishops (including Archbishop Æthelnoth), four earls, four abbots and eight *ministri*, and S 971 six bishops (including Æthelnoth), three earls, three abbots and twelve *ministri*, while the four earls and four *milites* in the first column of the list in S 977 are matched by eight abbots in the second. More important, witness lists can throw up slight but significant discrepancies. Bishop Æthelric of Selsey signs S 964 of 1032, although his predecessor Ælfmær appears in S 969 of 1033. Possibly one is a forgery, but slips could occur in charters evidently not fabrications in the normal sense.

Two of Cnut's grants to laymen, S 963 and 971, are apparent originals written in 1031[30] by the same scribe. He was careless, and in S 963 gave the indiction as the fourth when it was actually the fourteenth. This suggests that he accidentally omitted the x from xiv when copying an exemplar. More significant, Æthelnoth of Canterbury is given in the witness list as archbishop of York, 'I, Æthelnoth eminent archbishop of the church of York, have confirmed this royal gift.'[31]

[29] Likely forgeries are S 957–59, 965, 980–81, 989; suspect are S 951–54, 962, 966, 976, 982, 984–88, 990–92. Forgeries are usually identifiable because they include questionable features, such as dating errors or witnesses not alive at the time, or make grants which seem implausible, or concerning matters known to have later been disputed. Skilled fabricators were possibly capable of avoiding the more obvious errors; if so, the number of forged documents could well be greater than we realise.

[30] S 971 is not dated 1033, as given in *Anglo-Saxon Charters*, ed. Sawyer; this has been corrected in the *Electronic Sawyer*.

[31] Pointed out by Chaplais, 'The Authenticity of the Royal Anglo-Saxon Diplomas of Exeter', 24. Keynes, 'Cnut's earls', p.50, suggests that the witness lists of S 963 and 971 were both copied from that of a charter issued between about 1026 and 1030.

This too implies that the scribe was copying an exemplar, and accidentally jumped from Canterbury's name to York's subscription. Moreover, his exemplar for the witnesses was not very new, as they include Earl Hakon who died in 1030.[32] By the time he wrote S 971 he was better informed. Hakon has disappeared, although the three earls who do sign are the same and in the same order as in S 963, while the latter's eight bishops and four abbots are now six and three respectively. One can guess some of what happened. News arrived that Hakon was dead. This decreased the number of earls by one and so the abbots and bishops were also reduced to keep the proportions the same — six, three, three, as against eight, four, four. Perhaps to compensate, the number of *ministri* was increased. S 971 has twelve compared with the eight of S 963, but these numbers too show symmetry with the rest. Both lists are in this respect artificial, and the errors on Æthelnoth and Hakon suggest that they were copied from exemplars.[33] The anachronistic listing of Ælfmær of Selsey in S 969 (see above) may have arisen similarly. In other words, scribes did not always either know or care exactly who had been present at a grant, and relied on extant lists of great men, doubtless sometimes copied from earlier charters.

Land transactions did not always involve documents. When Cnut's henchman Tofi the Proud made a grant to Waltham, an oral declaration seems to have been followed by the donor girding his sword round the image on a crucifix.[34] The sword was evidently the token of gift in a ceremony perhaps similar to that in which King Edgar granted privileges to Glastonbury by placing on the altar an ivory horn, which he ordered to be cut in half and preserved so that it could be offered as testimony in future.[35] Although both events are known from twelfth-century sources, they are likely to reflect genuine practice. York Minster still preserves the Horn of Ulf, by which it claims to have received lands from a local magnate during the eleventh century, and tenure by horn was known even later.[36] But just as important as the token of gift was the witnessing of a transaction by good men and true. This was no doubt why land transfers were often arranged at meetings, to

---

[32] The entry in the *Chronicle* C text under 1030 might be a year out, but later Scandinavian sources favour 1029 for Hakon's death; *Encomium*, p.72.

[33] S 971's list cannot have been copied from S 963, because Ælfwig, bishop of London, appears in the former but not the latter, and the *ministri* are not identical.

[34] *De Inventione Sanctae Crucis* 12, ed. Stubbs, pp.11–12

[35] WM *Glaston.*, pp.122–23.

[36] See the articles in *Archaeologia*, iii (1775), 1–23. A mixture of old and new is represented by the twelfth-century document, preserved in the archives of Durham cathedral, which has tied to it the knife handle which served as the symbol of conveyance in the transaction; Major, 'Blyborough Charters', pp.203–05.

which they were announced.[37] Sometimes they were publicised at more
than one assembly. A mortgage by Bishop Eadnoth of Crediton from 1018
(S 1387) is said to have been declared to the borough meetings of Exeter,
Totnes, Lydford and Barnstaple. Moreover, a witness had obligations. In the
event of dispute he had to give testimony, whose value often seems to have
been related to his rank. In Æthelred's reign those who testified to the
authenticity of one disputed land transaction included the archbishop of
Canterbury, a bishop, an earl and the king's mother. It is worth noting that
the account of this case (S 1454) says nothing about the production of a
charter as evidence. Equally, when Bishop Æthelstan of Hereford was
involved in litigation over an estate in Cnut's time, it was ordered (S 1460)
that the boundaries be retraced, and this the bishop did together with the
man who had sold him the land and the witnesses. He had had a charter
drawn up, which presumably contained a boundary clause, but this seems to
have been less significant than the authority of the witnesses. Nevertheless,
it is clear that charters were often important in determining ownership,[38] as
the quantity in which they were produced implies, and that boundary
clauses could be taken very seriously. That this part of the text was usually in
the vernacular hints at its role as the most functional element, and care was
often taken over its drafting. In eleven of Cnut's grants the Latin introduction to the boundaries is followed not by the first set of bounds but by an
introduction in Anglo-Saxon.[39] This may mean that it was common for the
bounds to be noted on site, and then sent to wherever the charter was
drafted, and that in these instances the scribe copied in the Anglo-Saxon
heading. One of the originals from Cnut's reign (S 974) looks as though the
boundary clause was added later than the main text, for there is a distinct
gap between its last word and the beginning of the dating clause.

Furthermore, about forty wills, of laymen and women as well as ecclesiastics, have survived from the tenth and eleventh centuries, and with a range
of other texts suggest that the use of written records extended well beyond
simply the recording of estate boundaries. After a shire-meeting in
Herefordshire in Cnut's day had declared that lands belonged to Leofflæd
,her husband Thorkell the White rode to Hereford cathedral and had it
recorded in a gospel book.[40] Other documents imply the existence of lay

---

[37] See, for example, S 1216, 1473; Robertson, *Charters*, pp.106–07, 192–93.
[38] See, for example, S 1445, 1457; *SEHD*, pp.30–32; Robertson, *Charters*, pp.122–25.
[39] S 950, 960, 962–63, 967–68, 970 (has a phrase in Anglo-Saxon without a Latin introduction), 971–72,
    974, 977.
[40] S 1462; Robertson, *Charters*, pp.150–53.

archives, and this is hardly surprising in a world in which there may have been considerable literacy in Anglo-Saxon. When Brihtric's daughter was wooed by Godwin, the agreement made at Kingston in Cnut's presence was recorded in triplicate: one copy was deposited at Christ Church Canterbury, and the second at St Augustine's, but Brihtric himself kept the third.[41] Likewise, a lawsuit over a disputed estate in Worcestershire in Cnut's time ended with copies of the judgement destined for Worcester cathedral, Hereford cathedral and the holders of the land.[42]

Still, it is largely left to material from church archives to suggest the use of records in the vernacular on a considerable scale. Eleventh-century additions in English to blank leaves in the York Gospels include surveys of three of the archbishopric's estates, an inventory of church treasures at Sherburn-in-Elmet, and a list of sureties in a legal case involving one Ælfric,[43] while a Durham copy of Bede's *Lives* of St Cuthbert received an inventory of church possessions including a kettle and sixteen ornamented horns.[44] From the monastery of Ely we have farming memoranda which list and value livestock, seed, tools and other commodities supplied to Thorney Abbey, provide an inventory of animals on Ely estates, and catalogue the rent payable in eels (some 26,000) from various locations in the Fens. This item is a rarity, extant on three strips of parchment which miraculously escaped the destruction of monastic records in the sixteenth century.[45] Generally, as with the York and Durham texts mentioned above, such ephemera often only exist today when entered into formal manuscripts whose own chances of survival were relatively good. It can plausibly be taken to indicate the original existence and subsequent disappearance of large, and perhaps very large, quantities of similar material.

OTHER SOURCES

Yet not all such sources have been completely lost, for the historian of Cnut, so ill-served by contemporary records, is more fortunate in those produced after his death, and especially in the late-eleventh and twelfth centuries. From the immediate post-Conquest period come Domesday Book, the output of the hagiographers Goscelin and Osbern, and Hemming's

[41] S 1461; Robertson, *Charters*, pp.150–51.
[42] S 1460; Robertson, *Charters*, pp.162–65; similarly, S1391, 1402–03, 1470–71, 1473, 1476.
[43] See Keynes, 'The Additions in Old English'.
[44] Robertson, *Charters*, pp.250–51.
[45] Robertson, *Charters*, pp.252–57; see also Backhouse *et al.*, *The Golden Age of Anglo-Saxon Art*, No. 150.

valuable account of the estates of the bishopric of Worcester. Among numerous works from the flowering of historical writing in the twelfth century, those of John of Worcester, Henry of Huntingdon and William of Malmesbury stand out. The latter, in addition to recording the histories of Anglo-Saxon kings and churchmen, chronicled that of Glastonbury Abbey at the request of its monks, and several other monasteries, including Abingdon, Ely, Evesham, Peterborough and Ramsey, also had histories written at about this time. One can be confident that those responsible for such productions sometimes had access to valuable oral and written information which no longer survives. For example, the account of Cnut's visit to Sherborne in Goscelin's *Life* of St Wulfsige is very likely based on Sherborne tradition, as Goscelin, a monk of St Omer, came to England at the invitation of Bishop Hermann of Sherborne, probably spent time in the community there, and was writing at Hermann's request. Similarly, his work for St Augustine's Canterbury was assisted by a lengthy stay there, while his *Life* of St Edith of Wilton, written for the nuns whose testimony he cites as an authority, contains details which suggest that he was familiar with their house, its traditions, and possibly records in Anglo-Saxon.[46] Just as Goscelin claims to have listened to a monk who had known St Wulfsige of Sherborne (d.1002), Osbern of Canterbury says that as a boy he heard an account of the translation of the relics of St Ælfheah in 1023 from a monk who was involved in it.

Historians were as willing as hagiographers to use oral tradition. Henry of Huntingdon had in his youth heard very old men speak of the slaughter of Danes in England during the massacre of St Brice's Day in 1002,[47] but neither he, nor his contemporaries John and William of Malmesbury, relied solely on such evidence. All three researched and wrote their histories carefully. Henry had copies of the *Anglo-Saxon Chronicle* identifiable with our C and E,[48] and went to some trouble to reorder his material so that his account of early English history was clearer than that of his sources;[49] John helped his readers by prefacing his work with lists of bishops of English sees and genealogies of English royal dynasties. He compared different sources on the same event, indicates when they cannot be reconciled, supplies cross-references, and edits his material to increase its clarity. He had a copy of Cnut's

---

[46] On Goscelin, see *The Life of King Edward*, ed. Barlow, pp.133–49; Gransden, *Historical Writing*, pp.107–11; Ridyard, *The Royal Saints of Anglo-Saxon England*, pp.38–40.

[47] Henry, *Historia*, vi. 2, pp.340–41.

[48] *ASC*, ii. lv–lviii.

[49] Campbell, *Essays in Anglo-Saxon History*, pp.212–13; also on Henry, Partner, *Serious entertainments*, pp.11–50.

Letter of 1027, and his additions to the eleventh-century *Chronicle* have usually to be taken seriously.[50] For example, he names Eadric Streona's father and six brothers, and all but one can be found in the witness lists of Æthelred's charters.[51] William of Malmesbury was a formidable, widely-read and extensively-travelled scholar and researcher.[52] A careful user and comparer of sources, he often draws attention to discrepancies between them, and sometimes criticises their reliability, noting, for example, that Cædwalla of Wessex's confirmation of a Glastonbury grant was signed with a cross although he was a pagan at the time. His work on Glastonbury was assisted by research there, and in preparing his histories of English kings and bishops, the *Gesta Regum* and the *De Gesta Pontificum,* both of which appeared in 1125 and were revised subsequently, he seems to have visited most of the major cathedrals and abbeys in England, examining their archives and listening to their oral traditions. As noted above, those archives very probably contained documents, now lost, which were also available to others. The Ramsey chronicle of about 1170 for example, claims to have used charters, some written in English, while there is good reason to think that the historian of Ely Abbey did have access to records compiled in Anglo-Saxon in the late tenth century and translated into Latin in the early twelfth.[53] Some churches also long possessed objects given to them by Cnut, which occasionally bore inscriptions to that effect, like the reliquary for the remains of St Vincent which he presented to the monastery of Abingdon.[54]

Of the broadly contemporary foreign writers, the German bishop Thietmar of Merseburg, who died in 1018, is mainly valuable on the Danish conquest, while Adam of Bremen, working about forty years after Cnut's death, is a major source on his dealings in Scandinavia and with the German empire, even if his reliability can be questioned, as we noticed when dealing with his story of Swegen Forkbeard's exile from Denmark. The Norman chroniclers William of Jumièges and, to a lesser extent, William of Poitiers, also have significant, but not necessarily trustworthy, material. The former seems to have written most of his Norman ducal history, the *Gesta*

[50] Darlington and McGurk, 'The *Chronicon ex Chronicis* of "Florence" of Worcester and its Use of Sources for English History before 1066', 194. My comments are drawn from their work and Campbell, *Essays*, pp.213–14.

[51] Keynes, *The Diplomas of King Æthelred 'The Unready'*, pp.212–13. It is not certain that the names are identifiable with Eadric's relatives, but Professor Keynes thinks them so.

[52] For what follows, Thomson, *William of Malmesbury*, especially pp.1–38, 72–75; see also Gransden, *Historical Writing*, pp.166–85.

[53] *Chron. Rams.*, p.4; see Gransden, *Historical Writing*, pp.273–75; *Lib. El.*, pp.ix–x, xxxiv, li–liii.

[54] Below, p.126. Melted down in a famine in the time of Abbot Ingulph (1130–59), its value of sixty pounds of silver was given to the poor, *Chron. Ab.* ii. 291.

Normannorum Ducum, in the 1050s[55] after Edward the Confessor had promised the English throne to Duke William in 1051–52, and this is doubtless
why he describes Anglo-Norman relations under Æthelred and Cnut, and
comments on Edward's exile in Normandy. As a Jumièges monk, some of
his information may have derived from its former abbot, Robert, who
became bishop of London and then in 1051 archbishop of Canterbury, but
fled England during the political crisis of 1052, subsequently returning to
Jumièges, where he died. William of Poitiers used the *Gesta Normannorum
Ducum* when working on his history of William the Conqueror in the
1070s, but the beginning of his *Gesta Guillelmi* has not survived, and it now
opens with events just after Cnut's death. There are no contemporary
Scandinavian written sources apart from rune stones. Later Danish histories
include the mid-twelfth-century Roskilde *Chronicon* and the works composed by Swegen Aggeson and Saxo Grammaticus about 1200. Denmark
had in Cnut's day only recently been converted to Christianity, and these
authors are unlikely to have possessed much in the way of early documentary material, although like English historians they fairly clearly knew oral
traditions which need not always have been groundless.[56] However, the
most important sources available to later northern writers were the poems
attributed to the professional skalds who visited princely courts and were
paid to celebrate the achievements of patrons like Cnut, King Olaf
Haraldsson of Norway (St Olaf) and Earl Eric of Lade. These were first
written down maybe in the twelfth century, but now survive, often in a
fragmentary state, only in the Icelandic prose sagas of the thirteenth century
and later, the most famous of which is *Heimskringla*, a series of lives of kings
of Norway by Snorri Sturluson (d.1241). Few historians today place much
trust in the sagas (which apparently included a lost work on Cnut written
around 1200)[57] as sources for the eleventh century, but the verses which
they quote are another matter.[58] It may seem incredible that they could
have been remembered accurately for many decades, but the construction
of skaldic verse was complex, and features such as the binding of pairs of
lines by alliteration, and rhyme and consonance within lines, perhaps

---

[55] See the comments of van Houts in her edition of WJ, i. xxxii–v.
[56] On Saxo, see Campbell, 'Saxo Grammaticus and Scandinavian Historical Tradition', and the detailed
notes in the edition by Mr Christiansen.
[57] *Encomium*, ed. Campbell, pp.83–84; Saxo, ed. Christiansen,i. 156.
[58] For outlines of the nature of skaldic verse, see *END*, pp.255–72; Turville-Petre, *Origins of Icelandic
Literature*, pp.26–47; Turville-Petre, *Skaldic Poetry*; Foote and Wilson, *The Viking Achievement*,
pp.359–69; Frank, *Old Norse Court Poetry*, pp.21–89. Frank, 'King Cnut in the verse of his skalds', and
Townend, 'Contextualising the *Knútsdrápur*', deal specifically with poems about Cnut.

facilitated the correct transmission of individual words. Even so, this does not preclude the possibility that whole verses were varied or fabricated later, or associated by the saga writers, who sometimes misunderstood this material,[59] with the wrong poet and/or wrong leader. Alastair Campbell, for example, thought that a verse supposedly from Thord Kolbeinsson's *Eiríksdrápa*, which connects Earl Eric of Lade with the battle of Ringmere in 1010, is a fabrication,[60] and that lines about an attack on Norwich said by the thirteenth-century *Knytlinga Saga* to be from Ottar the Black's *Knútsdrápa* probably came from a different poem on Swegen, who is known to have sacked the town in 1004.[61] Nevertheless, skaldic verses are usually taken as authentic works of the poets to whom they are attributed,[62] although their original order is frequently unclear, and manuscript variations sometimes call the correct reading of individual words into question. Of course, even if accurately transmitted the reliability of this poetry is still open to doubt. Ottar, for example, seems not to have composed his *Knútsdrápa* until after 1025, at least ten years later than the campaigns of 1015–16 which it largely describes, and it is therefore possible to query details not confirmed by the *Anglo-Saxon Chronicle*. But the *Chronicle* itself is not comprehensive enough to make such doubts irresistible (see below), and skaldic poetry is sometimes a valuable supplement to our other sources, especially on the fighting of Æthelred's reign and Cnut's activities in Scandinavia. Moreover, poems produced at Cnut's behest (Thorarin Praise-Tongue was paid fifty marks for his *Tøgdrápa*), although obviously biased in his favour, can imply much about the ways in which he wanted to be seen.

Naturally, no source, especially those written later than the period they describe, can be trusted implicitly. Just as Goscelin's statement that Cnut was devoted to St Edith sits somewhat ill with a remarkable tale reported by William of Malmesbury,[63] and may simply reflect what the Wilton nuns wanted people to believe, churchmen writing the histories of their own

---

[59] Frank, 'Viking atrocity and Skaldic verse: The Rite of the Blood-Eagle', 335.

[60] *Encomium*, p.71. He later (*Skaldic Verse and Anglo-Saxon History*, p.15) accepted the verse as genuine, but argued that Thord was ill informed on Eric's English campaigns. See above, p.33, for the possibility that Eric was at Ringmere.

[61] Campbell, *Skaldic Verse and Anglo-Saxon History*, pp.3–4, 13. Poole, 'Skaldic Verse and Anglo-Saxon History', 276–80, thinks both verses genuine, and that Cnut attacked Norwich and Eric fought at Ringmere in 1016; see also Townend, 'Contextualising the *Knútsdrápur*', 160.

[62] Campbell, *Encomium*, p.66, n. 3, noted that the authors of the kings' sagas seem to give the verses in good faith, and unlike other saga writers apparently did not fabricate verses which they then attributed to their chief characters; similarly, Foote, *Aurvandilstá*, pp.223–24. See also Turville-Petre, *Skaldic Poetry*, pp. lxvi–lxxiv.

[63] Below, pp.114–115; and for other reservations about Goscelin's work on Edith, Ridyard, *The Royal Saints of Anglo-Saxon England*, pp.40–44.

foundations tended to be prejudiced. For example, Hemming's account of lands disputed between the bishopric of Worcester and Evesham Abbey does not accord with other evidence, and nor does the Ramsey chronicle's version of the difficulties experienced by their abbot early in Cnut's reign.[64] There were other causes of distortion too. When John of Worcester draws elements of his account of the battle of *Assandun* in 1016 from Sallust he is revealing quite a lot about the classical interests of twelfth-century historians, but also raising doubts about his own reliability, and William of Malmesbury, whose methods so often find favour with modern scholars, nevertheless records miracle stories which his critical faculties ought to have led him to doubt, and perhaps did;[65] and like historians of all periods, William, John and their colleagues were at the mercy of the bias and inadequacy of their sources, as well as their own prejudices and errors. Fortunately, none of this means that their work can simply be tossed overboard, for two examples should suffice to prove the contention that writers subsequent to Cnut's day sometimes had access to important evidence.

The first concerns taxation. Later authors, Hemming on the bishopric of Worcester, Hugh Candidus on Peterborough, and William of Malmesbury on Glastonbury and Malmesbury, record that those who could not pay their taxes under Cnut were likely to suffer temporary or permanent losses of estates. Domesday Book shows that this could indeed be eleventh-century practice, and there are what look like references to it in Wulfstan's legal text II Cnut and the rubric of one of Cnut's charters.[66] Moreover, not only do these sources tend to confirm each other, they collectively explain how Cnut was able to raise the very large sum of £82,500 in 1018. Church archives and traditions recorded and remembered losses of lands, as is hardly surprising: William's claim that his evidence on Malmesbury came from documents in English is entirely credible. The second example is even more striking.[67] In the 1130s the Anglo-Norman poet Gaimar, who was based in Lincolnshire, wrote a history of the English in French verse. He appears to have had a copy of the *Anglo-Saxon Chronicle* similar to E, but the later part of his work is filled with romance, and might seem to belong to what has been called the twelfth-century fictionalising history best exemplified by Geoffrey of Monmouth's *Historia Britonum*.[68] When he describes the foreign

---

[64] Below, pp.134–35.
[65] Thomson, *William of Malmesbury*, pp.22–25; Campbell, *Essays*, pp.222–23.
[66] Above, p.64; below, pp.174–79.
[67] For what follows, Lawson, 'Aspects of the reign of Cnut', pp.35–39; Poole, 'Skaldic Verse and Anglo-Saxon History', 275–76, 292–98.
[68] Campbell, *Essays*, pp.221–22.

exile of Edmund Ironside's sons Edmund and Edward, for example, Gaimar misnames them Edgar and Æthelred, and tells a rousing, romantic tale of their adventures, complete with dialogue.[69] Yet the popular traditions from which such stories presumably came were not always totally fictitious, and cannot be simply ignored. Gaimar also says that Æthelred II had a brother named Edmund who desired to take his kingdom and was supported in this by the Welsh, as he was married to the daughter of one of their kings. He assisted Edmund Ironside against Cnut, but died and was buried in Hereford, while the Ironside himself took the sister of a Welsh king, and received the support of the Welsh beyond Severn from Lancaster to Malvern.[70] Now although the only known brother of Æthelred named Edmund died in the early 970s, when Thietmar of Merseburg describes events in England in 1016 he tells how, after a battle in which Edmund was killed, the Danes fled from before London because they had heard that help was on the way from Edmund's brother Æthelstan and the *Britannis*.[71] This account too contains some blunders, for it is likely that it was Æthelstan who was killed in battle, at Sherston,[72] and that Edmund brought the relief, but when Thietmar wrote *Britannis* he was not thinking of Englishmen, whom he always describes as *Angli*. Obviously it is impossible to be sure whom he meant by it, and Freeman, who noticed this long ago, suggested that he was indicating troops levied mainly within the western shires.[73] Taken with Gaimar's story, however, it is more likely that these men were the Welsh of Wales. There is further evidence in the poem *Liðsmannaflokkr*,

---

[69] Gaimar, *L'Estoire,* ed. Bell, pp.142–48; translated Hardy and Martin, ii. 142–47.

[70] Gaimar, *L'Estoire,* ed. Bell, pp.130, 134; translated Hardy and Martin, ii. 130, 133–34.

[71] Thietmar, *Chronicon,* vii. 41, pp. 448–49.

[72] Christ Church Canterbury celebrated Æthelstan's death on 25 June, Keynes, *The Diplomas of King Æthelred 'The Unready',* p.267. ASC, i. 149–50, says that Sherston was fought 'after midsummer', i.e. after 24 June. Gaimar (ed. Bell, p.134) dates it to the morrow of St John (25 June), and Roger of Wendover (ed. Coxe, i. 454) to 25 June. Although both perhaps guessed from the *Chronicle*, this may be the date which its now obscure phrase was intended to denote. John of Worcester states that the first day of the battle was a Monday, as 25 June was in 1016. It is not unlikely, therefore, that Æthelstan was killed at Sherston, and that Thietmar, or his informant, confused him with Edmund. His will has been dated to 1014 by Professor Keynes, who thinks that he died on 25 June 1014, but although he thanks his father for sending him 'on the Friday after the feast of midsummer' permission to make the will, this may mean that it dates from July 1015 or slightly later. His last genuine charter signature is from 1013, but there is no real difficulty in believing that he lived for another three years, apart from a note in a Christ Church Canterbury manuscript in which Æthelred says that he survives his son and confirms Æthelstan's grant to them (Keynes, *Diplomas*, p. 267). However, this is probably not contemporary, being entered immediately after a copy of S 914, a spurious charter in Æthelred's name. Perhaps a scribe familiar with and attempting to strengthen the Canterbury copy of the will assumed from its content that the father outlived the son. If they in fact died within two months of each other the error would have been easy. Keynes, 'Cnut's Earls', p.71, n. 156, is not convinced by these arguments.

[73] *FNC*, i. 684.

apparently composed in Cnut's army around 1017, which mentions the sword ringing on *brezkum* byrnies. The word *brezkr* may mean something as general as British, but seems usually to denote the Welsh.[74]

If Edmund Ironside's involvement with the Welsh is not thought sufficiently established by this evidence, it can also be fitted into a plausible historical context. At some point, he and Eadric Streona of Mercia became enemies. Possibly the latter had supported Queen Emma in plans that one of her sons, rather any of the offspring of Æthelred's first consort, should succeed him. The *Life* of Edward the Confessor, written some fifty years later, claims that, when she was pregnant with him, all the men of England took an oath to accept the child as king should it be a boy, while the Norman *Inuentio et Miracula Sancti Vulfranni* of around 1053–54 alleges that he was anointed and consecrated king as a boy.[75] However that may be, it is unlikely to be coincidence that Eadric first defected to Cnut only shortly after Edmund's takeover of the Five Boroughs in the east midlands in 1015, and marriage to the widow of the Siferth whom Eadric had recently had murdered. The latter's relations with his Welsh neighbours cannot always have been good, for the *Annales Cambriæ* say that in 1012 he led an expedition against St David's. Depending upon when Edmund's Welsh alliance was made, it may have been an additional factor in persuading Eadric to change his allegiance, or a move to put pressure on him once he had deserted. Moreover, Edmund's association with the Welsh may also cast light on why Ottar the Black's *Knútsdrápa* apparently refers to the battle of *Assandun* being followed by another at *Danaskógar* (*skógr* = wood, forest). If, as seems likely, this is the Forest of Dean,[76] it would further explain why Cnut and Edmund eventually made peace in Gloucestershire.

There is much that is important about all this. The *Anglo-Saxon Chronicle* is detailed on the events of 1016, but clearly it omitted at least one important aspect of the fighting. Edmund's Welsh alliance has to be pieced together from a twelfth-century poet, a contemporary German bishop, and two skaldic poems. All sources, especially late ones, are likely to get things wrong, sometimes spectacularly so, but that does not mean that everything

---

[74] Poole, 'Skaldic Verse and Anglo-Saxon History', 292–94; see also on this poem, Poole, *Viking Poems on War and Peace*, pp. 86–115.

[75] *The Life of King Edward*, ed. Barlow, pp. 12–13; The *Inuentio* is printed by van Houts, 'Historiography and Hagiography at Saint-Wandrille', 251. See further Stafford, 'The Reign of Æthelred II', pp. 36–37.

[76] Lawson, 'Aspects of the reign of Cnut', p. 39; Poole, 'Skaldic Verse and Anglo-Saxon History', 275–76. *Danaskógar* was identified with the Forest of Dean in *Corpus Poeticum Boreale*, ed. Vigfússon and Powell, ii. 156; but it is conceivable, as Poole says, that Ottar intended all his comments in this verse to refer to *Assandun*, which he believed to be near *Danaskógar*.

in them can simply be swept aside as nonsense. Even tales such as Gaimar's on the two Edmunds and the Welsh can contain grains of truth. Scepticism is an essential part of our approach to sources: so too is an open mind. There is no need to make a desolation and call it scholarship.

In all, the scarcity of contemporary material is such that Cnut's personality and many of his activities will remain forever unknown. The inadequacies of the *Anglo-Saxon Chronicle* and the surviving charters, even when supplemented by such other fragments as the skaldic poetry and the Letters of 1019–20 and 1027, make it impossible to construct a decent chronology of his reign, while Wulfstan's legal texts are far from straightforward as guides to his administration. But Cnut was considerably more fortunate in the sources produced within 150 years of his death, for the explosion of literary activity which began shortly after the Norman Conquest, and which was to ensure that no future reign would be as badly documented as those of Cnut and his sons, also cast its light back to his period. For all their limitations, later works have valuable insights to offer, especially on Cnut's relations with the English Church. Without them, much of what follows would be impossible.

3

CNUT, ENGLAND AND NORTHERN EUROPE,
1017-35

Cnut inherited from his royal Scandinavian and English predecessors relations of an often threatening as well as potentially profitable sort with a very wide range of territories. Once in control of Denmark (possibly from 1019, see below), he became concerned, like Swegen, Harald Bluetooth and probably Gorm the Old before him, with Norway, Sweden, the German empire and the Slav peoples east of the Elbe, including the Poles. Both Harald and Swegen had taken Slavonic consorts and thought it desirable to subjugate Norway. Swegen also had dealings with the Swedes, and involved himself with Normandy and in the Irish Sea, perhaps selling his ill-gotten gains and fraternising not only with Duke Richard II in Rouen, but also the rulers of Norse settlements in Ireland such as Dublin, Wexford, Waterford, Cork and Limerick. King Æthelred II too had troubles with the Irish Sea and Normandy, sending expeditions against both, marrying Richard's sister Emma, and going into exile with her kin in 1013. He may have asked for Norman help against his enemies in 1009, and a continental source records that he at some point appealed to the French monarch Robert the Pious for assistance, conceivably in the hope that he could exert pressure on the Normans.[1] Like other English kings, he had relations with the Welsh and the Scots too. We have seen the former being raided by Eadric Streona in 1012 and fighting for Edmund Ironside in 1016, while the latter are said to have attacked Durham in 1006, and by Æthelred's death King Malcolm II was planning a further incursion. Hence, Cnut's inheritance was international and many-faceted: there were numerous opportunities to be taken, pitfalls to be avoided and problems to be

---

[1] Above, p.33; Ralph Glaber, *Historiarvm Libri Qvinqve*, iii. 8, ed. France, p.110. I owe this reference to Campbell, *Essays in Anglo-Saxon History*, p.198.

overcome, both at home and abroad, before his dominion and influence extended over much of the northern world, and merited the title by which his fellow Scandinavians know him today: Knut den store – Cnut the Great.

THE EARLY YEARS IN ENGLAND

According to John of Worcester, shortly after Æthelred died in April 1016 certain English churchmen and nobles elected Cnut king, came to him at Southampton, swore fidelity and repudiated all Æthelred's progeny; in return, he vowed to be a good lord in matters both church and lay. As late Anglo-Saxon rulers were often required to give undertakings of this sort at their coronations, Cnut was possibly crowned and anointed at this time. His involvement in such a ceremony after the death of Edmund Ironside is even more likely. John says that he held a meeting at London, and asked the witnesses of his agreement with Edmund whether the latter's brothers and sons were entitled to succeed him. They replied that Edmund left no claim to his brothers and had wanted Cnut to support and protect his sons until they were old enough to rule, and they also swore that they wished to elect Cnut king, humbly obey him, and pay tribute to his army. Finally, after he had given them a pledge supported by the oaths of Danish leaders, they completely rejected Edmund's brothers and sons and denied that they were kings. Whether or not they lied in describing the agreement with Edmund, as John claims, Cnut's use of it (assuming that the Worcester chronicler can be trusted thus far) to legitimise his position is interesting, because it suggests that right of conquest was not thought title enough. The meeting was obviously intended to establish him as sole king, and may have led directly to the coronation in London by Archbishop Lyfing reported by a twelfth-century dean of St Paul's.[2] That Cnut's earliest coin type, *Quatrefoil*, is the first since Edgar's *Bust Crowned* issue to show a king wearing a crown[3] could be some indication of its importance.

Having established his rule over the English at least in name, another pressing need was the reward of his army. The *Chronicle* says that the agreement with Edmund included the fixing of a tribute and that London bought peace from the enemy too, and we have seen that the later meeting there reaffirmed that a tribute would be paid. Cnut's men had fought hard,

---

[2] Ralph of Diceto, *Abbreviationes Chronicorum*, ed. Stubbs, i. 169; also Gervase, *Gesta Regum*, ed. Stubbs, ii. 55.

[3] Backhouse *et al.*, *The Golden Age of Anglo-Saxon Art*, pp. 174–81. Æthelred sometimes wears a diadem, but not a crown.

and doubtless expected to be remunerated accordingly. Failure to meet these expectations would have been dangerous, especially as his army consisted partly of the forces of independent warlords like Thorkell the Tall and the Norwegian Earl Eric of Lade, whose loyalty could not be taken entirely for granted. Collection of the very large sum of £72,000 therefore almost certainly went on throughout 1017 and into 1018, when it was handed over, along with £10,500 from London. Some of the Scandinavian ships then went to Denmark, and Danes and English came to an agreement at Oxford. This may indicate that no final reconciliation could take place until after the payment had been made. Conditions in England while the tax was being gathered are likely to have been grim, considering the devastation caused by the recent fighting, and that the tribute came on top of the large amounts levied in Æthelred's reign.

Cnut divided the country in four in 1017, keeping Wessex for himself and giving East Anglia to Thorkell, Mercia to Eadric, and Northumbria to Eric. Neither the precise purpose nor the duration of this move are clear, but it was probably largely intended to provide an interim military government, facilitate the collection of taxation, give Cnut's chief supporters the impression that their efforts were proving worthwhile, and hold the country down. The continuance of large-scale English resistance may have been unlikely, but there were sources of danger to be neutralised.

One was Eadric of Mercia himself. He had played a successful hand under Æthelred, and maintained his position in the fighting of 1015–16, but Cnut, perhaps with the encouragement of his consort Ælfgifu of Northampton,[4] who retained some sort of recognised position even after his marriage to Emma of Normandy, and whose father Eadric had overthrown, clearly decided that he was too powerful and dangerous to be tolerated further. The Encomiast has him beheaded by Earl Eric personally, while John says that he was killed in London at Christmas 1017 and that Cnut ordered the corpse to be left unburied.[5] The *Chronicle* too mentions his death, and also those of Northman of Mercia and the West Saxons Æthelweard and Brihtric, although there are indications that the blood-letting went further still. Executions are easily exaggerated, but the Encomiast's statement that many English leaders were killed with Eadric, and that of the later Evesham chronicle that many of his soldiers died too, are quite plausible, given that he would have had

---

[4] As suggested by Kirby, *The Making of Early England*, p.118; see also above, p.51. On Ælfgifu, see below, pp.123–24.

[5] Similarly, Hemming, i. 281. *ASC* F agrees that it happened in London. For later accounts, see *FNC*, i. 720–22.

powerful henchmen whom it was doubtless politic to eliminate.[6] More generally, the Norman William of Poitiers, writing just after the Conquest, claims that Cnut cruelly slaughtered the noblest of England's sons, young and old, to ensure the dominion of himself and his children.[7] Others were banished, including Eadwig, 'king of the ceorls', who had quite likely been the leader of a peasant rising. Conditions late in Æthelred's reign could well have resulted in such a movement, for apart from the effects of famine and enemy harrying, those landowners with dependent peasantry may often have expected them to shoulder much of the tax burden, and that burden had been particularly heavy between 1011 and 1014. Eadwig, who bore, or affected, a royal name, looks like a significant figure, and John says that he was eventually reconciled with Cnut.

Surviving members of the English royal family were an obvious focus for opposition, as Cnut's desire to deny Edmund's relatives their rights at the London meeting shows. John reports under 1016 that English counsellors decided upon the exile of the much-respected ætheling Eadwig, Æthelred's only surviving son by his first consort, and that Cnut, exulting at their abandonment of him, plotted his murder by promising honours, dignities and favour to the nobleman Æthelweard in return for Eadwig's head. However, Æthelweard, who was of the finest English stock, and may well have been the man of that name executed by Cnut in 1017 (see above), dissembled by undertaking what he had no intention of performing, and the *Chronicle* records the ætheling's eventual banishment in 1017. He seems later to have returned; possibly an attempt on the throne was being planned when he died, for the C text's statement that Cnut afterwards had him killed is followed by John, who adds that he was betrayed by those he held dearest.[8]

The history of Edward and Edmund, the infant sons of Edmund Ironside, is almost totally dark until Edward's eventual return from Hungary in 1057. John says that Eadric advised Cnut to kill them, but that he was ashamed to do so in England, and despatched the boys for the purpose to

[6] *Encomium*, ii. 15, pp. 30–32; *Chron. Eve.*, p. 84. Likewise, the execution of Uhtred of Northumbria in 1016 was accompanied, according to the late-eleventh-century Durham tract *De Obsessione Dunelmi*, by that of forty of his followers; ed. Arnold, i. 218. See Meehan, 'The siege of Durham, the battle of Carham and the cession of Lothian', 10, 12, who thinks that this source's comments on Uhtred came from an oral saga, and that the forty men are exaggeration. See Meehan, 'The siege of Durham, the battle of Carham and the cession of Lothian', 10, 12, who thinks that this source's comments on Uhtred came from an oral saga, and that the forty men are exaggeration.

[7] William of Poitiers, *Gesta Guillelmi*, ii. 32, ed. Davis and Chibnall, pp.156–57.

[8] William of Malmesbury, *GR*, ii. 180, ed. Mynors *et al.* i. 318–19, says that he was buried at Tavistock. The date of his death is not known: the 'afterwards' of *ASC* C may mean after 1017, although John of Worcester took it to refer to that year.

his ally the king of Sweden, who sent them to Hungary.[9] The twelfth-century poet Gaimar's tale that they went first to Denmark, and that there was a plot to restore them, may not be complete nonsense.[10]

This left Edward and Alfred, Æthelred's sons by Emma. Obscure as they are, one can be confident that relations with Normandy were an important aspect of Æthelred's reign: he is known to have made a treaty with Richard I, married his daughter, and gone into exile there in 1013, and reported to have both sent a military expedition against it and in 1009 asked Duke Richard II for help.[11] Scandinavian forces left England for Normandy in the summer of 1000, and Swegen Forkbeard allegedly made an agreement with Richard II in Rouen in around 1013[12] According to Thietmar of Merseburg, Emma was in London during the siege of 1016, and she may be the lady referred to in the poem *Liðsmannaflokkr*.[13] William of Jumièges says that Cnut married her after having her brought from the city before the siege ended and giving her weight in gold and silver before the whole army,[14] but his chronology here is suspect, as he places the battle of *Auxendunum* (presumably *Assandun*, 18 October) before Æthelred's death on 23 April, and the more contemporary *Chronicle* date of mid-1017 for the marriage is preferable. Despite the Encomiast's tale of how Cnut's men, searching far and wide for a suitable wife, eventually found her in Normandy, it may be, as Keynes has argued, that Emma had remained in England throughout.

The prime motive behind Cnut's desire for the union was almost certainly to prevent her sons gaining Norman military assistance, and it may well have occurred in mid-1017 because the preceding months were occupied by negotiations with her brother Richard.[15] The Encomiast mentions the exchange of emissaries, and Ralph Glaber, writing in Dijon before about

[9] Adam, *Gesta*, ii. 53, p.114, reports time spent in Russia, while in *ASC* D for 1057 Cnut dispatches them directly to Hungary; see further on the æthelings, Keynes, 'The Crowland Psalter and the sons of King Edmund Ironside'.

[10] Gaimar, *L'Estoire*, ed. Bell, pp.142–47; translated Hardy and Martin, ii. 142–46. The mention of Portchester as the point of departure for the ship intending to return them to England may mean that Gaimar employed here the Hampshire traditions which he used elsewhere; see Bell's introduction, p. x.

[11] Campbell, *Essays*, pp.198–200; Van Houts, 'The Political Relations between Normandy and England before 1066 according to the "Gesta Normannorum Ducum"', pp. 86–87; above, pp.42, 81.

[12] Above, p.33.

[13] Poole, 'Skaldic Verse and Anglo-Saxon History', 290–91.

[14] WJ, v. 9, ed. van Houts, ii. 20–21.

[15] Keynes, 'The Æthelings in Normandy', judges differently. Van Houts, 'The Political Relations', p.88, citing Wulfstan's legal texts, thinks that the marriage was delayed because widows were supposed to remain unmarried for twelve months; but whether a contract of such importance was hindered by strictures of this type seems very doubtful, especially bearing in mind the blatant irregularity of Cnut's relationship with Ælfgifu of Northampton (below, pp.123–124). Van Houts, 'A note on Jezebel and Semiramis', suggests that the enigmatic Latin poem *Semiramis*, apparently written in Richard II's Normandy, is a satire on Emma's marriage to Cnut, which van Houts believes occurred without Norman approval.

1030, thought that the marriage followed an agreement with Richard, and that Cnut at some stage sent the Normans military help, while the *Inuentio et Miracula Sancti Vulfranni*, written in the Norman abbey of St Wandrille around 1053–54, says that the match had Richard's consent and support.[16] The latter two sources are of uncertain reliability, while the Encomiast's suppression of Emma's previous marriage to Æthelred makes one suspicious of his entire treatment of the affair, but it is inherently likely that negotiations did take place, for Cnut was shrewd enough to appreciate that gaining Emma's assistance against her sons without Richard's goodwill would have been to leave the job half done. That he later troubled to marry his sister Estrith to Richard's successor Robert (see below) probably also implies that his wife's co-operation was not alone thought sufficient. Her previous experience as queen of England conceivably added to her attractions, and Swegen's treaty with Richard may have facilitated the discussions, especially if, as is quite likely, Cnut was present when it was made. The Encomiast has Emma stipulating that a son of hers, rather than any of his other progeny, should be given the succession, and in the circumstances this seems a plausible feature of the deal, especially as she had evidently earlier required the English to guarantee that her son Edward would succeed Æthelred.[17] Now, however, he, Alfred and their sister Godgifu were abandoned to what must have looked like permanent exile in the Norman court; Edward was doubtless on his way there when he visited the monastery of St Peter's Ghent in December 1016 and, according to a charter, promised them English lands should he become king.[18] Cnut still had a difficult road to travel, but by the end of 1017 some major obstacles already lay behind him, and his position in England was much more secure than it had been twelve months earlier.

Apart from the meeting and coronation in London, and Cnut's presence there at Christmas 1017 for Eadric's execution, little is known of his whereabouts very early in the reign. In 1018 Thietmar of Merseburg says that he destroyed the crews of thirty pirate ships,[19] and he perhaps visited Canterbury to initiate his important and generally good relations with the archbishopric.[20] Archbishop Lyfing is likely to have recently returned from Rome, where he received his pallium and letters of exhortation for Cnut from

[16] *Encomium*, ii. 17, pp.32–34. Ralph Glaber, *Historiarvm Libri Qvinqve*, ii. 3, ed France, pp.54–56. For the *Inuentio*, see van Houts, 'Historiography and Hagiography at Saint-Wandrille', 251.

[17] Above, p.78.

[18] The document, probably drawn up in the 1040s, is not certainly authentic, but see the excellent discussion in Keynes, 'The Æthelings in Normandy', 177–81; printed, 201.

[19] Thietmar, *Chronicon*, viii. 7, pp.502–03.

[20] Below, pp.141–142.

Pope Benedict VIII. The charter S 950 is a grant to him from 1018, and so is S 952, which alleges that Cnut gave Christ Church freedom, and may be connected with the report (S 985) that he confirmed their liberties by placing their charters on the altar.[21] A contemporary Christ Church gospel book records the entry of Cnut and his brother Harald into confraternity with the community,[22] and although Cnut could simply have given them Harald's name,[23] it is possible that he was in England in 1016, as Thietmar says, remained with Cnut, went to Canterbury, and returned to Denmark with part of the fleet after the payment of 1018.

If a Canterbury visit did occur in 1018 it may have been while Cnut and his men were waiting for the £82,500 to be handed over, as the bulk of those who received it were doubtless based in and around London. Cnut subsequently retained forty ships in his service, and proceeded west for the meeting at Oxford where the *Chronicle* says Danes and English came to an understanding. Its nature is unknown, for the D text's statement that they agreed to observe Edgar's law was probably taken from the Letter of 1019-20, itself influenced by Archbishop Wulfstan of York, who drew up a document after the meeting which stated that the *witan* had decided to zealously observe Edgar's law. We have already seen that this may simply have been a way of saying that Wulfstan had secured an undertaking that they were going to abandon practices which he found displeasing.[24] However, Wulfstan does say that 'Cnut, with the advice of his councillors, fully established peace and friendship between the Danes and the English and put an end to all their former enmity'.[25] This implies, as does its appearance in the *Chronicle*, that the Oxford assembly was important, and that the payment of tribute and the departure of part of Cnut's fleet had prepared the way for an accommodation between the two sides. Like the meeting in London just after the death of Edmund Ironside, it hints at a realisation on Cnut's part that his rule would to a degree depend on English support. It will become evident in Chapter 5 that this was so.

From Oxford he may have travelled into the south-west. The charters S 951 and 953 are gifts in Cornwall purportedly made by him in 1018, although neither is of certain authenticity, and this was seemingly also the

---

[21] See Brooks, *The Early History of the Church of Canterbury*, pp.287–90.
[22] BL MS Royal 1 D. ix, f. 43v; printed Ker, *Catalogue*, p.317; see Backhouse *et al.*, *The Golden Age of Anglo-Saxon Art*, No. 52; Temple, *Anglo-Saxon Manuscripts*, No. 70.
[23] Suggested by A. Campbell, *Encomium,* p. lvii.
[24] Above, p.63.
[25] I use here the translation given by Kennedy, p.72.

date of his lost foundation charter for Buckfast Abbey in Devon.[26] Maybe
he wintered in the area, attempting to ensure the loyalty of the West Saxon
heartland where Æthelred's son Eadwig the ætheling may have recently
returned and died and where there was soon to be difficulty,[27] for in 1019
one of his men, Agemund, received a Dorset estate by S 955, and the dubious Exeter charter S 954 bears the same date. By late March 1019 he is likely
to have been in Winchester: S 956 was granted in the royal presence to the
New Minster during the first week of Easter, and has a long witness list
which no doubt represents the gathering of the Easter court.

DENMARK c. 1014–19

Later in 1019, the *Chronicle* says that Cnut sailed for Denmark and stayed
there all winter. Events among the Danes are little known in these years.
The Encomiast alleges that Swegen Forkbeard took his elder son Cnut on
the conquest of England, leaving Harald, the younger, in Denmark, and that
after Swegen's death Cnut returned and asked Harald to divide it between
them, while offering him the eventual choice of Denmark or England if he
would assist in subjugating the latter; but Harald refused both requests and,
after jointly bringing their mother back from among the Slavs, Cnut sailed
for England alone.[28]

The Encomiast's reliability here is questionable. Thietmar of Merseburg
has Harald involved in the siege of London in 1016, and we have seen that
the Canterbury confraternity entry may also support his presence in
England. Numismatic evidence is relevant too. Mark Blackburn has shown
that the earliest Scandinavian coins inscribed *CNVT REX D* (Cnut, king of
Danes), and modelled on Æthelred's final *Last Small Cross* type, were struck
from dies probably made in Lincoln no later than 1015, and so could have
originated during Cnut's sojourn in Denmark in 1014–15.[29] This seems to
fit the Encomiast's evidence on his claim to the Danish throne, but throws
no light on what happened to Harald, or when.

Later sources claim to. The Danish mid-thirteenth-century *Annales
Ryenses* have him deposed in favour of Cnut for effeminacy, and Cnut then
replaced by Harald because of absence from Denmark, but restored after

[26] Above, p.67, n.26.
[27] Below, p.90
[28] *Encomium* i. 3–5, ii. 1–4, pp.10–20.
[29] Blackburn, 'Do Cnut the Great's first coins as king of Denmark date from before 1018?'.

Harald's death.[30] While this may be 'absurd',[31] there are other hints that the position was more complex than the Encomiast either knew or wanted to admit. A royal grant (S 952) of dubious authenticity to Christ Church Canterbury from 1018 is witnessed by a *Haldenne princeps regis* who also appears (as *Haldan princeps*) as a donor of land to them in later obituaries.[32] Now according to the mid-twelfth-century Roskilde *Chronicon*, after the death of Harald Bluetooth a certain Swegen invaded England and expelled King Æthelred, and his sons Gorm and Harthacnut attacked Denmark and killed King *Haldanus* and his sons. The one then took Denmark and the other England, as their father had died in the meantime. Whether *Haldanus* was the son of Harald Bluetooth is, it says, doubtful.[33] This story seems garbled and may be nonsense, but the coincidence between King *Haldanus* and the *Haldenne princeps regis* of the Canterbury material remains; possibly Cnut did have a relative or associate of this name, for the fact that his sister Santslaue occurs only in the *Liber Vitae* of New Minster Winchester indicates that his kin could have extended further than the threadbare sources reveal. Nor is it unlikely that some of them, or others, were interested in taking the Danish throne, and that the later stories about the killing of *Haldanus* and the expulsion of Harald reflect this, if in a distorted form. An alternative to thinking that Harald had been in England since 1016, and returned to Denmark with part of a disbanded fleet in 1018, might be that he had in the interval been expelled from it, and sailed with the fleet in 1018 in an attempt to regain control. But this is sheer speculation. What is tolerably certain is that he was still alive when he either entered into confraternity with Christ Church or Cnut gave them his name, and that when Cnut himself sailed for Denmark in 1019 it was to suppress trouble. The Letter of 1019–20 says that he intended to avert a threat to England, and succeeded in dealing with great dangers, so that the Danes would henceforth at need be able to assist the English. Little can be made of this, although the biographer of Edward the Confessor speaks of Danes preparing to rebel against Cnut early in his reign, and Henry of Huntingdon

<hr>

[30] *Annales Danici Medii Ævi*, ed. Jørgensen p.69. These annals were written in the Cistercian monastery of Ryd, near Flensborg Fjord.

[31] Campbell, *Encomium*, p.lvi, n.5; similarly, Lund, 'Cnut's Danish kingdom', n.11, who believes this account a garbled version of the events which actually followed Cnut's death in 1035.

[32] BL MS Cotton Galba E iii. f. 33v; BL MS Cotton Nero C ix. f. 15v. Dart, *The History and Antiquities of the Cathedral Church of Canterbury*, p.xxxix; Gerchow, *Die Gedenküberlieferung der Angelsachsen*, pp.290–91, 355. He died, somewhat curiously, on the same day (12 November) as Cnut, and may also be the Halfdan *dux* who witnesses S 954 of 1019.

[33] *Chronicon Roskildense*, ed. Gertz, i. 17–18. Cnut's brother Harald does not appear in this source.

thought that an English and Danish attack on the *Wandali* (the Wends, the Slav peoples on the southern shores of the Baltic) occurred in its third year.[34] The Letter is clearly concerned to give a favourable impression, but the situation was presumably fairly stable when Cnut returned to England in the spring of 1020. By then Harald is usually assumed to have been dead.

1020–24

A large meeting was held at Cirencester at Easter (17 April) 1020 and Ealdorman Æthelweard of Wessex outlawed. Cnut's absence had obviously seen unrest in the area, but unless it was connected with the return of the ætheling Eadwig (date unknown, see above) its nature is obscure. Later in the year, probably on the anniversary of 18 October, he went to *Assandun* for the consecration of the church which commemorated the battle of 1016.[35] This was performed by Archbishop Wulfstan of York, Lyfing of Canterbury having died on 12 June. It may have been at about the same time that monks were installed in the church of St Edmund at Bury.[36] Henceforth, knowledge of Cnut's activities deteriorates. The outlawing of Earl Thorkell of East Anglia on 11 November is his sole recorded action in 1021, and in 1022 the *Chronicle* says simply that he sailed out with his ships to *Wiht* (D reads *Wihtland*).

Both events merited fuller treatment. Thorkell's expulsion belongs to the ambivalent relations between Cnut and some of his powerful Scandinavian followers discussed more fully in Chapter 5, and may reflect considerable political difficulties, possibly linked to friction with some East Anglian and Fenland churches around this time.[37] Indeed, it is not unlikely that he at some point faced armed resistance in the Fens, as the *Liber Eliensis* mentions a siege of Ely.[38] Even so, that he was able to expel the powerful figure to whom he may have owed much of his victory in 1016 must say something about the effectiveness of the power base which he had succeeded in creating in England in the intervening years. If Thorkell had once dreamt of dominating the young king then he had dreamt in vain, although he soon proceeded to occupy a position in Denmark which would cause further problems within the next two years.

[34] *The Life of King Edward*, ed. Barlow, p.9; Henry, *Historia*, vi. 15, pp. 362–63.
[35] See further, below, pp.132–33.
[36] Below, p.132.
[37] Below, pp.132–35.
[38] Below, p.134.

The *Chronicle* annal for 1022 is thoroughly obscure. Elsewhere, its entries regularly use *Wiht* and *Wihtland* to denote the Isle of Wight; why Cnut needed a navy there at this date is less clear. Sandwich was better situated to meet a threat from Scandinavia; Wight, where Harold's ships awaited William the Conqueror long and unsuccessfully in the summer of 1066, implies a connection with the south or west, and perhaps particularly Normandy. If Ralph Glaber's information on the assistance sent to the Normans by Cnut is correct, it could have been a staging-post on a journey south. Indeed, if his (undated) grant to the abbey of Fécamp (S 949) is genuine, one might suppose that he visited the Norman coast at some time, and his generosity to a foundation which had been particularly favoured by the ducal family (in 1001 Richard II invited the celebrated monastic reformer William of Dijon to be its abbot) seems most likely to mean that his relations with them were still satisfactory. A move to Wight with hostile intent against the Normans in 1022 also appears the less plausible because the eventual worsening of Cnut's relations with the duchy (see below) is not known to have preceded Richard II's death in 1026. It is now thought to have been Richard, rather than his son Robert, who gave Godgifu, sister of the aethelings Edward and Alfred, in marriage to Count Dreux of the Vexin.[39] This implies that the exiles enjoyed a certain status in his court, but need not mean that he envisaged actively espousing their cause, or had become dissatisfied about Emma's union with Cnut. Nevertheless, Dudo of St Quentin's history of the Norman dukes, which is addressed to Richard II, claims that an English king, *Alstemus*, gave assistance to Richard's great-grandfather Rollo, and later invoked a pact between them to receive Rollo's help against English rebels, at the same time presenting the Norman with half of his kingdom and his property, which Rollo returned to him. Dudo also says that one of Richard I's enemies acknowledged that the English were subject to him.[40] Unfortunately, it is uncertain whether he was writing during Emma's marriage to Cnut or that to Æthelred, but these tales hint that one or both suggested to Richard II that a claim to England was worth recording, and that he wanted to keep his options open.

Even so, Cnut's journey to Wight in 1022 need have had nothing to do with the Normans. It could have been directed against a piratical descent of the sort which had happened in 1018 (see above), and would occur again in

[39] Bates, 'Lord Sudeley's Ancestors', p.36.
[40] Dudo, *De Moribus*, ii. 7–8, 17–19, 103, ed. Lair, pp.147–49, 158–60, 265. See Campbell, *Essays*, p.200; *Carmen de Hastingae Proelio*, ed. Morton and Munz, pp.57–58.

1047, when twenty-five ships harried Sandwich and Wight.[41] Furthermore, it is possible that the *Chronicle* entry for 1022 does not refer to the Isle of Wight at all. J.C.H.R. Steenstrup pointed out that an account of a northern voyage given to King Alfred, and incorporated into his translation of Orosius's *Histories against the Pagans*, mentions Witland as an area east of the Vistula (now north-east Poland), and judged that Cnut was operating on the southern shores of the Baltic.[42] Henry of Huntingdon's tale of fighting against the Slavs (see above) might also be relevant, and if Cnut did spend part of 1022 in the Baltic it would explain why the *Chronicle* C text records his return from Denmark in 1023 without, otherwise, having said that he had gone there. Against this theory is that the *Wiht* of C and E indicate that this was the annal's original reading rather than D's *Wihtland*, and that it seems very likely to mean Wight. Also, unless something particularly striking happened there, it is difficult to see why an English annalist should single out Witland from the various places which Cnut may have visited during a Baltic expedition.

At any rate, he was in Denmark early in 1023, making terms with Thorkell, whose position there had strengthened since his expulsion from England two years earlier to the extent that Cnut left it in his care and exchanged sons with him. Thorkell probably received one of Cnut's offspring by Ælfgifu of Northampton, as Harthacnut, who can at this date have been no older than five, was present at the translation of the relics of Archbishop Æltheah (see below) in June. Cnut brought Thorkell's son back to England. Osbern has his father killed by a lowly mob and thrown to birds and wild animals;[43] more reliable sources do not mention him again. Arguing from silence is dangerous, but had he played a significant role in Cnut's Scandinavian wars of about 1025–28 (see below) information about it might have been expected to survive, and so he perhaps did disappear from the scene soon after 1023. Possibly Cnut took active steps to rid himself of this dangerous figure for good. We do not know.

His return to England seems to have been accompanied by Bishop Gerbrand of Roskilde, who was to be consecrated by Archbishop

[41] *ASC*, i. 166–67.
[42] Steenstrup, *Normannerne*, iii. 322–25; Larson, *Canute the Great*, pp.157–58; the source is translated, *ASP*, pp.35–37.
[43] Osbern, *Translatio Sancti Ælfegi*, ed. Rumble, pp.298–99; William of Malmesbury, *GR*, ii. 181, ed. Mynors *et al.*, i.320–23, says of Thorkell that after his banishment, *statim ut Danemarkiae littus attigit a ducibus oppressus est.*

Æthelnoth of Canterbury,[44] and is among the witnesses of the charter S 958. Although this grant to Ely, dated 1022, is a likely forgery, its witness list could come from a genuine document of 1023, as Cnut may have visited the monastery on his return to deal with trouble involving the abbot, who had recently taken his case to Rome.[45] By early June he was in London for the translation from St Paul's to Canterbury of the body of St Ælfheah. As we shall see, this may well have been politically motivated to the extent that the relics of the archbishop so recently and brutally murdered by Cnut's countrymen were perhaps serving as a rallying point for discontent in the city. However that may be, they were removed, with the assistance of troops if Osbern can be believed, and accompanied from Rochester to Canterbury by Queen Emma and Harthacnut;[46] Cnut remained in London. S 961, a grant in Dorset to the Scandinavian Orc, is the only relic of his activities in 1024. At the same time, events across the North Sea were building to a crisis.

THE NORTHERN WARS

After the death of King Olaf Tryggvason of Norway at the battle of Svold in 999 it had been ruled by Earl Eric of Lade and his brother Swegen under the sovereignty of Cnut's father; according to later Scandinavian tradition, Eric married Swegen Forkbeard's daughter Gytha.[47] He may have fought in the army raiding England between 1009 and 1012,[48] and certainly assisted in Cnut's conquest of 1015–16, subsequently receiving the earldom of Northumbria. Norway he left under the control of his brother Swegen and son Hakon, but the former died shortly after being defeated by Olaf Haraldsson in around 1015 at the battle of Nesjar (in the Oslofjord); Olaf became king, and Hakon made his way to England. Cnut thus lost the control over Norway enjoyed by his father, and Olaf conceivably had some connection with whatever early difficulties he experienced in Denmark. In so far as these involved Thorkell after 1021 it is worth remembering that

---

[44] Recorded by Adam, *Gesta*, ii. 55, pp.115–16, who says that Cnut made him bishop of Zealand, and that while returning to Denmark he was arrested by Archbishop Unwan of Hamburg-Bremen, who knew that he had been consecrated by Æthelnoth and obliged him to promise fidelity to Hamburg. On relations between the English and Scandinavian churches in this period, see Abrams, 'The Anglo-Saxons and the Christianization of Scandinavia'.

[45] See the *Chronicle* E text under 1022; below, pp.133–34 and on S 958, below, p.215.

[46] Below, pp.130–132, 165–66.

[47] On Eric, see Encomium, pp.66–71. Thorarin Praise-Tongue's Tøgdrapa describes his son Hakon as Cnut's nephew.

[48] Above, p.33.

Olaf and he had been associates in the army of 1009–12, and that both had later served Æthelred. King Olaf of Sweden was also an ally, as well as step-son, of Swegen Forkbeard, and presumably the Swedish king who according to John of Worcester had a treaty with Cnut. Adam of Bremen confirms this, and recounts that with Olaf's help he intended to conquer both England and Norway.[49] Unfortunately, Olaf died in around 1022, to be succeeded by his son Anund Jacob, and Cnut's position in Denmark subsequently came under serious threat.

The *Chronicle* E text says under 1025 that he went to Denmark, to the Holy River, where he met Ulf and Eglaf with large Swedish naval and land forces, and that very many men, both Danes and English, fell on his side, and the Swedes had possession of the field. The next annal in E is not until 1028, and hence it is quite feasible that the 1025 entry has been dislocated by one or even two years. Later Scandinavian sources suggest a date of 1027 for the battle of Holy River,[50] but this is rendered implausible by Chapter 13 of the Letter sent by Cnut to England in that year, which mentions people who had tried to deprive him of his kingdom and his life, but whose power had been destroyed by God, and says that he is returning from Rome to Denmark to make peace with them. As the fighting was apparently over by the time he attended the German emperor Conrad II's imperial coronation in Rome in March 1027, the most likely year for Holy River therefore seems to be 1026,[51] or conceivably, if operations were protracted, 1025. Only if there was further trouble after the visit to Rome would 1027 be a plausible date.

Although Ulf and Eglaf are often identified with Ulf, the husband of Cnut's sister Estrith, and his brother Eglaf, this is not certain. Eglaf held an English earldom, and any rebellion must have been forgiven, if he fled England after Cnut's death as later Welsh chronicles say.[52] Even so, he last witnesses a dated charter (S 961) in 1024, which would fit well enough with his presence at Holy River. If his brother Ulf was involved, as stated by Saxo Grammaticus and possibly lost northern sources, he too must have made his peace with Cnut, who allegedly had him assassinated in a church at

---

[49] Adam, *Gesta*, ii. 52, pp. 112–13. WJ, v. 8, pp. 18–21, reports that after Swegen's death Cnut asked for the assistance of both Olaf of Norway and a Swedish king, Lacman.

[50] *Encomium*, p. 82.

[51] Similarly, Steenstrup, *Normannerne*, iii. 350; Moberg, *Olav Haraldsson, Knut den store och Sverige*, p. 160; Stenton, *Anglo-Saxon England*, p. 403; Moberg, 'Knut den store's motståndare i slaget vid Helgeå', 10–11; Gräslund, 'Knut den store och sveariket: Slaget vid Helgeå i ny belysning', 211.

[52] Below, p. 169.

Roskilde.[53] Obviously, he and Eglaf may have sided with those attacking Denmark, and one or both could later have been forgiven, but other candidates are available as Cnut's opponents at Holy River.[54]

The skald Sighvat's poem *Austrfararvísur* (Eastern Travel Verses) describes a journey to Sweden by its author on behalf of Olaf of Norway, and refers several times to a chieftain named Ragnvald, who appears once with 'the wise Ulf'.[55] Moreover, another of Sighvat's poems, *Erlingsflokkr*, on the Norwegian Erling Skjalgsson, mentions the marriage of one of his sisters to Ragnvald, father of Ulf, and verse 19 of *Austrfararvísur* includes an unnamed brother of Ulf.[56] The Icelandic saga writer Snorri Sturluson was by the early thirteenth century calling this brother Eglaf, and identifying Ragnvald as earl of Västergötland in Sweden. It might be doubted whether Ragnvald's sons, who were first put forward as Cnut's opponents at Holy River long ago,[57] would have been sufficiently well known in England for the *Chronicle* entry to be readily intelligible,[58] but this is not certain, and an annalist naming leaders of large Swedish forces may have thought it obvious that they were Swedes themselves. In all, identifying Ulf as the son of Ragnvald seems at least as plausible as believing that he was Cnut's brother-in-law Ulf. Whoever they were, Ulf and Eglaf are unlikely to have been the prime movers in the attack on Cnut.

The campaign which included the fight at Holy River was probably a joint enterprise of Olaf of Norway and Anund Jacob of Sweden, who perhaps both felt threatened by the strength of Cnut's position in England and Denmark, and hoped to profit by his absence from Scandinavia. Sighvat's *Knútsdrápa* apparently composed shortly after Cnut's death, has

[53] Saxo, *Historia*, x, 16, ed. Christiansen, i. 31–34; see further, *Encomium*, pp.82–86; *FNC*, i. 727–29. Adam, *Gesta*, ii. 54, p.114, mentions Ulf's marriage to Cnut's sister Estrith, whom he calls Margaret, but not until the Roskilde *Chronicon*, vii, ed. Gertz, i. 21, do we get the tale that this occurred without Cnut's knowledge, that he banished and then forgave them, and shortly afterwards had Ulf killed in a Roskilde church. He was presumably dead by the time Estrith married Robert of Normandy (below, p.105).

[54] For what follows, see Moberg, 'Knut den store's motståndare', 13–15.

[55] See the Select Bibliography of Primary Sources under Sighvat and on *Austrfararvísur*, Turville-Petre, *Skaldic Poetry*, pp.76–83, where some verses are translated. Their original order is uncertain, but Ragnvald appears in those numbered 12, 17, 20 and 21 in Jónsson's edition. Ulf is mentioned in verse 20: Jónsson's BI version of this alters *Spakr lét Ulfr* into *Sunr lét Ulfs*, thus making Ragnvald Ulf's son, but this has no authority, see Jónsson AI and Kock.

[56] Jónsson BI prints *Ulfs bróður-lið*, meaning that Olaf got Ulf's brotherly help, but as the hyphen seems unwarranted (Jónsson AI; Kock; Moberg, 'Knut den store's motståndare', 15), he was in fact indebted to the help of Ulf's brother.

[57] *FNC*, i. 742–43; Moberg, *Olav Haraldsson*, p.164; Moberg, 'Knut den store's motståndare'. Rejected by Campbell, *Encomium*, p. 86; Sawyer, 'Knut, Sweden and Sigtuna', p.93.

[58] *Crawford Collection*, ed. Napier and Stevenson, p.142.

Olaf[59] taking a fleet south from the river Nid (in the Trondheim area) to Zealand, and Anund leading a Swedish force against the Danes. But, says Sighvat, they were unable to subdue Denmark, and one of them, the destroyer (*hlöðr*) of the Danes, harried Skåne. There is no doubt that Cnut disposed of this threat, but where Holy River fits in is unclear. Sighvat's poem is known to be incomplete, but surviving verses do not mention the battle, and Ottar the Black's *Knútsdrápa* says that Cnut opposed or threw back (*hnekðir*) the Swedes there, and describes him as their withstander (*þengvir*), neither of which is resonant of overwhelming victory. Indeed, if Holy River was known only from the *Chronicle* entry one would think it a defeat, but Ottar is unlikely to have included a famous reverse in a list of Cnut's achievements, and the royal title used in the 1027 Letter (see below) suggests that he did eventually claim suzerainty over some Swedes.[60] Also, coins seem for a time to have been minted in his name in Sigtuna (on Lake Mälar, near modern Stockholm) with the title *REX SW* (king of Swedes), by a moneyer who had earlier struck for Anund Jacob. However, the significance of this is questionable, as extant specimens all emanate from a single obverse die.[61] Holy River is usually identified with that still called Helga Å, which enters the sea near Kristianstad in southern Sweden, and then lay roughly on the eastern border of the Danish province of Skåne.[62] This is plausible enough, although Bo Gräslund has recently contended that a watercourse near Stockholm once bore the name too, and that a battle there would provide a better historical context for the Sigtuna coinage and

---

[59] Freeman (*FNC*, i. 743) suggested and Campbell (*Encomium*, p.86) agreed, that the Eglaf of the *Chronicle* might be an error for Olaf. On the *Knútsdrápa*, see Fidjestøl, *Det norrøne Fyrstediktet*, pp.119–20. Townend, 'Contextualising the *Knútsdrápur*', 153–56, favours a date of about 1027 for the composition of the poem.

[60] William of Malmesbury, *GR*, ii. 181, ed. Mynors *et al.*, i. 322–23, says that Cnut was at first unsuccessful against the Swedes, but later put them to flight and forced the kings Ulf and Eiglaf to make peace; but this may well be inference from the *Chronicle*. Moberg, *Olav Haraldsson*, p.170 (followed by Gräslund, 'Knut den store', 213) argued that Cnut won Holy River, and that the *Chronicle* says that the Swedes possessed the field because they lay dead upon it. This is not convincing: *heafdon weallstowe ge weald* is a stock *Chronicle* phrase for possessing a battlefield; see Sawyer, 'Knut, Sweden and Sigtuna', p.89. Townend, 'Contextualising the *Knútsdrápur*', 159–61, raises the possibility that the verse was not originally part of the *Knútsdrápa* (which he is inclined to date to about 1016), if indeed it is by Ottar at all.

[61] Sawyer, 'Knut, Sweden and Sigtuna', p.92, who doubts whether such coins reflect political reality. Of the two iron dies needed to strike coins, the obverse bore the king's portrait and title. The Sigtuna obverse with Cnut's Swedish title shows him with a fleur-de-lis sceptre, which probably means that it was not struck until after this feature appeared on his English *Short Cross* type, maybe introduced about 1029; Lagerqvist and Dolley, 'The Problem of the "Fleur-de-lis" sceptre on the Sigtuna coins of Cnut'; Lagervist, 'The Coinage at Sigtuna in the names of Anund Jacob, Cnut the Great and Harthacnut'. Jonsson, 'The coinage of Cnut', pp.228–29, shows fairly conclusively that these coins 'cannot be taken as evidence that Cnut ruled in Sweden', and suggests that the part of the country taken by him after Holy River was the province of Blekinge, to the east of Skåne.

[62] See Christiansen's note on the area, Saxo, *Historia*, i. 196.

Cnut's claim to rule some of the Swedes.[63] This may or may not be so. Professor Sawyer has drawn attention to rune stones in Denmark and Västergötland raised in honour of men accorded the English epithet thegn, and concluded that the latter area was the part of Sweden controlled by Cnut, through agents who received a title borne in England by royal subordinates. Seven instances or variations of the place-name Thegnaby in the coastal area between Oslo and Göteborg could be part of this picture too, and hint at a considerable degree of organisation.[64] Cnut's supremacy over part of Sweden may be obscure; it need not have been ineffective.

Sighvat's *Knútsdrápa* indicates that he had sailed from England to deal with the threat posed by Olaf and Anund Jacob, and mentions his visit to Rome. He was certainly present there at the imperial coronation of Conrad II at Easter (26 March) 1027,[65] and the Letter states his intention of returning to Denmark to make peace. By this time, if not before, he must have been preparing to overthrow Olaf of Norway. The Letter calls him king of all England and Denmark and the Norwegians and of some of the Swedes, which if genuine implies that he already claimed Olaf's throne,[66] and John of Worcester says that in 1027 he heard that some Norwegians were discontented, sent them large quantities of gold and silver, and secured an undertaking of future support. But he returned to England before launching his campaign, almost certainly to marshal his resources.

The *Chronicle* C text records that in 1028 Cnut sailed from England to Norway with fifty ships; D and E add that he drove Olaf away and took it for himself. The skaldic poetry is more helpful. Sighvat was in Olaf's service at the time, and his *Vestrfararvísur* (Western Travel Verses) name Earl Hakon, son of Earl Eric of Lade, as acting with Cnut, and speak repeatedly of money offered to Olaf's men, while the *Tøgdrápa* of Thorarin Praise-Tongue, who apparently sailed with Cnut's fleet, indicates that he went first to Denmark to assemble his ships in the Limfjord in Jutland, and then proceeded north along the Norwegian coast to Trondheim. Olaf's major followers had seemingly not only been seduced by Cnut's cash, but also angered, according to Adam of Bremen, by the king's tendency to

---

[63] Gräslund, 'Knut den store'.

[64] Sawyer, *När Sverige blev Sverige*, pp. 53–55. It should be noted that the rune stones cannot be dated, and that there are some bearing the word thegn in the area south of Lake Mälar in eastern Sweden.

[65] His participation at the Easter meeting with Conrad and Pope John (XIX) is mentioned in chapter 5 of the Letter, and this was in 1027, at Conrad's imperial coronation; see *FNC*, i. 729–31; *ASC*, ii. 206–07; below, pp. 99–100, 104–05.

[66] But the title may have been altered at some time to reflect later events; copies of the Letter survive no earlier than in the Latin works of John and William of Malmesbury.

apprehend their wives for sorcery.[67] He was able to mount no effective resistance and withdrew, while Cnut put Norway under Hakon's control. If Thorarin is reliable this was also the point at which he entrusted Denmark to one of his sons. Sighvat's *Knútsdrápa* implies that he had a son there at the time of the joint attack by Olaf and Anund, possibly the one given to Thorkell in 1023. The *Chronicle* D and E texts assign Cnut's return to England to 1029. Either in that or more likely the following year[68] Earl Hakon was drowned at sea,[69] and Olaf took the opportunity to return to Norway. In 1030 he was killed at the battle of Stiklestad (near Trondheim) by his own people, and Cnut then put his consort Ælfgifu of Northampton and their son Swegen in charge there.

Swegen Forkbeard had ruled Denmark, controlled Norway, and been allied with King Olaf of Sweden. Cnut inherited this alliance, but Norway was lost to Olaf Haraldsson as he was conquering England, and Denmark may have had to be left to his brother Harald. It hence took time to recreate his father's empire. His position in England had to be secured, and early difficulties in Denmark, Thorkell, Olaf of Norway and Anund Jacob of Sweden all had to be overcome; thus, not until 1028 did Cnut's position in Scandinavia rival Swegen's in 1013. But this is not to deny his achievement, which was fairly clearly founded on political, military, administrative and diplomatic skills of a high order, and his own sense of it is indicated by his adoption around this time of a crown modelled on that worn by the German emperors.[70] His considerable standing in the northern world is also reflected by his good relations with the emperor Conrad II, which culminated in the betrothal of his daughter Gunnhild to Conrad's son (see pages 104–05). He seems to have intended to rule Norway, like Swegen, through the earls of Lade, and his dominion there would doubtless have been more secure if Earl Hakon had not died prematurely and without issue. Still, the return of Olaf's son Magnus to Norway, and expulsion of Ælfgifu of Northampton and her son, lay in the future in 1030, when Cnut was perhaps at the zenith of his power.

[67] Adam, *Gesta*, ii. 61, p.120. On the date of the *Tøgdrápa*, see Townend, 'Contextualising the *Knútsdrápur*', 156–57.
[68] The *Chronicle* gives 1030 but later Scandinavian sources may favour 1029; see *Encomium*, p.72.
[69] John of Worcester reports that Hakon was exiled because Cnut feared treachery, and killed on Orkney.
[70] Below, pp.127–28.

ROME AND SCOTLAND

Nothing is known of his other activities in that year (but see below) and 1031 brings a further set of problems. The *Chronicle* C text is blank here, while D and E record visits to Rome and Scotland. 1031 for the Rome visit may be a scribal error for 1026 (*MXXVI* having become *MXXXI*),[71] for as Cnut was certainly in Rome in March 1027 his journey could have started late the previous year. All the same, he possibly did visit it twice. According to Goscelin's account of the translation of the relics of St Mildred from Thanet to St Augustine's Canterbury, written in the late eleventh century, Cnut went to Canterbury as he was setting out for Rome and promised that he would allow the translation if he returned safely. Sure enough, St Augustine saved him from shipwreck on the way back, he agreed to the translation, and ordered Ælfstan, abbot of St Augustine's, to come to him at Whitsuntide. Ælfstan anticipated events by receiving the royal assent on the Saturday, and arrived in Thanet on Whit Sunday itself. Knowing the likely unpopularity of his mission, he concealed its purpose from the island's inhabitants, and withdrew from their banquet early, with the excuse that he had been tired by the journey; later, when they had gone exhausted to their beds, he entered Mildred's church accompanied by selected monks and the soldiers he had prudently brought with him. Much of the night passed in vain attempts to open the tomb, but an appeal to the saint herself worked wonders (a common feature of such tales) and the party made for its ships with the precious plunder. Narrowly escaping the hostile intentions of the awakened populace, they eventually bore Mildred into Canterbury amid great rejoicing. This translation, says Goscelin, took place in 1030, on 18 May, when Benedict was pope, Henry emperor, Cnut king of England, Æthelnoth archbishop of Canterbury, and Ælfstan abbot of St Augustine's. Apart from the fact that the pope at this time was John XIX and the emperor Conrad, these details are consistent. Whitsuntide was 17 May in 1030, and as the saint's body was raised during the following night, it would have entered Canterbury on 18 May.[72] Now if Goscelin was correct in believing that the translation occurred immediately after Cnut's return from Rome, this seems unlikely to be the visit of 1027. Moreover, the story of Cnut's presence in Canterbury before and after the Rome trip, and of the

---

[71] *FNC*,i.731.
[72] Goscelin, *Translatio Sancte Mildrethe Virginis*, x–xvii ed. Rollason, 167–76. There seems no need to follow Professor Rollason in emending the year to 1035, when Whitsuntide was 18 May, and Benedict IX was pope.

storm and near shipwreck, also occurs in his account of the miracles worked by St Augustine. This omits the details on Mildred, but adds, in a way reminiscent of Chapter 5 of the 1027 Letter, that Cnut was most accept-able to the emperor, and says that on landing he hurried to St Augustine's to offer them rich gifts – no doubt including the gold plate which he took from his treasures and held aloft to attract the saint's attention during the storm.[73]

One hesitates long before accepting such details from a hagiographer writing some sixty years later, not least because by Goscelin's time the canons of St Gregory's Canterbury were claiming that they, not St Augustine's, had Mildred's remains.[74] However, the most notable feature of these accounts is not so much their dating, as the apparent belief in St Augustine's, where Goscelin spent the last years of his life, that Cnut visited them both on the way to and from Rome. This may be invention, for the propaganda value of possessing a saint courted thus by a king renowned for his piety is obvious; but if not, and taken together with the Encomiast's statement that Cnut vis-ited St Omer while on pilgrimage to Rome, a journey in which he embarked from somewhere near Canterbury (maybe Sandwich) and sailed to Flanders seems a distinct possibility. It is not readily identifiable with the 1027 trip (even though Goscelin's mention of the emperor in the second story seems to refer to it), as the Letter says that he had arrived in Rome from Denmark and intended returning there. The evidence is inconclusive, but a further visit to Rome, perhaps in 1030, cannot be completely ruled out.

Although the date, like that for the Rome trip, should not be pressed, the *Chronicle* E text (D is less detailed) says that in 1031 Cnut went to Scotland and received the submission of three kings, Malcolm (II, 1005–34), Mælbæth and Iehmarc. There has been doubt whether Mælbæth is identifiable with Shakespeare's Macbeth, who deposed Malcolm II's grandson Duncan in 1040, and whose name is given clearly enough as Macbeoðen by D under 1054. Even so, B.T. Hudson has recently stressed that a spelling in D is irrelevant to one in E, and used twelfth-century evidence (and E is a twelfth-century manuscript) to show that in any case Mælbæth is a con-vincing English version of Macbeth,[75] whose family ruled, conceivably by the early eleventh century with the title king, an area around the Moray Firth as far north as Sutherland and Caithness. Iehmarc may have been

[73] Goscelin, *Liber de Miraculis, Acta Sanctorum Maii*, vi. 399–400.
[74] See *Writs*, pp.191–95. The probably spurious writ S 990 purports to record Cnut's gift of Mildred's relics to St Augustine's.
[75] Hudson, 'Cnut and the Scottish Kings'.

Echmarcach Ragnallson, later king of Dublin (see below), but who possibly in 1031 controlled part of Galloway and maybe the Isle of Man.[76]

Ralph Glaber reports that Cnut fought a long war against Malcolm and the Scots, that they were eventually reconciled through Emma and Richard of Normandy, and that he received Malcolm's (otherwise unknown) son from the baptismal font.[77] Written before about 1030,[78] this must if correct refer to events prior to Richard's death in 1026, and perhaps to the aftermath of the battle of Carham. Early twelfth-century works attributed to Symeon of Durham mention Carham (on the Tweed) twice. The *Libellvs de exordio* (a history of the church of Durham) says that the English were heavily defeated there by the Scots in 1018, and the *Historia Regum* that it was a great battle fought in 1018 between Earl Uhtred of Northumbria and Malcolm king of Scots, supported by Owain king of Strathclyde.[79] Unfortunately, the *Anglo-Saxon Chronicle* has Uhtred killed on Cnut's orders in 1016. Either this date is wrong, and he died later, or Carham was in 1016 or earlier, or it was in 1018 and the *Historia Regum* is mistaken about Uhtred's presence there. The late-eleventh-century Durham tract *De Obsessione Dunelmi* states that after his death Eadwulf, his brother and successor as earl of Bernicia, surrendered Lothian (i.e. territory beyond the Tweed) to Malcolm, but yet another Durham work, the *De Primo Saxonum Adventu*, has Lothian given to the Scots by Edgar.[80]

The *De Obsessione* says that Malcolm assaulted Durham and was driven off by Uhtred during Æthelred's reign, and the Irish *Annals of Ulster* record fighting between Scots and English in 1005 (*recte* 1006).[81] It would not be surprising if Malcolm renewed his efforts in around 1016–18, considering the likely state of England at the time, and Cnut could well have acted

---

[76] I follow Dr Hudson here, although he informs me that the death of a Suibhne king of Galloway is recorded by the *Annals of Ulster* under 1034; he also rejects the idea that Echmarcach was son of Ragnall land brother of Ragnall I (d. 1035), kings of Waterford.

[77] Ralph Glaber, *Historiarvm Libri Qvinqve* ii. 3, ed. France, pp. 54–56. Ralph was in Italy in 1028, and it may be, as Dr France says, that he acquired this information from people who had spoken to Cnut's entourage the year before.

[78] Ralph Glaber, *Historiarvm Libri Quinqve*, ed. France, p. xlv.

[79] Symeon, *Libellvs de exordio*, ed. Rollason, pp. 154–57; Symeon, *Opera Omnia*, ed. Arnold, ii. 155–56; see Gransden, *Historical Writing in England*, pp. 114–21, 148–51.

[80] In Symeon, *Opera Omnia*, ed. Arnold, i. 218, ii. 382. Meehan, 'The siege of Durham, the battle of Carham and the cession of Lothian', 4–5, 17, argues convincingly that Lothian was indeed ceded by Edgar; see also Stenton, *Anglo-Saxon England*, p. 370. A possible refinement is that the Scots recovered after Carham a part of Lothian which they had lost during their incursion into northern England in 1006; Kapelle, *The Norman Conquest of the North*, p. 22. On the *De Obsessione*, see Morris, *Marriage and Murder*, pp. 5–12.

[81] In Symeon, *Opera Omnia*, ed. Arnold, i. 215–16. Meehan, 'The siege of Durham', 15–17, contends that this is a mistaken duplication of the siege of Durham in 1040, but see Duncan, 'The battle of Carham, 1018', 20. *Annals of Ulster*, ed. Mac Airt and Mac Niocaill, pp. 436–37.

against him once free to do so. Ralph Glaber may thus be correct in referring to hostilities before 1026. However, the 1031 visit itself, assuming that it is not misdated, suggests further trouble. A verse by Sighvat says that famous princes have brought their heads to Cnut from Fife to buy peace; where this fits in is not clear, although as it also refers to St Olaf, and in the past tense, his death in 1030 had evidently occurred before it was composed.[82]

RELATIONS WITH THE WELSH AND THE IRISH

A verse attributed to Ottar the Black[83] greets the ruler of the Danes, Irish, English and Island-dwellers. The reference to the Irish not only brings to mind Swegen Forkbeard's putative activities in the Irish Sea and Adam of Bremen's story of his stay with a *rex Scothorum* (? king of the Irish),[84] but can also be linked to the possibility that the Iehmarc who submitted in 1031 was Echmarcach Ragnallson, who replaced Sihtric Silkbeard as king of Dublin in 1036. Hudson has concluded that Cnut received the submission of the Scots in 1031 in Strathclyde, during a naval expedition into the Irish Sea, and whether or not Echmarcach did rule in Galloway and the Isle of Man at this time (see above), his presence at the meeting could be relevant to Cnut's relations with the Irish. Similarly, the plundering of Wales by the Foreigners (i.e. Scandinavians) of Dublin and the English, recorded by the Irish *Annals of Tigernach* under 1030, may have been a joint expedition,[85] and there is a faint possibility that Dublin's first bishop was consecrated by Archbishop Æthelnoth of Canterbury in Cnut's time, with whatever implications that might or might not have.[86] As for Wales, a charter forged in Llandaff in the twelfth century claims that the Welsh ruler Rhydderch ab Iestyn (d.1033), whom it calls king, confirmed Bishop Joseph of Llandaff in possession of all the see's lands and charters, with the support of Archbishop Æthelnoth and letters from Cnut. Opinion is divided on whether this document was forged on the basis of a record made in Joseph's time.[87] If so,

[82] *Lausavísur*, ed. Jónsson AI, pp.269–70; BI, p.249; Kock, i. 129. This is Dr Hudson's point.
[83] *Lausavísur*, ed. Jónsson AI, p. 299; BI, p.275; Kock, i. 141. See further Townend, 'Contextualising the *Knútsdrápur*', 157–59.
[84] Above, pp.31–32.
[85] *Annals of Tigernach*, ed. Stokes, p.370. I owe this suggestion to Dr Hudson.
[86] Gwynn, 'The origins of the see of Dublin'; Gwynn, 'The First Bishops of Dublin'; and recently and sceptically, Flanagan, *Irish Society*, pp.8–18. Barlow, *The English Church 1000–1066*, pp.232–33, thinks that the occasional consecrations of bishops from Scotland, Ireland and Wales by English archbishops had little political significance.
[87] Davies, *The Llandaff Charters*, p.126; rejected by Maund, *Ireland, Wales and England in the Eleventh Century*, pp.188–89. Printed, *The Text of the Book of Llan Dâv*, ed. Evans and Rhys, pp.253–55.

Cnut's power would seem in some sense to have extended into Wales. As so often, there is much here that is both tempting and tenuous. One would like to know more, for example, of the circumstances in which Olaf, son of the Dublin monarch Sihtric Silkbeard, was killed by Englishmen on his way to Rome in 1034, and about the death of Caradog, son of Rhydderch ab Iestyn, at the hands of the English in 1035.[88] Still, it is far from unlikely that both Swegen and Cnut did have relations with the Scandinavian colonies in Ireland, and there is just enough evidence to suggest that when the Encomiast named among the latter's dominions not only England, Denmark and Norway, but also *Brittania* and *Scothia*, he was not necessarily exaggerating.[89] Cnut was well able to raise powerful fleets, which may have been effective not only in Scandinavia, but also against Scotland and Wales, and in the Irish Sea. Claims to suzerainty over the Scots, Irish and Welsh are thus far from unlikely, and may for a time have enjoyed a foundation in reality.

Nor need these relations have owed everything to his father. Æthelred's expedition into the Irish Sea in 1000 implies difficulties there, and earlier Anglo-Saxon kings had frequent contacts with the Welsh, whose border was no doubt often troubled. Eadric Streona's raid on St David's in 1012 was not the first English incursion of Æthelred's reign, and Cnut had been opposed by Welsh allies of Edmund Ironside in 1016, and felt it necessary to settle several Scandinavian earls in the west midlands, one of whom, Eglaf, ravaged Dyfed in 1022;[90] it is Welsh, not English, sources which record his flight from England after Cnut's death. In 1039 Earl Leofric of Mercia's brother Edwin was killed in battle by Gruffydd ap Llywelyn, king of Gwynedd and Powys (north and mid-Wales), who was to extend his power over all his countrymen before meeting his death during Harold Godwinsson's Welsh campaign of 1063. King Æthelstan, whose lordship over various Welsh princes is implied by their witnessing of his charters, also invaded Scotland in 934, and the Scots were among the enemies he defeated at *Brunanburh* three years later. The control of the Northumbrian kingdom, first established by Æthelstan in 927, brought his successors too into regular contact with the Scots, and notably Edgar, who in 973 was consecrated at Bath in a ceremony perhaps intended to celebrate his lordship of all Britain. Shortly afterwards, he probably ceded Lothian to the Scottish king Kenneth, and received his submission and that of other princes, including

[88] *Annals of Ulster*, ed. Mac Airt and Mac Niocaill, pp.472-73. Maund, *Ireland, Wales and England*, p.122.
[89] *Encomium*, ii. 19, p.34.
[90] *Annales Cambriæ*, ed. Williams ab Ithel, p.23; see also below, p.169.

the kings of Gwynedd and Strathclyde.[91] Cnut's taking of a second, imperial, crown may well have been stimulated not only by a position in Scandinavia which emulated that of Swegen, but by achievements in Britain which lay firmly in a tradition established by the greatest of his royal Anglo-Saxon predecessors.

GERMANY AND NORMANDY

Two other areas, Germany and Normandy, were particularly important late in Cnut's reign. His Danish border with Germany, and evident desire to emulate its rulers,[92] must have stimulated mutual contact, although nothing is known of relations with the emperor Henry II(1002–24). By his day the sort of German pressure on Denmark experienced by Harald Bluetooth was a thing of the past, for Henry was fully occupied with campaigns in Italy and Lotharingia, and especially against Cnut's uncle Boleslav of Poland, and may have troubled little about Swegen and Cnut, who were presumably happy to leave the Germans largely to their own devices while they were subjugating England. Even so, one could guess that his wars against the Poles (peace was made in 1018) led to coldness with Boleslav's nephew, and that Cnut's attitude to the Germans improved when first Henry and then Boleslav (1025) died. Adam of Bremen's statement that he and Henry's successor, Conrad II (1024–39), made peace through the mediation of the archbishop of Hamburg-Bremen hints at initial difficulties, but the only certainty is that good relations existed by March 1027, when Cnut attended Conrad's imperial coronation.[93]

   His pride in doing so is clear from the Letter of 1027, and no doubt extended to his other contacts with Conrad. Adam, who is conflating events from various dates here, reports that Conrad asked for the marriage of Cnut's daughter (Gunnhild) to his son (Henry), and ceded Schleswig and territory north of the river Eider (south of Hedeby) as a token of their treaty of friendship.[94] However, the marriage negotiations are likely to have been after 1027. Conrad had sent an embassy to Constantinople to arrange Henry's union with a daughter of the emperor Constantine VIII, who had

[91] Nelson, *Politics and Ritual*, pp.296–303; Stenton, *Anglo-Saxon England*, pp.369–70.
[92] Below, pp.127–28.
[93] Wipo, *Gesta Chuonradi*, xvi, ed. Bresslau, p.36. Stafford, *Unification and Conquest*, p.75, contends that uppermost in Cnut's mind in Rome in 1027 were the exiled English æthelings in Normandy and Hungary; this seems rather unlikely.
[94] Adam, *Gesta*, ii. 56, pp.116–17.

CNUT, ENGLAND AND NORTHERN EUROPE, 1017–35

no male heir. Constantine's death in November 1028, and the marriage of the fifty-year-old Zoe to Romanus Argyrus, who thus gained the Byzantine throne, brought this to nothing, and it was probably in 1029 or later that a stronger link with Cnut became attractive.[95] Adam says that Cnut's valour secured a firm peace among the Slav peoples east of the Elbe,[96] and Conrad perhaps gained military assistance against those troubling eastern Saxony, and Cnut's neutrality during the German campaigns which led to the submission of his cousin Mieszko II of Poland in 1032. Gunnhild's betrothal to Henry occurred in 1035, and the marriage itself in 1036; she died of pestilence in Italy two years later.

Relations with Normandy were as important at the end as at the outset of Cnut's reign, because his marriage to Emma ultimately failed to maintain the good relations with her kin necessitated by their sheltering of Edward and Alfred, her sons by Æthelred. Her brother Duke Richard II, with whom the union had almost certainly been negotiated in 1017, died in 1026, to be succeeded by his sons Richard III (1026–27) and Robert (1027–35). Adam of Bremen states that Cnut's sister Margaret (usually known by her other name, Estrith) married Duke Richard, who repudiated her, and set off on pilgrimage to Jerusalem to escape Cnut's wrath. This is confused: it was Robert who went on pilgrimage to Jerusalem, dying on the return journey in 1035, and Ralph Glaber says clearly that it was he who married and divorced Estrith.[97] The diplomacy which must have preceded this match, and Cnut's desire for it, imply worries about Robert's attitude which were to prove well founded. William of Jumièges alleges that he treated the æthelings Edward and Alfred with honour, adopted them as brothers, and sent messengers to Cnut asking that they be restored to their own. On Cnut's refusal, he commanded the construction and assembly of a large fleet at Fécamp. This sailed for England, was driven by a gale to Jersey, made its way to Mont St Michel, and was then used in a campaign against Count Alan III of Brittany. Nevertheless, envoys subsequently arrived from Cnut offering to restore half of England to Æthelred's sons and establish peace, as he was gravely ill, whereupon Robert decided to postpone his expedition and go to Jerusalem.[98] Professor Keynes

[95] As suggested by Bresslau, 'Ein Beitrag zur Kenntnis von Konrads II Beziehungen zu Byzanz und Dänemark'.
[96] Adam, *Gesta*, ii. 66, p. 125. Mr Christiansen thinks (Saxo, i. 186) that Cnut may have borne sway over the Slavs of Holstein and Mecklenberg, in association with Duke Bernard of Saxony and Archbishop Unwan of Hamburg-Bremen.
[97] Adam, *Gesta*, ii. 54, pp. 114–15; Ralph Glaber, *Historiarvm Libri Qvinqve*, iv. 20, ed France, p. 204. Adam, apparently wrongly, thought that Estrith's Norman match preceded her union with Ulf.

has shown that Norman charter evidence seems to support important elements of this account.[99] Edward and Alfred appear together in only two of
Robert's grants, one dated 1033 to the abbey of St Wandrille, and another, to
the abbey of Fécamp, probably from that year. Indeed, similarities in their
formulae suggest that both were drawn up at Fécamp in 1033. Also, a further
grant by Robert to Fécamp from the early 1030s, which survives on its original single sheet of parchment, is witnessed by Edward as king, and in yet
another charter, witnessed by Robert, Edward 'king of the English' makes a
grant to Mont St Michel. It looks as though Robert may well have assembled a fleet at Fécamp, seemingly in 1033, and that it visited Mont St Michel,
where Edward made a gift to the monks. Another witness of the charter to
St Wandrille dated 1033 is King Henry I of France, who is known from other
sources to have been briefly in exile with Robert at Fécamp, and according
Edward the title 'king of the English' would presumably have done Robert's
prestige no harm at all, as he would thus have been entertaining two exiled
monarchs at the same time.[100]

    Whether his ships ever sailed against England, as William of Jumièges
claims, is another matter. Mont St Michel is known to have been disputed
between Brittany and Normandy at about this date,[101] and Robert's fleet
may from the first have been intended to operate against it and the Bretons.
Furthermore, William of Jumièges was probably writing in the 1050s, after
Edward the Confessor had promised the English throne to Robert's son
William, and it was fairly clearly this which led him to repeat Dudo of St
Quentin's story of the English king who entered into a pact with the
Normans and later received Rollo's assistance against rebels, to include
accounts of Anglo-Norman relation in the days of Æthelred and Cnut, and
to end his description of Cnut's conquest of England and marriage to
Emma by stating that he had wished to explain King Edward's origins to
those who were ignorant of them.[102] At much the same time (around

[98] WJ, vi. 9, 11, ed. van Houts, ii. 76–81.
[99] What follows is drawn from Keynes, 'The Æthelings in Normandy'. See also FNC, i. 466–73; Van
Houts, 'The Political Relations between Normandy and England before 1066 according to the "Gesta
Normannorum Ducum"', pp.89–92. The Carmen de Hastingae Proelio, written either just after the
Conquest or in the early twelfth century, says that Robert 'set the necks of the English under the
yoke', line 332, ed. Barlow, pp.20–21.
[100] But it should be noted that Edward does not witness the grant to St Wandrille as king.
[101] Bates, Normandy before 1066, pp.70–71.
[102] WJ, ii. 1, 7, v. 9, ed. van Houts, i. 32–33, 58–61, ii. 20–23. William names the king assisted by Rollo as
Athelstanus, who is possibly to be identified with the viking Guthrum, who ruled in East Anglia in
the late ninth century and took the name Athelstan on his baptism.

1053–54), a monk of St Wandrille was similarly including in his *Inuentio et Miracula Sancti Vulfranni* an account of how Edward and Alfred took refuge in the Norman court, were welcomed by Richard II, and treated as his sons.[103] Edward was clearly, and not surprisingly, of considerable interest in Normandy at this date, and William of Jumièges would have had a motive for inventing Robert's expedition against England, to increase Edward's debt to the Normans in general and William's father in particular. Nevertheless, it is not certainly fictitious, for the paucity of English sources on the later years of Cnut's reign makes their silence inconclusive, and Robert may have been moved not only by feeling for the æthelings and his apparent friendship for their sister Godgifu's husband, Count Dreux of the Vexin,[104] but also by memories of his rift with Cnut's sister Estrith. If it did sail against him, Cnut presumably took appropriate measures, and contrary winds need not have been the only force responsible for its repulse. William of Jumièges's statement that he later offered the æthelings a share of England is very difficult to credit; it may owe something to Dudo's story of the offer made to Rollo, or result from confusion with the events of 1041, when Edward returned to England at Harthacnut's invitation and according to the *Chronicle* C text was sworn in as king.[105]

These events across the Channel had something of a postscript after Cnut's death. William of Jumièges, elaborated by William of Poitiers, reports that Edward set sail with forty ships, crossed to Southampton, defeated a large English force, and returned to Normandy after realising that he needed more men to obtain the kingdom. Meanwhile, Alfred sailed from Wissant to Dover, went inland, and was betrayed to death by Earl Godwin.[106] The *Chronicle* C text for 1036 also records his arrival and death, which an *obit* in an Ely calendar shows occurred on 5 February.[107] As Cnut himself only died on 12 November 1035, it looks as though Alfred, and doubtless Edward too, were poised to act. If their friend Duke Robert had not died on his way back from Jerusalem these expeditions might have been better supported, and had a different outcome.

[103]Van Houts, 'Historiography and Hagiography at Saint-Wandrille', 251.
[104]Bates, 'Lord Sudeley's Ancestors', p.37.
[105]*ASC*, i. 162; *Encomium*, iii. 13, p.52.
[106] WJ, vii. 5–6, ed. van Houts, ii. 104–07; William of Poitiers, *Gesta Guillelmi*, i. 2–3, ed. Davis and Chibnall, pp.2–5.
[107]Dickins, 'The day of Byrhtnoth's death', 15; Gerchow, *Die Gedenküberlieferung der Angelsachsen*, p.344.

THE END IN ENGLAND

Obscure as they often are, more is known of Cnut's foreign relations than
his later years in England. He may have visited Glastonbury on 30 November
1032,[108] and the five charters from 1033 (S 967–70, 972) are the most to
survive from any year of his reign. 1034 has only one (S 973) and 1035 three
(S 974–6). Of these, S 975, to the monks of Sherborne, is of some interest. It
expresses Cnut's wish that the gift of transitory earthly riches will secure
eternal rewards in heaven, the redemption of his soul, and absolution from
his crimes. Such sentiments are common in charters, but this one goes further. The monks are always to offer prayers to almighty God, and daily to
beseech God by singing psalms and celebrating masses for his sins, so that
after his death through God's mercy and their holy intercession he will
come to the heavenly kingdom. It looks as though Cnut was already mor-
tally ill when he made this grant. He died at Shaftesbury on 12 November
1035 and was buried in the Old Minster Winchester. [109] That he knew of
death's approach and had time to prepare for it, and that others knew and
were preparing too, is implied not only by S 975 but also the rapidity of the
ætheling Alfred's actions late in the year. How far Cnut used the time available to determine the succession is not clear. Harthacnut, no older than
seventeen, had been in Denmark for some years by 1035. According to the
Encomium, John and later Norse tradition, he was its king, and he evidently
struck coins as *REX* before his father's death.[110] Swegen, probably Cnut's
eldest son, had since 1030 been ruling Norway with his mother Ælfgifu of
Northampton. John says that Cnut made him king of Norway, but he was
expelled by Olaf's son Magnus in around 1034, and died shortly afterwards
in Denmark. Harthacnut chose to remain there, presumably because he was
exercised by the threat which Magnus posed to his own position, and this
left Harold Harefoot, Cnut's other son by Ælfgifu of Northampton, to dispute the English throne with his half-brother's supporters, headed by
Queen Emma and Earl Godwin.

Accepted first as regent, he was in 1037 recognised as king, and Emma
went into exile. Adam of Bremen reports that Cnut had intended Swegen

[108] Below, p.129.
[109] This is the *Chronicle* date, with which most church calendars agree, although one gives 11 and
another 13 November; Gerchow, *Die Gedenküberlieferung*, pp.335, 338, 341, 343, 349, 355. For the
suggestion that Cnut was buried near the grave of St Swithun, and the subsequent history of his
bones, which may still lie within the cathedral, see Crook, "'A worthy antiquity'".
[110] *Encomium*, iii. 1, p.38; Becker, 'The Coinages of Harthacnut and Magnus the Good at Lund
c.1040–c.1046', p.121; Becker, 'Studies in the Danish coinage at Lund during the period c.1030–c.1046',
p.459.

to rule Norway, Harthacnut Denmark, and Harold England, and the *Historia Regum* attributed to Symeon of Durham that he made Harold the English king, but the *Encomium* says that he not only promised Emma that any son of hers should be heir, but later on oath pledged the whole kingdom subject to him to Harthacnut, who received oaths of loyalty from English nobles.[111] Obviously, this was what Emma wanted to read, but one would have expected her to take advantage of her rival Ælfgifu of Northampton's absence from England to press Harthacnut's case with his father, and it seems significant that both the *Chronicle* C and E texts consider Harold's claim and identity questionable,[112] that the Oxford meeting which followed Cnut's death decided that he should hold the country for himself and his brother, and that Emma was allowed to reside in Winchester with Harthacnut's housecarls to keep Wessex for him. Harthacnut was thus evidently thought to have a claim, which his housecarls (if they were not simply inherited from his father) were perhaps in England to safeguard. The irregularity of Cnut's relationship with Harold's mother possibly influenced some: the Encomiast claims that Archbishop Æthelnoth refused to crown him, although he does not connect this with Harold's birth.[113] Nevertheless, he had much support, especially north of the Thames and among the troops in London, and suggestions that he was not Cnut's son are likely to be false. The Encomiast's tale that he was born to another woman and smuggled into Ælfgifu of Northampton's bed at least implies that he was generally recognised as son of Cnut and Ælfgifu,[114] and Adam calls Gorm the Old *Hardecnudth Vurm*,[115] which if correct makes it feasible to believe that Cnut named Swegen and Harold from his father and grandfather, and Harthacnut, evidently the third-born, after his great-grandfather. Whatever his intentions about the succession, it was almost certainly not the confusion which actually occurred. Probably, like other strong rulers (Charlemagne, for example), he faced strife within his own family which

[111] Adam, *Gesta* ii. 74, p.134; Symeon, *Historia Regum*, ed.Arnold, ii. 158; *Encomium*, ii. 16,19, iii. 8, pp. 32–34, 48. Campbell (p.lxii) thought that Cnut's promise to Harthacnut was made before he conquered Norway, which he was then free to give to Swegen.

[112] D follows C and is no independent witness here. It is conceivable that the conclusion of E's annal for 1036 (*recte* 1035), which says that many thought it incredible that Harold was Cnut's son by Ælfgifu, is a later addition: it earlier makes no bones about his being Harthacnut's brother. John of Worcester admits that certainty is impossible, but recounts various rumours about the parentage of Swegen and Harold, which can be connected with the idea that their mother is the Ælfgyva who appears in puzzling circumstances on the Bayeux Tapestry; see McNulty, 'The Lady Aelfgyva in the Bayeux Tapestry'.

[113] *Economium*, iii. 1, p.40.

[114] *Econonium*, iii. 1, pp.38–40.

[115] Adam, *Gesta*, i. 55, p.56.

proved difficult to resolve. Sending Ælfgifu and Swegen to Norway perhaps had its advantages here, and maybe Harold Harefoot was not allowed to live at court, which might partly explain alleged doubts about his identity. If so, such expedients failed, for Ælfgifu was soon back in England supporting her son,[116] and he may well have owed his popularity in the midlands partly to her Mercian kindred.

Thus, Cnut's reign ended, like that of Edgar, one of the greatest of his Anglo-Saxon predecessors, with the king's early death and a succession dispute between his sons. The complex legacy which he had inherited in 1016 had been well utilised, a considerable number of its problems solved (for a time, at least), and many of its opportunities taken. After some early difficulties, his grip on England apparently became firm enough, and its magnates committed to the Danish dynasty: nobody seems to have taken the claims of the æthelings Edward and Alfred seriously in 1036. Like other powerful English rulers, he may also have been recognised as overlord by the Welsh and Scots, and possibly some of the Irish. He combined this with achieving a position in the Scandinavian world which rivalled and in some respects surpassed that of his father. Not since Æthelstan a century earlier had an English king married a female relative to the German imperial heir; no Danish monarch had ever done so. He had gone to Rome once, maybe twice, and his relations with continental potentates were doubtless more extensive than we can now know. The Aquitanian chronicler Adémar of Chabannes says that Cnut sent Duke William the Great of Aquitaine yearly embassies with costly gifts, and received even more costly ones in return.[117] If this looks like the tip of a diplomatic iceberg, it at least indicates Cnut's international standing, which his evidently extensive gifts to foreign churches[118] were surely intended to foster.

That the dominions which he had so laboriously assembled fragmented upon his death (indeed, his position in Norway had collapsed before it) is a pointer to Cnut's abilities, and of how individual, and hence transitory, political achievement could be. Within seven years all his sons were dead too, and the West Saxon dynasty, in the person of Edward the Confessor, sat once more upon the throne of England.

[116] Stevenson, 'An Alleged Son of King Harold Harefoot', 115–16.
[117] Adémar, *Chronique*, iii. 41, ed. Chavanon, p.163. See further Beech, 'England and Aquitaine in the century before the Norman Conquest'.
[118] Below, p.146.

4

CNUT AND
THE ENGLISH CHURCH

Not the least of the problems which Cnut faced as king of England was
an important and complex relationship with the English church. Its
importance arose from the extent to which Christianity had by the early
eleventh century become part of political and national life, its complexity in
part from the complex nature of church affairs themselves. If it occasionally
had Cnut in difficulties, it also offered him considerable opportunities, and
it is no less generous to the historian, who is better informed upon it than
any other aspect of Cnut's rule.

The Anglo-Saxons accepted Christianity in the seventh century, and in
some respects its progress thereafter was spectacular. Within a hundred years
of the missionaries' arrival many English men and women had enthusiasti-
cally adopted the monasticism which was considered the purest form of the
Christian life and the surest way to salvation, and which had spread
throughout Western Europe in the fifth and sixth centuries. Northumbria
quickly produced, in the monk Bede (d.735), one of the great scholars of
the early Middle Ages, and by the time of his death English missionaries
were themselves at work attempting to convert the continental Germans.

Elsewhere, progress was slower. The early English bishoprics were large,
and Bede complained that there was insufficient preaching, while Latin, the
language of the church, probably always remained the province of well-
educated monks and higher clergy. Bede supplied ignorant clerics with
English translations of the Creed and Lord's Prayer, and King Alfred was
concerned to provide vernacular versions of key works, such as Pope
Gregory the Great's *Pastoral Care*, a handbook for bishops. In the tenth and
eleventh centuries the texts produced for the education of parish priests
were still in English. By then, however, the number of priests and church
buildings had greatly increased. Some of the earliest English churches,

minsters containing communities of secular (i.e. non-monastic) priests, were responsible for the spiritual welfare of a sizeable surrounding area, perhaps sometimes as large as fifteen modern parishes. In time these were joined, and often had their jurisdiction diminished, by large numbers of churches served by single priests and founded by private individuals, frequently nobles, for whom their own place of worship was a source of financial as well as religious benefit. By the late eleventh century village churches are likely to have been fairly common: it is known that there were over 400 in Kent.

This is not the only indication of considerable interest in religion. Surviving rules of gilds of laymen suggest that most such associations had a spiritual aspect; in tenth-century Exeter gildsmen assembled 'for the love of God and for our souls' need, having regard both to the prosperity of our life and also to the days thereafter which we wish to be allotted to us at God's Judgement', and gave any member going on pilgrimage overseas five pence from each of his colleagues.[1] A pilgrim, whether bound for Rome, or Jerusalem, or simply one of the many shrines in England, would have expected to see the relics of the saints. These holy men, whose sanctity was often clear from the miracles which God had allowed them to perform in life, had in death entered his presence. They could therefore intercede with him for the living, to whom they might appear, and for whom they might still work miracles. Their activities were thus not only believed to be tangible proof of the truths of Christianity, but were also an essential link between men and a somewhat remote but terrifying god. A church could derive both prestige and wealth from possessing the relics of a major saint, whose devotees were expected to be generous in their donations of land and precious metal. Moreover, English interest in saints, like that of the French, seems to have been particularly intense in the second half of the tenth century and early decades of the eleventh, when many saints' lives were written[2] and a number of relics were transferred to new shrines.[3] One of two surviving copies of a list of saints' resting places in England was produced in New Minster Winchester in Cnut's time.[4] Relics were also important in the contemporary French peace movement,[5] being prominently displayed at the large and enthusiastic public gatherings organised by

---

[1] *EHD*, p.605; on the gilds, Barlow, *The English Church*, pp.196–98.
[2] Rollason, *Saints and Relics in Anglo-Saxon England*, pp.174–75.
[3] Rollason, 'List of saints' resting places in Anglo-Saxon England', 65–66.
[4] Ibid., 61.
[5] Cowdrey, 'The Peace and the Truce of God in the Eleventh Century', 49.

bishops in an attempt to improve the state of public order; they possibly found similar use in England, where the national assemblies of Æthelred II may occasionally have resembled continental peace meetings.[6]

CHURCH WEALTH

In view of all this, it is hardly surprising that Domesday Book reveals a country in which the church was in places a mighty landowner. The two richest foundations were the sees of Canterbury and Winchester, the former with a revenue of about £1,750, the latter with over £1,000. Yet all other bishoprics were surpassed by the greater monasteries – Glastonbury, Ely, Bury St Edmund's, and St Augustine's Canterbury. In total, monks and nuns disposed of between a sixth and a seventh of all Domesday landed value.[7] Bury, reformed in Cnut's reign, and Westminster, patronised by Edward the Confessor, may have gained much of their endowment during the eleventh century, but otherwise the Domesday picture was probably very similar to that which faced Cnut on his accession. Ely, for example, had already received the bulk of the lands it held in 1086,[8] and the same may well have been true of other foundations such as Glastonbury, Abingdon and the Old and New Minsters in Winchester.[9] These churches had gained many of their possessions from wealthy laymen as a result of the noble piety which characterised the monastic reform movement of the tenth century, when substantial numbers of new monasteries were created and old ones re-established. Some leading families were closely associated with particular foundations. In Æthelred's reign Ramsey was patronised by Ealdorman Æthelwine of East Anglia and his relatives, Ely by Ealdorman Brihtnoth and his kin. The foundation of Tavistock by Ordulf, the king's uncle, was completed, the creation of Burton by Wulfric Spott, and of Cerne and Eynsham by Ealdorman Æthelmær, undertaken. Gifts could comprise not only land, but also money and precious objects, including jewellery.[10]

Nevertheless, the religious state of the country in 1017 was one of some diversity, especially geographically. The monastic reform movement, so important in the south, had at this date penetrated no further north than

[6] Above, pp.60–62.
[7] Corbett, 'The Development of the Duchy of Normandy and the Norman Conquest of England', pp.509–11; Knowles, *The Monastic Order in England*, pp.702–03.
[8] Miller, *The Abbey & Bishopric of Ely*, p.23.
[9] See the comments of Knowles, *Monastic Order*, p.59.
[10] See, for example, *Wills*, Nos. X and XI; and for Anglo-Saxon wealth in precious metals, Dodwell, *Anglo-Saxon Art*, pp.188–215.

Burton in Staffordshire and Crowland in south Lincolnshire. The lands to the north and east of a line joining these two houses had in the ninth century been conquered and to some degree settled by pagan Scandinavians, who had destroyed the existing monasteries and several of the bishoprics, and such evidence as there is suggests that the Christianity practised within them retained aspects upon which the stricter kind of churchman would have frowned. Stone monuments from tenth- and eleventh-century Northumbria sometimes contain scenes from pagan myth and legend. The stories of Sigurd and Wayland seem to have been particularly popular, and while, as R.N. Bailey has argued, such carvings could have been attempts to link pagan with Christian belief, one is still driven to the conclusion that they 'may have appealed to tastes and interpretations which were based more on the traditions of Scandinavia than the Christian Fathers'.[11] That paganism itself was not completely extinct is indicated by the tract known as *The Law of the Northumbrian Priests*, probably compiled in Cnut's reign, which forbids heathen practices, witchcraft, idol worship, and the existence of sanctuaries around stones, trees and wells. It further reveals that a non-celibate priesthood was tolerated in Northumbria.[12] Differences between north and south cannot, however, be attributed solely to Scandinavian influence. The monastic reform movement did not reach north-west Mercia either, yet this area had not been much influenced by Scandinavian settlement, and it did eventually extend into East Anglia, which had to some degree been so affected. Possibly the West Saxon monarchy's links with the new monasticism had something to do with its lack of popularity in northern Mercia and Northumbria. At any rate, their bishoprics could not equal the territorial wealth, and so presumably to an extent the political influence, of some of their southern brethren. The archbishopric of York was poverty stricken compared with that of Canterbury, the communities of secular canons characteristic of north-west Mercia could not remotely approach the holdings of the great southern monasteries.[13]

KINGS AND THE CHURCH

No layman was expected to be more generous to the church, or was more intimately connected with it, than the head of this Christian society, the

[11] Bailey, *Viking Age Sculpture*, p.142.
[12] Chapters 47–54.1, 35; *Gesetze*, i. 382–83; *EHD*, pp.474–75.
[13] There were some secular colleges in the south, Hill, *An Atlas of Anglo-Saxon England*, p.153.

king. On his accession he was crowned and anointed by ecclesiastics. They believed that he held his kingdom from God, that it was his duty to provide peace and justice and to further Christianity, and that his life should be a fitting example to his people. As the tenth century wore on English church-men, like their counterparts in Ottonian Germany, were increasingly inclined to compare the king with Christ himself.[14]

Royal gift-giving to churches could be lavish. While on an expedition to Scotland King Æthelstan visited the shrine of the great northern saint Cuthbert at Chester-le-Street, and gave royal gifts (*regia munera*). They included two chasubles, an alb, a stole with a maniple, a girdle, three altar covers, a silver chalice, two dishes – one of gold, one of 'Greek work' – a silver censer, an ivory and gold cross, a royal cap of gold texture, two silver candelabra embellished with gold, a missal, two gospel books in gold and silver, a *Life* of St Cuthbert, three tapestries, four large bells, three horns fashioned in gold and silver, two standards, a lance and two gold rings.[15] King Eadred left two gold crucifixes and two swords with gold hilts to Old Minster Winchester in his will, together with £4,000.[16] His nephew Edgar gave Ely a cross with a gold front containing three golden images and pre-cious stones, the rest being of silver gilt; the silver base was in three parts with gilt embellishment. Other of his gifts included a gospel book, his royal cloak extensively covered in gold, and reliquaries from the royal chapel complete with relics.[17] He also seems to have donated his belt and hose, as a twelfth-century account of their treasures lists a girdle made from the one and an alb decorated with gold thread from the other.[18]

The frequent appearance of objects of gold and silver is striking. So is the range of the gifts, which included not only items of direct utility to a church, such as the ecclesiastical vestments and bells received by St Cuthbert, but also objects whose chief characteristic was that they had belonged to the king, like Æthelstan's cap and Edgar's cloak. The presence of such items in a church may have been intended to increase popular respect for the monarchy.

Yet gift-giving was not the only connection which these kings had with religion. Æthelstan was an assiduous collector of relics and had a probably genuine concern for the salvation of his soul. Edgar promoted the monastic reform movement, and two of his children, Edith and Edward the Martyr,

---

[14] See E. John in Campbell *et al.*, *The Anglo-Saxons*, pp.188–89; John, 'The World of Abbot Aelfric', p.309.
[15] *Historia de Sancto Cuthberto*, ed. Arnold, i. 211.
[16] *SEHD*, pp.34, 64.
[17] *Lib. El*, ii. 50, p.117.
[18] *Lib. El*, iii. 50, p.293.

were soon regarded as saints.[19] So was Ælfgifu, wife of King Edmund I, and Eadburg, daughter of Edward the Elder.[20] The royal saint, beginning with the Northumbrians Edwin and Oswald in the seventh century, had been a recurrent and important Anglo-Saxon phenomenon, and tended to reinforce the fusion of monarchy and church. Nor, if Cnut and his advisers sought models for his kingship, need they only have looked to the English past: there was also the European present. The French king Robert the Pious (996–1031) allegedly delighted in generosity to the poor, in acts of humility, such as when he washed the feet of 160 clerics with his own hair, and in making gifts to churches.[21] Humility and displays of emotion were not considered unkingly. Wipo, the biographer of Emperor Conrad II of Germany, says that he burst into tears after hearing a sermon delivered to him at his coronation in 1024.[22]

Naturally, kings did not treat all churches alike. Some were richer and more prestigious than others, and their favour presumably the more worth having. Also, their inmates may often have come from the ranks of the noble and landowning class. Monasteries, hopeful of future gain, could frequently have preferred their entrants to be from wealthy families. The relatives of both Leofsige, abbot of Ely from 1029 to 1044, and of Ælfwine, bishop of Elmham in Cnut's reign, granted estates in Norfolk, Suffolk and Cambridgeshire to Ely when their sons entered the monastery, and the *Liber Eliensis* says that it was Leofsige's own policy to accept no monk who was not well-educated and of good birth, so that the church might be enriched by liberality.[23] Consequently, it is not surprising that senior churchmen were sometimes related to each other. Brihtheah, the nephew of Archbishop Wulfstan, was abbot of Pershore and later bishop of Worcester,[24] while Bishop Brihtwine of Sherborne was succeeded by his brother,[25] and Brihtwold of Cornwall was the uncle of Lyfing, abbot of Tavistock and subsequently bishop of Crediton, Cornwall and Worcester.[26] Family influence must have secured some of these appointments, and family loyalties were not forgotten in the

[19] Ridyard, *The Royal Saints of Anglo-Saxon England*, pp.140–75; Rollason, *Saints and Relics in Anglo-Saxon England*, pp.139–40, 142–44.

[20] Ridyard, *Royal Saints*, pp.170, 16–37, 96–139; Rollason, *Saints and Relics*, pp.137–39.

[21] Helgaud, *Epitoma*, ed. Bautier and Labory; generosity to the poor, chapters v, viii, ix, xi, xxi, pp.62–64, 68–72, 76, 102–06; humility, chapters xiii, xxi, pp.78–80, 102–06; generosity to churches, chapters xv, xxii, xxviii, pp.84–90, 106–14, 128–32.

[22] Wipo, *Gesta Chuonradi*, iii, ed. Bresslau, p.23.

[23] *Lib. El*, ii. 74–75, 84, pp.143–45, 152, 424.

[24] JW, ii. 518–19.

[25] Goscelin, *De Vita Sancti Wlsini*, xvi, ed. Talbot, p.82.

[26] JW, ii. 512–13; *GP*, ii. 94, pp.200–01.

service of the church. Bishop Oswald of Worcester granted church land to his relatives in the late tenth century, and his successors Wulfstan and Brihtheah followed suit.[27] Such gifts were doubtless useful in providing reliable support for episcopal authority. Hemming says that Brihtheah's were made because he was from Berkshire and had no relatives in Worcestershire,[28] and in Edward the Confessor's time Bishop Hermann complained that nobody could hold the see of Ramsbury without the help of kinsmen.[29]

THE CHURCH AND POLITICS

Churchmen must always have been aware of family loyalties, and when these became involved in politics there may often have been a strong temptation to give active support. The family of Bishop Eadnoth of Dorchester, who had been both monk and abbot of Ramsey, and whose rich brother gave land to the monastery,[30] was possibly allied with that of Æthelstan Half-King, the powerful ealdorman of East Anglia in the mid-tenth century, whose sons were great patrons of Ramsey. Eadnoth was, at least, killed fighting at *Assandun* in 1016 along with his successor at Ramsey, Abbot Wulfsige, and Æthelstan's grandson, Æthelweard. Personal ambition was doubtless another factor which tended to enmesh ecclesiastics in politics. Bishop Lyfing of Crediton is said by John of Worcester to have been accused of being associated with Earl Godwin in the murder of the ætheling Alfred in 1036, and one of his accusers was Archbishop Ælfric of York, who had designs on the bishopric of Worcester, given to Lyfing by Harold Harefoot as a reward for his support.[31] If such machinations are seldom heard of in this period it is unlikely to be because they were rare. These factors – the noble connections of churchmen and the extent of their involvement in the secular world – meant that the king's attitude to them could be determined not only by the importance of their spiritual role in a society in which religion mattered, but also by an intricate web of personal political allegiances and aspirations deeply rooted in lay affairs.

[27] Oswald's surviving grants to kinsmen are S 1308, 1315, 1326, 1340, 1345, 1348, 1355, 1361, 1363, 1370; S 1384 is a lease of land by Archbishop Wulfstan to his brother; for Brihtheah's gifts to relatives, see Hemming, i. 255, 266–67, 269. His brother Æthelric held the church of St Peter's Worcester; Hemming, ii. 342–43.

[28] Hemming, i. 266.

[29] *GP*, ii. 83, p.182.

[30] *Chron. Rams.*, p.111.

[31] JW, ii. 530–31; see Barlow, *The English Church*, pp.73–74.

This was one reason among many why kings and churchmen could sometimes be at odds. To be sure, the latter did not always approve of royal actions, for even the most pious rulers occasionally transgressed. Henry II of Germany incurred ecclesiastical disapproval by entering into an alliance with heathen Slavs against Christian Poles, while his French contemporary Robert the Pious repudiated his first wife and took a second who was within the forbidden degrees of kinship. Æthelred II was perhaps not the most pious of kings,[32] but even if he was, his relations with churchmen could be stormy. Ecclesiastical wealth could be a sore temptation, and in his youth Æthelred misappropriated (in their view) the lands of several churches.[33] He also had difficulties with Bishop Ælfstan of Rochester, whose diocese he ravaged in 986, and Bishop Æthelsige of Sherborne, who incurred the king's anger, was expelled from his see, and went abroad never to return.[34] Perhaps some of his churchmen allowed personal ambition and family loyalties to involve them in the political divisions of the reign, and so may have welcomed a change of dynasty in 1016. No doubt still more simply welcomed peace.

Yet if not all of them necessarily regarded Cnut with disfavour on his accession, it is likely that there were quarters in which he had to face considerable initial hostility. Not only may churchmen have lost kinsmen in the recent fighting, but enemy harrying had almost certainly resulted in extensive damage to church lands and possessions. The abbey of Tavistock was burnt in 997,[35] and that of Cerne later despoiled by Cnut,[36] while St Mary's church in Exeter was seemingly destroyed in the sack of 1003,[37] and the nunnery at Minster-in-Thanet at some stage in Æthelred's reign.[38] Worst of all, Christ Church Canterbury was burnt in 1011[39] and its archbishop

[32] It may be significant that there seem to be fewer recorded instances of gifts of precious objects to churches by Æthelred than by kings such as Æthelstan and Edgar; but he did give a large cameo to St Albans; Dodwell, *Anglo-Saxon Art*, pp. 109–10.

[33] Keynes, *Diplomas*, pp. 177–80.

[34] *Chron. Eve.*, p. 80. This story occurs in the section of the thirteenth-century Evesham chronicle probably drawn from a history written around 1100; Gransden, *Historical Writing in England*, pp. 89–90, 111–12. Æthelsige's see is not named, but from the accompanying detail he is very likely to have been Æthelsige II of Sherborne; Kirby, *The Making of Early England*, p. 216.

[35] *ASC*, i. 131.

[36] The spoliation of Cerne, which may have happened during Cnut's ravaging of the area in 1015, was mentioned in a *Life* of St Eadwold consulted by John Leland, *Collectanea*, ed. Hearne, iii. 67.

[37] See the text of the doubtful charter S 954.

[38] Goscelin, *Translatio Sancte Mildrethe Virginis*, v, ed. Rollason, pp. 160–61, describes an attack on Kent by a 'massive army of Danes and other barbaric peoples intent not only on plunder, but on subjugating the whole British kingdom'. During it, the church at Minster was burnt down. This may well have occurred during the harrying of 1009–11, for *ASC*, i. 141, reports the capture of Abbess Leofrune at the taking of Canterbury and John of Worcester (ii. 468–69) calls her abbess of St Mildred's.

[39] Osbern, *Vita S. Elphegi*, ed. Wharton, ii. 136; Eadmer, *Historia Novorum*, ed. Rule, p. 4; Brooks, *The Early History of the Church of Canterbury*, p. 285.

murdered the following year after refusing to be ransomed.[40] Churches which escaped are likely to have paid for the privilege: the raiders had threatened to destroy Christ Church in 994 unless they were given a sum promised them by Archbishop Sigeric.[41] Small wonder that some of their prey did not mince their words. In his *Life* of St Oswald, Brihtferth of Ramsey described the Danes as accursed (*nefandi*) and accomplices of Beelzebub, while Archbishop Wulfstan's *Sermo Lupi* (Sermon of the Wolf) equates the imminent Scandinavian conquest of England with the reign of Anti-Christ.[42] Wulfstan quickly changed his tune once Cnut was king, but in 1017 memories of the destructive wars of the previous three decades must still have been very fresh, among churchmen as well as their lay brethren. Moreover, there is much to suggest that Cnut's reign was itself a difficult time for some churches.

Heavy taxation was a major factor here, as various sources (discussed in Chapter 5) are at pains to stress, and Dr Gem has argued that there was a recession in church building as a result.[43] Some foundations had to melt down precious objects and sell off estates, and even the wealthier, such as the abbey of Glastonbury, were occasionally in difficulties. As early as 994 Archbishop Sigeric of Canterbury was forced to borrow £115 from Bishop Æscwig of Dorchester to prevent the raiders burning his cathedral to the ground, giving in return an estate in Buckinghamshire.[44] Sigeric's successor, Ælfric, recovered it, but Professor Brooks has pointed out that other losses would have left no trace in the Canterbury records if they were not regained,[45] and Thietmar of Merseburg says that Archbishop Ælfheah was unable to ransom himself in 1012 because of dire poverty.[46] Of course, the picture may not have been quite as bleak as all this might suggest. Donations by pious laymen doubtless continued, and Glastonbury and Canterbury not only survived, but did so as wealthy churches. The seventy-five years preceding 1066 were a time of great activity in the Canterbury scriptorium, which produced a number of magnificently illustrated gospel and service-books, as well as many more mundane volumes apparently intended to form a new cathedral library.[47]

[40] *ASC*, i. 142, presumably representing a common belief, says that he refused to be ransomed; Thietmar, *Chronicon*, vii. 42, pp.448–50, that he promised them money but could not obtain it.
[41] Below, n. 44.
[42] *Vita Oswaldi*, ed. Raine, i. 455; see also Lapidge, 'The *Life of St Oswald*', pp.51–57; Hollis, 'The thematic structure of the *Sermo Lupi*', 185, 194.
[43] Gem, 'A Recession in English Architecture during the early eleventh century'.
[44] S 882; see Lawson, 'The collection of Danegeld and Heregeld', 728.
[45] Brooks, *Early History*, p.283.
[46] Above, n. 40.
[47] Brooks, *Early History*, pp.266–78. For the possibility that fine volumes were commissioned by Cnut, see below, p.126–27.

Even so, there are signs that its inmates were under pressure from the king and his officials. Eadui Basan, a well-known Canterbury scribe who worked on several surviving *de luxe* manuscripts, forged S 914, which purports to be a re-founding of the monastic community by Æthelred, possibly as some sort of safeguard at a time when Cnut was trying to force upon them, in his royal priest Eadsige, a non-monastic archbishop.[48] It may be significant that it was almost certainly Eadui who also wrote the oldest surviving copy of S 22, an alleged grant of the Kentish king Wihtred (d.725) apparently forged in Canterbury in the early ninth century.[49] His motive was probably connected with the part of the text which says that the estates of Christ Church and other Kentish churches are henceforth to be free of all secular service and royal debt. If this had been implemented, taxation of church land in Kent, which was extensive, would have ceased. Moreover, Brooks has stressed the verbal similarities between S 22 and S 985, which records an alleged gift by Cnut and was copied by Eadui into a Christ Church gospel book in the form of a royal writ.[50]

It describes how Archbishop Lyfing spoke to the king about the freedom of his church, and then rejected Cnut's offer of a new charter of freedom with the complaint that he had plenty such charters if only they were good for anything. Cnut then laid the charters on the altar and freed Christ Church in the same terms as his predecessors. It is not impossible that S 985 is simply a forgery concocted by Eadui to protect his church from the demands of royal officials. If, on the other hand, it records a genuine act by Cnut, Lyfing's complaint about the uselessness of existing charters may well be an allusion to the activities of those same officials. It was not to be the last. In S 987, a writ from 1035, Cnut declares that he will not permit wrong to be done to Canterbury no matter who may be reeve (presumably of Kent) – a clear indication that it was still suffering from the attentions of his men.

There were thus many reasons, grounded in both Æthelred's reign and his own, why individual churchmen may have harboured resentment against Cnut, and it will be suggested below that this could take a religious form. Generally, however, they must have been concerned to persuade him to become an amenable ruler. Archbishop Wulfstan of York had done his best under Æthelred to rectify social conditions worsened by ravaging, taxation and famine, and produced for the 1018 meeting of Danes and English

[48] Brooks, *Early History*, pp.257–59.
[49] Ibid., pp.193–97.
[50] Ibid., pp.288–90.

at Oxford a text 'devised according to many good precedents' and intended
to be of 'advantage in religious and secular matters'[51] which he later used as
a basis for his more extensive legal material in Cnut's name. Archbishop
Lyfing of Canterbury, returning from Rome with his pallium, also brought
letters and messages from Pope Benedict VIII, who evidently urged Cnut to
'everywhere exalt God's praise and suppress wrong and establish full security'.[52] At his coronation he probably promised to preserve true peace,
prohibit all iniquities and show equity and mercy in all his judgements.[53]
The same year (1017) he married Emma, herself a generous giver to
churches,[54] whose previous experience as Æthelred's wife ought to have
made her a fount of good advice on English churches and churchmen and
how they were best dealt with.

CNUT'S RELIGIOUS BACKGROUND

Cnut must have needed it. Danish Christianity went back only to his
grandfather Harald Bluetooth, and according to Adam of Bremen
Christians were for a time persecuted by Swegen Forkbeard. However, if
this occurred at all it is unlikely to have lasted long. Adam also says that
Swegen destroyed idolatrous rites, commanded the Norwegians to receive
Christianity, and appointed a bishop who had come from England to teach
in Skåne.[55] The skald Thorleif Rauthfeldarson has him bloodying swords in
England with God's help, and he was eventually buried, perhaps first in York
Minster, but later in a church at Roskilde, according to the Encomiast in a
tomb which he had prepared himself.[56] Hence it is fairly clear that Cnut,
who received the name Lambert at his baptism,[57] was a Christian when he
acquired the English throne, and the same was probably true of most of his
major followers. Certainly, some were later prepared to patronise English
churches. On the other hand, the rank and file of his army of conquest of
1016, comprising Norwegians and Swedes as well as Danes, doubtless contained a fair number of heathens, and it is very unlikely that the Danish

---

[51] Kennedy, p.72.
[52] Letter of 1019–20, chapter 3; *Gesetze*, i. 273; *EHD*, p.453.
[53] Nelson, *Politics and Ritual*, pp.369–70.
[54] See *Encomium*, pp. xlvii–xlviii.
[55] Adam, *Gesta*, ii. 29–30, 39, 41, pp.90–91, 99–101.
[56] *Encomium*, ii. 3, p.18. His burial in York Minster is given by Gaimar, *L'Estoire*, ed. Bell, p.132; translated
Hardy and Martin, ii. 132.
[57] Adam, *Gesta*, scholium 37, p.112; an *obit* in the Leofric Missal records the death of *Landberti piissimi
regis* on 11 November, Gerchow, *Gedenküberlieferung*, p.338. This may mean that Cnut was baptised on
the feast day of St Lambert of Liège on 17 September, as Dr Gerchow has said.

church had yet permeated national life as deeply as that of the English. In particular, Cnut, unlike William the Conqueror, whose Norman duchy contained a vigorous church, was not in a position to start replacing English personnel with continentals on any scale. In matters of religion he was largely obliged to play an English game, with English men, and by English rules.

Although, as will shortly be evident, he became extravagantly pious, he retained some of the values and attitudes of a pagan past. A warrior king, he patronised Scandinavian skalds who celebrated his victories in poems which had their roots in the world of the pagan gods and heroes. To Cnut and some of his contemporaries this world still mattered, and evidence of this has been found where it might have been least expected. Professor Biddle has proposed that a stone fragment unearthed in excavations of Old Minster Winchester in 1965, which may depict part of the story of Sigmund (father of Sigurd), of the Volsung family, originally formed part of a decorative frieze in the church commissioned by Cnut.[58] The presence of this pagan tale in a cathedral is strikingly reminiscent of Sigurd's appearance in Christian contexts on sculptures in northern England, and the possible positioning of the frieze near Cnut's tomb may imply that he was inviting comparison of his own exploits with those of the Volsungs.[59]

All the same, it is not obvious that he differed much from his English predecessors in this sort of area, for the Anglo-Scandinavian background outlined in the Introduction again becomes relevant here: King Edgar was criticised for inviting heathens into the country, some of whom were possibly poets, while Æthelred evidently patronised the skald Gunnlaug, and it was probably during his reign that the surviving manuscript of Beowulf, with its story of pagan Scandinavia, was written.[60] The poet praises Beowulf by linking his killing of the monster Grendel with the feats of Sigmund, who was clearly expected to be familiar to an English audience. Also, English kings too could hear their military prowess extolled by poems which gloried in slaughter in ways not dissimilar to those on Cnut, as is demonstrated by that which celebrates Æthelstan's great victory at

[58] Biddle, 'Excavations at Winchester 1965', 329–32. The fragment cannot be dated more precisely than between about 980 and the demolition of Old Minster in 1093–94. See also Backhouse et al., The Golden Age of Anglo-Saxon Art, No. 140, and for further evidence on the Scandinavian presence in Winchester around this time, Yorke, Wessex in the Early Middle Ages, pp. 143–4, and Townend, 'Contextualising the Knútsdrápur', 168–72.

[59] Bailey, Viking Age Sculpture, pp. 123–25, shows that the Volsungs were often invoked in tributes to great men, and concludes that some of their achievements could readily have been linked with Christianity.

[60] Above, pp. 11.

Brunanburh in 937.[61] Nor, of course, did the Church always disapprove of war – the English coronation service made clear to the king that he must protect his people, and symbolised this with the gift of a sword.

CNUT AND ÆLFGIFU OF NORTHAMPTON

But it must have disapproved of Cnut's marital practices. His relationship with Ælfgifu of Northampton may well have begun before he married Emma of Normandy in 1017. She was the daughter of Ealdorman Ælfhelm of Northumbria, and Cnut's association with her was probably intended to secure her family's support.[62] Hence, it is likely that she was openly acknowledged as his consort, and was present when he was chosen as king in 1016. By this time she could already have borne him their two sons, Swegen and Harold. Nor is it likely that either she or her children were set aside when he married Emma, although she was possibly provided with an establishment in her own part of the world, perhaps Northampton, and expected to stay there. This may explain why in 1035 Harold's claim to be Cnut's son was greeted by some with incredulity.[63] Nevertheless, the probability that early in 1023 Thorkell the Tall was willing to accept one of Ælfgifu's sons in exchange for his own when he and Cnut were reconciled[64] strongly implies that the boy was openly acknowledged by Cnut. That after the conquest of Norway Swegen was put in charge of it under his mother's tutelage reinforces this conclusion. Although it may have been a convenient way of getting her out of the country, this also indicates that Ælfgifu had previously enjoyed a recognised position. Entries in the *Liber Vitae* of Thorney Abbey, a record of the names of church friends and benefactors which survives in a hand of around 1100, seem to confirm this. After the names of Cnut, Harold and Harthacnut appear those of 'Imma Regina. 7 Ælfgifu. Ægelnoð archiepiscopus. 7 Æðericus episcopus.' It is noteworthy that Ælfgifu is not called queen, but that she nevertheless occupies a position next to Emma and before the archbishop of Canterbury. This suggests that she is Ælfgifu of Northampton,[65] and that her status, in Thorney at least, was considerable. Although she was absent from England late in the

[61] *ASC*, i. 106–10; see Frank, 'Did Anglo-Saxon Audiences Have a Skaldic Tooth?'; Niles, 'Skaldic Technique in *Brunanburh*'.

[62] Above, p.51; John of Worcester, ii. 520–21, calls her *Northamtunensis Alfgiue*.

[63] Above, p.109.

[64] Above, p.92.

[65] BL MS Additional 40000, f. 10r; see Gerchow, *Gedenküberlieferung*, pp.186–97, 326.

reign, Cnut was before that in the position of having two consorts. This clearly contravened church teaching: in II Cnut 54.1 Archbishop Wulfstan forbids a priest to minister to a man who has both a rightful wife and a concubine. The church also disqualified the offspring of concubines from inheriting, but in allowing Swegen to rule Norway Cnut recognised that he had a claim.[66] How far laymen would have disapproved of his behaviour is another matter, for concubinage of a type whereby a married man could also have a relationship with a woman who had a recognised position and whose children might share in the inheritance had been common among Germanic peoples, and may still have existed in England in Cnut's day.[67] Indeed, several tenth-century royal consorts are shadowy figures of doubtful legitimacy, and it is possible that Æthelred's first, who like Ælfgifu of Northampton never witnesses charters, was not a fully-married wife.[68] Even so, churchmen must have disagreed with Cnut's behaviour, although perhaps many did so diplomatically, that is to say, silently. However much Cnut may have played the Christian king, he was, like other rulers, willing to turn a blind eye to church teaching when it suited him.

THE USES OF RELIGION: CNUT, PIETY AND CHRIST

All the same, most of the time it was expedient to follow where the church led. His coronation, for example, must have been important in giving his regime a much-needed aura of legitimacy. The point is made in the contemporary depiction of Cnut and Emma giving a cross to New Minster Winchester, preserved in its *Liber Vitae*. A hovering angel places a crown on Cnut's head, while pointing upwards to a seated Christ. Once crowned, his position had divine sanction, was regarded by the church as sacrosanct,[69] and so was considerably strengthened. The Letter of 1027 reports that he visited Rome to pray for the redemption of his sins and the security of his subjects, and tells how he had negotiated with the Pope a reduction in the sums paid by English archbishops when they went for the pallium. This is

---

[66] A point made by Stafford, *Unification and Conquest*, p.77.

[67] Ross, 'Concubinage in Anglo-Saxon England'.

[68] *FNC*, i. 671–73. Barlow, *Edward the Confessor*, pp.28–29, concludes that 'it was probably a legal marriage'.

[69] Bethurum Loomis, '*Regnum* and *sacerdotium*', pp.132–33. But see also Godden, 'Ælfric and Anglo-Saxon Kingship', who argues that Ælfric's well-known statement that a consecrated king could not be deposed refers to practical rather than moral problems. The New Minster drawing (*Liber Vitae*, ed. Keynes, pl. v; Backhouse *et al.*, *The Golden Age of Anglo-Saxon Art*, p.77) is discussed by Gerchow, 'Prayers for King Cnut'. Keynes suggests that the *Liber Vitae* was produced in 1031 and the cross given by Cnut in the 1020s.

Cnut the caring Christian king and diplomat, vowing to amend what has hitherto been done amiss through negligence or the intemperance of youth, and stressing the generosity of his reception by the emperor to enhance his own prestige. Good religion could be good politics, good politics could require good religion, and there can be no question that Cnut threw himself into certain aspects of his role with zest.

There is the Encomiast's eye-witness account of his lavish gifts to the monasteries and poor of St Omer when on the way to Rome, and of the tears and breast-beating which accompanied them.[70] This makes it easier to accept such later stories as that of Symeon of Durham, who says that he walked barefoot for five miles before reaching the church of St Cuthbert.[71] There may also be a basis of fact, in a planned act of piety, behind the famous story of how Cnut attempted to turn back the waves and then used his failure to demonstrate to his followers the weakness of his power compared with that of the king of heaven. After this, says Henry of Huntingdon, he placed his crown on the head of a crucifix and never wore it again.[72] Similarly, Goscelin says that one Easter at Winchester Cnut refused to wear his crown and put it on a crucifix, with the explanation that the king of kings was more worthy of it than he.[73]

Such displays of humility are not only reminiscent of those of Robert the Pious in France, they may also reflect the teaching of Cnut's own churchmen. As Eric John emphasised, early-eleventh-century kings were invited to identify not with Christ in majesty, but with the suffering Christ, and drawings of the crucifixion survive from this period in which his suffering on the cross is made very explicit;[74] perhaps the cross which Cnut gave to New Minster, which bore an image of the crucified Lord,[75] did so too. Abbot Ælfric stressed Christ's humility, describing in his homily *The Exaltation of the Holy Cross* how an angel reminded the seventh-century Byzantine emperor Heraclius that he 'would not encircle his head with a

---

[70] *Encomium*, ii. 20–21, p.36.

[71] Symeon, *Libellvs de exordio*, ed. Rollason, pp.166–67.

[72] Henry, *Historia*, vi. 17, pp.366–69. Dr Greenway (p.368, n.95) points out that, while the story of Cnut and the waves is to be found in all versions of the *Historia Anglorum*, that on the crown did not appear until the third version of around 1140. Henry's words suggest that Cnut really thought he could stop the rising tide, but this may be an understandable later distortion of a planned act of piety. Gaimar, *L'Estoire*, locates it on the banks of the Thames and dispenses with the throne which figures in Henry's account; ed. Bell, pp.149–50; translated Hardy and Martin, ii. 148–49. Gransden, *Historical Writing in England*, pp.197, 200, 210, notes Henry's liking for stressing the transitory nature of earthly power, and thinks the story a fable.

[73] Goscelin, *Translatio Sancte Mildrethe Virginis*, vi, ed. Rollason, p.163.

[74] In Campbell *et al.*, *The Anglo-Saxons*, p.206.

[75] William of Malmesbury, *Historia Novella*, ed. Potter, p.59.

golden crown, but with one of thorns', and that before the crucifixion 'he
was not clothed in purple, nor adorned with a royal crown, nor rode he...
upon a horse but upon the back of an ass'. In response, Heraclius 'took off
his purple... then went he with naked feet and took the Cross, praising God
with the shedding of tears'.[76] The tears, the bare feet, and the rejection of
royal insignia have enough in common with Cnut's behaviour to indicate
that he responded to what he heard preached. He was eager to imitate
other rulers, and not least the king of kings himself, in continuance of the
tradition which likened earthly kings to Christ. Even his Icelandic skalds
understood this, and adapted their products accordingly. Thorarin Praise-
Tongue's *Höfuðlausn* and Hallvard's *Knútsdrápa* both have Cnut defending
his land as God does heaven. Paradoxical as it may seem, his acts of humility
were really statements about the elevated nature of his power.

With this extravagant behaviour, as the Encomiast says, went lavish gifts
of precious objects. The New Minster *Liber Vitae* shows the cross he gave
them as large, no doubt correctly. It contained relics, and when melted
down in the twelfth century yielded 500 marks of silver, and thirty of
gold.[77] Similarly, Cnut and Emma gave to Abingdon a reliquary for the
remains of St Vincent which bore upon it the inscription 'King Cnut and
Queen Ælfgifu commanded the making of this reliquary from 230 gold
mancuses, refined by fire, and two pounds of silver of great weight'.[78]

He also ordered a gold shrine to be made for St Edith at Wilton which
required the skills of three goldsmiths,[79] while Westminster Abbey received
an arm of St Cyriacus, bought for 100 marks and clad in gold and silver. It
could still be seen there in the fourteenth century.[80] Clearly, gifts of precious metal were something in which Cnut delighted, and it has recently
been argued that the magnificently illustrated gospel books which have survived from this period, and others which have not, were commissioned by
Cnut and Emma for donation to favoured individuals and churches.[81] He

---

[76] Ælfric, *Lives of Saints*, ed. Skeat, ii. 150–51. I owe this reference to John, 'The World of Abbot Aelfric',
p.311.
[77] See n.75 above.
[78] *Chron. Ab.*, i. 433. It was broken up in the twelfth century, above, p.73. The mancus was worth thirty
silver pennies.
[79] Goscelin, *Vita S. Edithe*, ii. 13, ed. Wilmart, p.280.
[80] Richard of Cirencester, *Speculum Historiale*, ed. Major, ii. 185. The value of the mark may have been
two thirds of a pound, below, p.163, n.66.
[81] Heslop, 'The production of *de luxe* manuscripts and the patronage of King Cnut and Queen Emma'.
Manuscripts involved include the Copenhagen Gospels, the Arenburg Gospels, the York Gospels, the
Trinity Gospels, the Eadui Gospels and the Bury Gospels; Temple, *Anglo-Saxon Manuscripts*, Nos. 47,
56, 61, 65, 67, 75; Backhouse *et al.*, *The Golden Age of Anglo-Saxon Art*, Nos. 48, 47, 54, 49, 56, 58.

may, for example, have given the York Gospels, produced in Canterbury, to Archbishop Wulfstan.[82] Such giving lay not only in the tradition of church patronage established by his royal Anglo-Saxon predecessors, but must have come naturally to him anyway. Ostentatious displays of wealth in gold and silver were very much a part of the secular as well as the ecclesiastical world.[83] Not least, they were a part of military splendour. Weapons were often embellished with precious metal, and the Encomiast describes the magnificence of Cnut's invasion fleet, and the gold and silver decoration of its ships.[84]

Gift-giving and Christ-like displays of humility are unlikely to have been the only aspects of religion which Cnut found attractive. The story of how he left his crown on a crucifix is of great interest here. The giving of crowns and other regalia to churches was not uncommon. A crown now on the head of a Madonna in Essen may be that of the child Otto III, while another on the head of a crucifix in Vercelli has been thought a gift of his.[85] Nor were donors always royalty: the wife of Cnut's henchman Tofi the Proud adorned a crucifix at Waltham in Essex with a crown, as well as decking it with other ornaments.[86] Moreover, the Winchester crown need not have been the only one that Cnut gave away, as Christ Church Canterbury seems also to have received one.[87] All the same, there was perhaps rather more to this matter than initially meets the eye. Goscelin says that he put his crown on the Winchester crucifix when he had supremacy over four kingdoms. If correct, this apparently means that it was after the conquest of Norway in 1028 and therefore after he attended the imperial coronation of Conrad II of Germany in Rome in 1027.

It may be that he took new insignia after the subjugation of Norway, and that he left his old crown in Winchester, in much the same way that Henry II of Germany had, at his imperial coronation in 1014, hung his

---

[82] Alternatively, Wulfstan could have received it from Archbishop Æthelnoth, whom he consecrated in 1020.

[83] Dodwell, *Anglo-Saxon Art*, pp. 188–213.

[84] *Encomium*, ii. 4, pp. 18–20; see also John of Worcester's account (ii. 530–31) of the ship and crew given by Earl Godwin to Harthacnut.

[85] Schramm, *Herrschaftszeichen und Staatssymbolik*, iii. 910–12; Schramm and Mütherich, *Denkmale der deutschen Könige*, i. 37, 147.

[86] *De Inventione*, 12, ed. Stubbs, p. 12.

[87] S 959, of doubtful authenticity, says that Cnut laid his crown on the altar for their benefit. Whether this means that he gave it, or put it on the altar as a token of his gift of Sandwich, seems uncertain. However, Gervase, *Gesta Regum*, ed. Stubbs, ii. 56, says that he gave Sandwich *cum aurea corona capitis sui*, and a list of Christ Church donations written around 1400 (printed Dugdale, *Monasticon Anglicanum*, i. 97) adds that Cnut's crown adorned a large crucifix in the nave.

former crown above the altar of St Peter's, where Cnut would almost certainly have seen it thirteen years later.[88] Possible similarities between Cnut's (lost) seal and Conrad II's imperial seal perhaps belong in this context too,[89] as may his willingness to allow his son Harthacnut to become king of Denmark, conceivably in imitation of the crowning of Conrad's son Henry (III, born in 1017) at Aachen in 1028. There are also resemblances between the drawing of Cnut in the New Minster *Liber Vitae*, usually dated around 1031, and two pictures of Henry II. In a sacramentary he is shown being crowned by Christ, and in a book of pericopes (biblical extracts) which he gave to the cathedral of Bamberg, Christ is crowning Henry with one hand and his wife Kunigund with the other, while the patron saints of Bamberg, Peter and Paul, look on.[90] Cnut is being crowned and Emma is apparently being given a veil by angels pointing to Christ, who is flanked by the patron saints of New Minster, the Virgin Mary and Peter. More significant still, Cnut's crown in the New Minster drawing is a lily crown, very similar to that which appears on his first *Quatrefoil* coin type, but with an additional arched bar spanning its centre. This resembles the bar which Conrad II added to the imperial crown probably made originally for the coronation of the emperor Otto I in Rome in 962.[91] In other words, the crown which the *Liber Vitae* depicts Cnut as wearing late in his reign looks like a German imperial crown.[92] Of all continental rulers, the German emperors may have been the ones Cnut was most eager to imitate, for in the second half of his reign he perhaps wished to see his own position in the northern world as emulating theirs in Europe. However, there may also have been English precedent and inspiration for the adoption of a second crown – notably in Edgar's second, 'imperial', coronation at Bath in 973.[93]

[88] Thietmar, *Chronicon*, vii. 1, pp.396–99. I am grateful to Professor K.J. Leyser for drawing my attention to this.

[89] *Writs*, pp.100–01.

[90] Schramm and Mütherich, *Denkmale der deutschen Könige*, i. 156–57. Cnut is not known to have had direct relations with Henry II, although the latter used religion to protest his legitimacy in a not dissimilar way (Mayr-Harting, *Ottonian Book Illumination*, i. 179–201) and could have been a model.

[91] Schramm and Mütherich, *Denkmale der deutschen Könige*, i. 141, 170. Conrad's bar was probably a replacement for an earlier one.

[92] This was pointed out by Marion Archibald in Backhouse *et al.*, *The Golden Age of Anglo-Saxon Art*, p.180.

[93] Above, p.103.

RELIGION AND POLITICS:
CNUT, EDMUND IRONSIDE AND EDWARD THE MARTYR

Another example of the rich and regal possibilities which religion offered Cnut is provided by a visit which he made to Glastonbury on 30 November of a year which may have been 1032, when William of Malmesbury says that he laid a cloak decorated with peacocks on the tomb of Edmund Ironside.[94] The peacock appears in other English contexts – together with the Tree of Life on a finger-ring bearing the name of the ninth-century West Saxon king Æthelwulf, and on the lid of the eighth-century Mortain casket. In Christian belief it was a symbol of the resurrection of the flesh, and may have been significant in Scandinavian paganism too, for the bones of a peacock were found within the ninth-century ship-burial from Gokstad in Norway, whereas all other animal remains lay outside it. All the same, peacock decoration is known on surviving Byzantine silks, and it may be that the cloak which Cnut gave Edmund was one of the precious cloaks (*pallia*) which Conrad II presented to him in 1027.

This visit to Glastonbury must have been an impressive occasion, but there was probably more to it than simply pomp and piety. William of Malmesbury says that Cnut honoured the brotherly corpse with pious lamentations, and that he was accustomed to calling Edmund his brother. The fact that the visit took place on the anniversary of Edmund's death, together with the peacock cloak, suggests that Cnut was expressing concern for Edmund's salvation. But he may also have intended to remind those present that he had come to the throne as a result of the treaty he had made with Edmund, which according to John of Worcester established peace, friendship and brotherhood between them. John further says that witnesses of the agreement later declared that Edmund left no portion of the kingdom to his brothers should he die, and agreed that Cnut should be the protector of his sons until they came of age. After his death, however, Edmund's sons were set aside.[95] This account of the treaty may, as John claims, have been a lie, but it, or something like it, could well have been what Cnut preferred people to believe, for he may have been aware that it had not been unusual within the West Saxon dynasty for brother to follow brother: it was the succession of King Æthelwulf's sons in turn which

---

[94] *GR*, ii. 184, ed. Mynors *et al.*, i. 330–31; WM *Glaston.*, p.132. William connects the visit with the charter S 966, which may be spurious, but is dated 1032.
[95] JW, ii. 492–95; above, p.82.

brought Alfred to the throne in 871, despite the fact that his brother Æthelred I had male issue. Favouring Edmund, stressing their brotherhood, and bringing their treaty to the fore diminished the extent to which Cnut looked a usurper.

He perhaps promoted the cult of Edward the Martyr for similar reasons. An injunction that his feast day is to be observed appears in the legal texts which Wulfstan drafted for him, and if the same clause in surviving copies of Æthelred's laws is a later interpolation, as Patrick Wormald has contended,[96] then Cnut's interest in Edward, implied by his apparent gift of relics of this saint to Westminster Abbey,[97] would be all the more striking. It was possibly connected with a desire to discredit Æthelred, whose followers had murdered Edward, and who had acquired the throne as a result. Professor Stafford thinks that Cnut may have reinforced this by encouraging the cults of other murdered princes, such as Wigstan, a ninth-century Mercian, whom he had translated from Repton to Evesham.[98] Alternatively, as Æthelred had himself patronised his half-brother's cult, it could be argued that Cnut was stressing the continuity of his regime with his predecessor's, and generally enhancing the prestige of kingship.[99] His interest in Edmund Ironside and Edward the Martyr is thus the first of several indications that attitudes to religion in his reign may have had distinct political overtones. Nor was this always to his advantage. If, as suggested above, he faced considerable initial hostility, and presided over a government which some churchmen found oppressive, religion could have been one way in which opposition was expressed.

RELIGION AND POLITICS:
THE CULTS OF ST ÆLFHEAH AND ST EDMUND OF EAST ANGLIA

It is, at least, in this context that two of the most popular cults of the day, those of Ælfheah and Edmund of East Anglia, can be considered. Archbishop Ælfheah of Canterbury was murdered in April 1012 by a Scandinavian army possibly associated with Cnut's father.[100] The entry of his feast-day in eleventh-century church calendars indicates that he became fairly widely

---

[96] I Cnut 17.1; *Gesetze*, i. 298–99; Wormald, 'Æthelred the Lawmaker', pp. 53–54; see also, Wormald, *The Making of English Law*, pp. 343–44.

[97] Below, p. 143.

[98] Stafford, 'The laws of Cnut and the history of Anglo-Saxon royal promises', 183.

[99] Ridyard, *Royal Saints*, p. 168.

[100] Above, p. 32–33.

venerated, and miracles were occurring at his tomb in St Paul's before the translation of his remains from London to Canterbury in 1023.[101] The translation merits attention, and fortunately two detailed accounts of it have survived, one by Osbern and a second in the D version of the *Chronicle*; both are discussed in more detail in Chapter 5. Osbern records the presence of royal housecarls to prevent interference by the Londoners, and this can be fitted into a credible historical context of popular hostility to the Danes in the city, arising from the fighting and sieges of Æthelred's time, the heavy taxation of 1018, and the probability that Cnut found it prudent to maintain a garrison there.[102] It is therefore likely that support for Æltheah's cult in London had a political as well as a religious aspect, and so the removal of his relic may indeed have been expected to provoke opposition. The use of a cult as a means of political expression would be far from unparalleled. The veneration of several murdered Anglo-Saxon royal saints, and especially of Edmund of East Anglia[103] and Edward the Martyr, almost certainly had overtones of this kind, and probably so too did the rapid growth of St Olaf''s cult in Norway in the 1030s, occasioned partly by the unpopular rule of Swegen and Ælfgifu of Northampton, who owed their position to his death. It may also not have been the least of Ælfheah's attractions to the people of London, heavily taxed in 1018, that he was murdered for being unable or unwilling to give money to the Danes; nor need it have made Cnut's position any easier that King Æthelred, too, lay buried in St Paul's.

Ælfheah's cult may therefore have presented him with considerable problems, and it is unlikely to be coincidence that the bishopric of London is known to have suffered at his hands.[104] Concerned to be an extravagantly pious king, and to take full political advantage of the elevated position enjoyed by Christian monarchs, the popular regard for an ecclesiastic so recently and brutally murdered by his countrymen may have been a source of considerable embarrassment. It would have been a way of criticising his regime which it was difficult to counter directly, and, in the short term perhaps most troublesome of all, it was possibly also a source of popular disorder. Certainly, if there was a degree of hostility to the Danes in London the anniversary of Ælfheah's death on 19 April would have been a time when feelings ran particularly high, for Cnut's England was clearly conscious of anniversaries of recent events, as awareness of the dates of the

[101] *English Kalendars before A.D. 1100*, ed. Wormald, Nos. 2, 4, 6–20; *ASC*, i. 143.
[102] Below, pp.165–66.
[103] Ridyard, *Royal Saints*, pp.214–23.
[104] Below, p.143.

battle of *Assandun*[105] in 1016 and the death of Edmund Ironside indicates. So
it may be significant that in 1023 the translation of Ælfheah's body began on
1 June,[106] only about six weeks after the anniversary. If 19 April 1023 saw
expressions of anti-Danish feeling, Cnut could have decided that it was time
for the situation to be defused by removing the body to Canterbury. He
then waited for the next major religious festival – Whitsuntide – and made
the translation into a great occasion, although with troops at hand in case of
trouble. Perhaps like Æthelred with Edward the Martyr, he attempted to
disarm the opposition by making much of the saint himself. He was, at least,
later believed to have given one of Ælfheah's fingers to Westminster
Abbey.[107] There were other advantages to the translation too. It must have
pleased the powerful church of Canterbury, with which he seems to have
wished to be on good terms, and been gratifyingly displeasing to that of
London. Religious affairs were complex, but pregnant with possibilities.

There are traces of a similar position in East Anglia – like London, a
locality which had received much recent attention from hostile armies, and
strongly resisted them. In addition to the slaughter of Ealdorman Brihtnoth
of Essex and his followers at Maldon in 991, East Anglian leaders were killed
fighting Swegen in 1004, while six years later Brihtnoth's son-in-law and
'many good thegns and a countless number of people' died at the battle of
Ringmere. The raiders then spent three months harrying and burning the
area. Among the casualties at *Assandun* in 1016 were several important East
Anglians and doubtless a large number of lesser people.

Cnut had a church built at the site of the battle, and it was consecrated in
1020, at about the same time that he allowed the replacement of clerics by
monks in St Edmund's church at Bury. According to Hermann,[108] working
in the late eleventh century, this happened because Edmund's popularity
was increasing, and this tends to be confirmed by the entry of his feast-day
in calendars produced in Winchester and Canterbury at about the same

---

[105] Below, p.133.
[106] I use Osbern's date here. The D version of the *Chronicle*, like Osbern, knows that the translation took
a week, but takes 8 June, when the translation was celebrated, as the date of removal from London,
rather than reburial in Canterbury.
[107] Below, p.143.
[108] Hermann, *De Miraculis*, 17, ed. Arnold, i. 47, dates the reform to 1020. However, the earliest evidence
is an entry against the years 1020–24 in an Easter Table in the Bury Psalter, a manuscript of around
1020–50; Temple, *Anglo-Saxon Manuscripts*, No.84. This says that Bishop Ælfwine (of Elmham) under
Earl Thorkell (exiled in November 1021) established a monastic rule in the church of St Edmund,
and that with the wish and licence of King Cnut it continues until the present. It therefore seems to
have been written before Cnut's death. Ælfwine's predecessor Ælfgar did not die until 1020x21 (see
Lib. El., p.143, n.1), but may previously have retired to Ely and been replaced by Ælfwine in
Æthelred's reign; *Lib. El.*, pp.143, 144, n.7.

time, and by the inclusion of a special mass for him in a sacramentary probably written in Ely.[109] Explaining this popularity is not difficult: Edmund
was himself killed by the Danes, and it was perhaps only natural that veneration for him should grow in the area which had formed his kingdom, and
seen a great deal of the renewed conflict between Danes and English. It thus
seems significant that there appears to have been a rumour that Edmund
was in some way responsible for the death of Cnut's father, after issuing a
vain warning that tribute should not be levied from his church's lands. As it
is not recorded until the work of Hermann and John of Worcester,[110] who
states that the saint speared Swegen from his horse, it would not be impossible to consider this story a reaction to taxation by the Normans; but if it did
originate earlier it too conceivably had something to do with Edmund's
increasing popularity, and if John's version was current in Cnut's time he
cannot have been flattered by the notion that Edmund had disposed of his
father in a similar way to that in which St Mercurius was believed to have
killed the emperor Julian the Apostate.[111]

In any case, there is a still stronger piece of evidence that Edmund's
popularity in Cnut's day was connected with the recent past. When the
new basilica of his church was consecrated late in the reign the day chosen
for the event was not his own feast-day of 20 November, but that of St Luke
on 18 October – the anniversary of the battle of *Assandun* in 1016.[112] If the
story of Edmund's connection with Swegen's death does date from Cnut's
time, it is interesting, and seems to hint at one of the most resented aspects
of Danish rule, that Edmund, like Ælfheah, had not only been martyred by
the Danes, he had also refused to give them money.

Indications that Cnut had difficulties with some Fenland ecclesiastics can
also be considered in this context. It is possible that the abbacy of Ely was
vacant from before Æthelred's death until 1019,[113] and clear that Leofwine,
the abbot next appointed, ran into some kind of trouble. The E version of
the *Anglo-Saxon Chronicle* says that he was unjustly driven from Ely and

[109] Gransden, *Historical Writing in England*, p. 11.
[110] Hermann, *De Miraculis*, 6, ed. Arnold, i. 36–37; JW, ii. 476–77.
[111] See Ælfric, *On the Assumption of the Blessed Mary, Catholic Homilies*, ed. Thorpe, i. 450–52.
[112] The date of the consecration is recorded by a calendar in the Bury Psalter; Temple, *Anglo-Saxon Manuscripts*, No. 84; that of *Assandun* by Roger of Wendover, *Flores Historianum*, ed. Coxe, i. 457, confirmed by a twelfth-century Ely calendar which gives 18 October as the *obit* of Bishop Eadnoth, killed at *Assandun* according to the *Chronicle*; Dickins, 'The day of Byrhtnoth's death', 21. An eleventh-century calendar from New Minster Winchester commemorates men killed on 19 October, but seems to have intended this to refer to the previous day, and so almost certainly to *Assandun*; ibid., 25. These obits are also printed by Gerchow, *Die Gedenküberlieferung*, pp. 334, 343.
[113] *Lib. El.*, pp. 411–12.

went to Rome to clear himself before the Pope of the charges brought against him. Unfortunately, we are told neither what the charges were nor who had brought them. Yet if they, or the possible abbatial vacancy, had any connection with the king, both may have stemmed from the unsuccessful attack which the *Liber Eliensis* records him as once having made on the monastery.[114] This was perhaps during the fighting of 1016.

There also seems to have been trouble at Ramsey. Abbot Wulfsige, killed at the battle of *Assandun*, was according to the twelfth-century Ramsey chronicle succeeded by a German, Wythman, who quarrelled with the monks and accused them of disobedience and negligence of monastic discipline before the diocesan bishop. The latter, however, visited the monastery unexpectedly, and found the accusations groundless. Shortly thereafter, Wythman left on pilgrimage, to be succeeded by a member of the community, Æthelstan.[115] The Peterborough chronicler Hugh Candidus tells a different tale, stating that in the days of Abbot Ælfsige of Peterborough (1006–42) the Ramsey monks were accused before the king 'for a certain reason', and that in the royal presence it was decided that the monastery should be destroyed and its monks expelled. The king, in great anger, ordered the immediate implementation of this judgement, but relented on the intercession of Abbot Ælfsige and Queen Emma, who argued that it was unjust to punish the whole community for the faults of a few. Ælfsige then appointed a new abbot from among the Ramsey monks.[116] It is difficult knowing how far to credit such stories in twelfth-century sources, although given that the Ramsey chronicle is recording the history of its own house, and that the Peterborough source refers to trouble there at the same time,[117] it is reasonable to believe that trouble of some sort there was. Moreover, unless Hugh is wildly inaccurate it seems to have gone beyond the simple quarrel between abbot and flock described by the Ramsey source. The flock are unlikely to have been as completely innocent as the latter suggests, and their guilt may well have had a secular aspect, for it might be doubted whether Cnut would have become involved with spiritual shortcomings. Nor need it have been completely unexpected, for the original appointment of a German, whom Cnut had possibly brought from Denmark, could, though need not, imply that he was concerned from the start about

[114] *Lib. El.,* ii. 109, p.190.
[115] *Chron. Rams.*, pp.121–25.
[116] Hugh, *Chronicle*, ed. Mellows, p. 50.
[117] This was the only vacancy at Ramsey during Ælfsige's tenure of Peterborough and Cnut's marriage to Emma. Hugh does not name the king involved in the affair, but has earlier mentioned Ælfsige's three years of exile in Normandy with Emma, and so is presumably referring to Cnut's reign.

the trustworthiness of the Ramsey abbot. It may be a coincidence that this affair, the consecration of the church at *Assandun*, and the introduction of monks at Bury all happened at about the same time. Even so, together with the problems at Ely, they may reflect a somewhat hostile attitude to Cnut in this area, perhaps exploited by Thorkell, its earl, who was banished in 1021. Not impossibly there was a resistance movement in the Fens, as later under William the Conqueror, and ecclesiastics became involved. If so, Cnut's attack on Ely may have been after 1016.

Nevertheless, the situation was probably of a complexity that cannot now be recovered. When considering events at Ramsey, for example, it should be remembered that Cnut allowed one of its monks to take the see of Dorchester not long after his accession. Nothing is known of Bishop Æthelric's connections, but it could be that if he had relatives they were among Cnut's supporters, or that as an individual he was prepared to back the king, for he is said to have enjoyed the royal favour.[118] His promotion should at any rate warn against over-simplification. As for Edmund, the Danes themselves may have supported his cult, as the Danish rulers of East Anglia came to do in the ninth century,[119] and if so he would eventually have become a means of reconciliation between the two peoples. The consecration of his new basilica on the anniversary of *Assandun* and the erection of a church on the battlefield could also have owed something to Danish interest. Their own losses in the battle may have been heavy, and they possibly wished to honour their dead and provide for their salvation. Cnut himself perhaps wanted to commemorate a great victory.

In so far as these religious matters were an expression of English resentment against their conquerors, such a Danish attitude would have tended to appease and disarm the opposition. This may have been one of the purposes behind some of Cnut's actions, as has been suggested in connection with his interest in Ælfheah. It is a pity that the extent of his involvement with the introduction of monks into Bury St Edmunds is uncertain, although it apparently occurred with his licence.[120] However, Hermann says that he was generous to them,[121] and the Bury Psalter and the Bury Gospels, both of which seem to have been produced in Christ Church Canterbury, were possibly commissioned by him as gifts.[122] The charter S 980, in favour of

[118] *Chron. Rams.*, p.126.
[119] Ridyard, *Royal Saints*, pp.216–18.
[120] Above, n.108.
[121] Hermann, *De Miraculis*, 16, ed. Arnold, i. 46.
[122] Temple, *Anglo-Saxon Manuscripts*, Nos. 84, 75.

Bury, could well be a forgery of the late eleventh century, although its donation of eels, fish, a fishery, and judicial rights may come from a genuine text.[123] Cnut is also said to have had the relics of saints Botulf and Jurminus translated there,[124] and a ditch dug round the abbey's lands to protect it from interference.[125] If his generosity was occasioned by concern at the growth of Edmund's cult, and its connection with Swegen and taxation, it may have been principally an attempt to mollify the opposition by making much of patronising the saint himself. Similarly, his patronage of Cerne was perhaps connected with his looting of the abbey during his campaign of conquest.[126] He had nothing to lose by ostentatious atonement for past sins; and St Eadwold, whose relics Cerne claimed to possess, was the brother of Edmund of East Anglia.

CHURCH APPOINTMENTS

If some ecclesiastics showed resentment against the Danes, many others were doubtless willing to make the best of the new regime. Promotions to abbacies and bishoprics were probably often the subject of competition between important families, and canvassing and intrigue may have taken place both locally and at court. Something of this can be seen in the Confessor's reign, when Earl Godwin supported one of his kinsmen, a Canterbury monk, in an attempt to obtain the archiepiscopacy.[127] Cnut may well have profited from this sort of process, for the sources are scanty and their silence on the matter of simony is not enough to rule it out. Æthelred, Harold Harefoot, Harthacnut and Edward may all have been guilty of it,[128] and there seems no reason why Cnut should have been an exception. An examination of his appointments hints at some of the other factors involved.

The sees of Ramsbury and Hereford did not fall vacant in his reign, while it is not known which king appointed Bishop Godwin II of Rochester. Of the promotions made under Cnut, nothing can be said of the origins of Ælfric II of Elmham, Leofgar of Lichfield, Brihtmær of Lichfield

[123] Writs, pp.433–34; Gransden, Historical Writing in England, pp.10–11.
[124] Memorials of St Edmund's Abbey, ed. Arnold, 1; 351–52, 361.
[125] GP, ii. 74, p.155.
[126] Below, p.139; above, n.36.
[127] The Life of King Edward, ed. Barlow, pp.30–31.
[128] Barlow, English Church, pp.42, 109–12. The way in which ASC C says that in 1044 Archbishop Eadsige feared that someone would become his suffragan 'either by asking or by purchase' implies that simony was not uncommon.

and Æthelric of Selsey, or of the reasons why Ælfric Puttoc, the *praepositus* of Winchester, was made archbishop of York in 1023. Others were appointed to sees from ecclesiastical establishments – monasteries in every case but one – within the diocese concerned. This was true of Lyfing of Crediton, who had been abbot of Tavistock; of Æthelric and Eadnoth II of Dorchester, both Ramsey monks; of Edmund of Durham; of Brihtwig of Wells, abbot of Glastonbury; and of Brihtheah of Worcester, abbot of Pershore. One might add Ælfwine of Elmham, a monk of Ely in the nearby diocese of Dorchester. These promotions may sometimes have resulted from family connections securing the nomination from Cnut, or from local influence being so important for a bishop that there was a natural tendency to choose a local man. The former rather than the latter could have been true of Brihtheah of Worcester, whose family was that of Archbishop Wulfstan of York and Worcester, but whose kinsmen lived in Berkshire,[129] while if Symeon of Durham's account of the election of Bishop Edmund is correct, Cnut simply confirmed a choice made in Durham.[130] Lyfing of Crediton doubtless owed his advancement largely to the influence of his uncle Brihtwold of Cornwall and to his own services to Cnut during the 1027 pilgrimage to Rome. The origins of the abbots appointed in Cnut's reign are seldom known. Internal promotion seems to have been frequent, and occurred with Ælfstan of St Augustine's Canterbury, Leofric and Leofsige of Ely, Æthelstan of Ramsey and Leofsine of Thorney. Perhaps many other abbots had also been monks of the houses they eventually ruled, and Cnut did not always take much interest in their selection. On the other hand, new men were occasionally brought in from outside. Brihtric of Burton and Ealdred of Tavistock were both Winchester monks, and Siward of Abingdon was from Glastonbury.[131]

This leaves a group of appointments which look like the deliberate insertion of royal supporters into important positions. The promotion of Æthelnoth to Canterbury in 1020 seemingly shows Cnut as willing to allow the Christ Church monks to elect their own dean. This may in part have been a political move, for if he was the son of Ealdorman Æthelmær of Wessex,[132] as is usually assumed, he came from a major West Saxon family, and had a brother, Æthelweard, executed by Cnut in 1017 and a brother-in-law (another Æthelweard) banished in 1020. He had a good later

[129] Hemming, i. 266.
[130] Symeon, *Historia Dunelmensis Ecclesiæ*, ed. Arnold, i. 85–6.
[131] On the Ely abbots, *Lib. El.*, pp. 143–44, 150; on the rest Knowles *et al.*, *The Heads of Religious Houses*.
[132] JW, ii. 506–07, calls him *nobilis uiri Ægelmari filius*.

reputation, and according to Osbern was very acceptable to Cnut because
he had given him holy chrism. Freeman suggested that this refers to participation in a ceremony of confirmation at Southampton in 1016, or to Cnut's
coronation by Archbishop Lyfing in 1017.[133] However that may be, Cnut's
considerable generosity to Canterbury[134] implies that he did have good relations with Æthelnoth, and this possibly made him the more determined to
control the selection of his successor. He evidently intended that this should
be the royal priest Eadsige, who took over some of Æthelnoth's duties in
1035 and succeeded him in 1038. As he became a monk at Christ Church as
a preliminary, it looks as though Cnut did not feel able to ride roughshod
over the church of Canterbury.[135]

Other royal priests raised to the episcopate were Ælfwine, who became
bishop of Winchester in 1032, and Duduc, who received Wells a year later.
These men must have been close to the king, and no doubt had considerable influence with him. There survives a copy of a letter sent to a priest
Ælf, almost certainly Ælfwine, which says that none of the royal councils are
hidden from him, and asks for his intercession with the queen so that the
writer might be given a fishery.[136] He also, according to Goscelin, helped
Abbot Ælfstan persuade Cnut to allow the translation of St Mildred's
remains to St Augustine's Canterbury.[137] His elevation to the wealthy and
important see of Winchester confirms his influence. Duduc had been given
lands at Congresbury and Banwell in Somerset and a *monasterium* in
Gloucester before he was promoted to Wells,[138] and another royal priest,
Stigand, received the new church at *Assandun* and became a major figure
under Edward the Confessor, eventually (and illegally) holding the great
sees of Winchester and Canterbury in plurality. Probably to be grouped
with the royal priests as a king's man is Ælfweard, allegedly a relative of
Cnut,[139] who became bishop of London in 1035 without relinquishing the
abbacy of Evesham, contrary to church law. Cnut's relations with the see of
London seem to have been poor,[140] and on the death of Bishop Ælfwig he
could well have wished it to be held by one of his own supporters. Also of

[133] *FNC*, i. 676.
[134] Below, pp. 141–42.
[135] Brooks, *Early History*, pp.295–96.
[136] See the Select Bibliography under Förster. The script is of the first half of the eleventh century and probably from Abingdon; Ker, *Catalogue*, pp.2–3.
[137] Goscelin, *Translatio Sancte Mildrethe Virginis*, ix, ed. Rollason, p.166.
[138] *Historiola*, ed. Hunter, p.15. The *monasterium* is said to have been St Peter's, but may have been St Oswald's; see Barlow, *English Church*, p.75, n.5; Finberg, *The Early Charters of Wessex*, p.249.
[139] *Chron. Eve.*, p.83.
[140] Below, p.143.

interest is Abbot Ælfmær of St Augustine's Canterbury. He may have co-operated with the Danes in some way at the siege of Canterbury in 1011,[141] and it was maybe in 1023 that he received the bishopric of Sherborne after the expulsion of Bishop Brihtwine.[142] Although Brihtwine was eventually reinstated after Ælfmær vexed the Sherborne flock, went blind and returned to Canterbury, one would gladly know more of what lay behind this. If Cnut was primarily responsible for the expulsion it would show that he sometimes dealt in a fairly high-handed manner with ecclesiastics who incurred his displeasure. Even so, the deposition of a bishop was not an expedient which was properly within his power, and Brihtwine's restoration may reflect this.[143]

CNUT'S PATRONAGE

Clearly, he might have been most willing to favour the foundations of churchmen with whom he got on well, or whose communities contained men connected with influential families. Before discussing his patronage, however, something must first be said about the sources. The survival of ecclesiastical records on this period is uneven, and the ones we have were often not put into their extant form until considerably later. The making of cartularies (books containing copies of charters), for example, does not seem to have been common before the twelfth century. Hence, there may well have been churches which received Cnut's generosity but whose records, if any were kept, have not survived to inform us of it. He is only known to have been a particular benefactor of the monastery at Cerne through the sixteenth-century antiquary John Leland,[144] and is likely to have given something to Thorney when he entered into fraternity there, but we know not what.[145] There is also the particular problem of the secular

[141] *ASC*, i. 141, says that he was released from the captives taken with the city. This would seem to mean that he was not held for ransom, perhaps because as St Augustine's lay outside the Roman walls upon which the defence was presumably conducted he had in some way mollified the besiegers to save it from destruction.

[142] Goscelin, *De Vita Sancti Wlsini*, xvi, ed. Talbot, 82. See Barlow, *English Church*, p.72, n.1.

[143] There may have been difficulties at Wells too. William of Malmesbury, *GP*, ii. 90, p.194, says that Bishop Æthelwine was ejected in favour of Brihtwine, restored and then ejected again. Other sources also report a Brihtwine of Wells, *Historiola*, ed. Hunter, p.15; Corpus Christi College, Cambridge MS 140 ff. 114v–115v (lists of bishops added to a Bath gospel book by a hand of around 1100, Ker, *Catalogue*, p.48). Æthelwine was certainly replaced by Brihtwig of Glastonbury in 1024, and if later writers confused the names Brihtwine may never have existed; charter signatures, as far as they go, would support this conclusion. There is also the possibility that Brihtwine of Sherborne acted as coadjutor in the neighbouring see, Knowles *et al.*, *The Heads of Religious Houses*, p.15.

[144] Leland, *Collectanea*, ed. Hearne, i. 66.

[145] BL MS Additional 40000, f. 10r.

colleges. Many of these originated as royal churches, and, as the favour shown to Waltham by Tofi the Proud and Harold Godwinsson, and the pre-Conquest wealth of the church of Bosham, once rated at 147 hides,[146] show, did receive royal bounty of which we are largely ignorant. However, it is known that four of the twenty hides held by the canons of St Milburg at Much Wenlock were freed of tax in Cnut's time,[147] although this may have owed something to the influence of Earl Leofric of Mercia, who was their patron. It is therefore necessary to be careful before using arguments from silence or partial silence to conclude that Cnut patronised some churches more than others.

The list of his gifts is long. While many foundations claimed that they had received land, it should be remembered that this may occasionally have been purchased from the king, or that he could have been confirming a gift made by someone else. Abingdon, for example, in addition to the reliquary for the remains of St Vincent and two great standards,[148] was granted an estate at Lyford, Berkshire and the *monasteriolium* of St Martin in Oxford by the charter S 964, but a note following the boundary clause suggests that Cnut was simply confirming a bequest by one Æthelwine. Two further grants to them, S 967 and 973, both give land at Myton, Warwickshire. The need for a second charter may mean that the estate was disputed; certainly the monks did not possess it in 1066.[149] However, Athelney still held land at Seavington, Somerset, granted to them by S 979,[150] and Buckfast, perhaps founded by Ealdorman Æthelweard in 1018,[151] their estate at Zeal Monachorum in Devon.[152] S 975 confirmed the monks of Sherborne in possession of Corscombe, Dorset,[153] and S 968 handed over a large estate at Patrington, Yorkshire to its archbishop, which his successor still held in 1086.[154]

Cnut was also generous to Durham, giving them sizeable lands at Brompton in Yorkshire and Staindrop in Durham,[155] and this fits with his

---

[146] Barlow, *English Church*, pp.190–91.

[147] *DB*, i. 252c.

[148] Above, p.126; *Chron. Ab.*, i. 443.

[149] DB, i. 239d, 241d. See also *Charters of Abingdon Abbey Part 1*, ed. Kelly, pp.542–43, 548–49, where S 964 is regarded as probably authentic and the problems attending S 967 and S 973 are discussed in detail.

[150] DB, i. 91b.

[151] Finberg, *'Supplement to "The Early Charters of Devon and Cornwall"'*, No. 52a.

[152] Finberg, *The Early Charters of Devon and Cornwall*, No. 57.

[153] See further on Sherborne, below, p.146–7.

[154] DB, i. 302b.

[155] *Historia de Sancto Cuthberto*, ed. Arnold, i. 213; Symeon, *Libellvs de exordio*, ed. Rollason, pp. 166-9 and n. 38. They held Brompton in 1086, DB, i. 304d. Domesday does not cover Durham, but Staindrop was in their possession in the twelfth century.

prominent display of piety when he visited St Cuthbert's shrine.[156] He was no less concerned to patronise the great northern saint, and please obdurate northerners, than his predecessor Æthelstan.[157] The abbey of Ramsey he favoured in a slightly different way, providing money from the royal treasury for the building of a second church, which he intended, in vain, but to the relief of the Ramsey chronicler, to turn into a nunnery. He also permitted Bishop Æthelric of Dorchester to transfer the relics of St Felix from the royal manor of Soham by boat to Ramsey; hostile naval intervention by the monks of Ely was frustrated by the miraculous descent of a very dense mist.[158]

Like Ramsey, Ely seems to have recovered from its initial difficulties with Cnut.[159] At least, the *Liber Eliensis* records how in the twelfth century it was still remembered that he had visited them, composing a song in English in response to the singing of the monks as he was rowed over the water towards them, and confirming their privileges by charter when he landed. Unfortunately, no such charter has survived, and the one which has, S 958, may be a forgery.[160] S 984, a grant of the site of the abbey of St Benet of Holme, which Cnut was later said to have founded,[161] may also be spurious, while S 953, a gift of privileges to St German's in Cornwall, is believed to have been concocted just after the Norman Conquest.[162] Yet even forgeries are not without interest, as it was probably his reputation for piety which led later churchmen to think that documents could plausibly be associated with Cnut.

He entered into fraternity with Christ Church Canterbury early in the reign,[163] gave Archbishop Lyfing land in Sussex by S 950 in 1018, and in S 1229 joined with Emma in granting them Newington (Oxfordshire), which had been forfeited to him, to provide food for the community. In 1023 Christ Church got the relics of St Ælfheah and probably rights within the important port of Sandwich.[164] They also claimed later through the charter S 981 that Cnut gave them the minster at Folkestone and its lands,[165]

---

[156] Above, p.125.

[157] Above, p.115. For the interest shown in northern saints by southern kings, see Rollason, *Saints and Relics*, pp.149–52.

[158] *Chron. Rams.*, pp.126–28.

[159] Above, pp.133–34.

[160] *Lib. El.*, ii. 84–85, pp.152–54; below, p.215[on S 958].

[161] See *St Benet of Holme 1020–1210*, ed. West, pp.190–91; and on S 984, below, p.215.

[162] Below, p.214.

[163] Above, p.87.

[164] However, S 959 is unlikely to be genuine as it stands, Brooks, *Early History*, pp.292–94; below, pp.213–14.

[165] But S 981 is a forgery, see Brooks, *Early History*, pp.300–01.

and at some time they received an arm of St Bartholomew[166] and maybe the remains of St Wendred.[167] This patronage seems to have been more marked than that of Cnut's immediate predecessors, perhaps for several reasons. One may have been geographical proximity to London, where the little that is known of the king's itinerary suggests that he spent a fair amount of time. Another was no doubt a good understanding with Archbishop Æthelnoth. Possibly more important, Canterbury was the richest of the English sees, and so presumably politically the most influential. Also, the wealthiest and most prestigious churches may have tended to attract the most noble inmates, both because of their status and of the benefits which might accrue from future promotion; Eadmer describes the pre-Conquest Christ Church community as living more like earls than monks. Worldly monks had worldly relatives, and Cnut's patronage may have been intended to please them.

Such factors could have influenced his attitude to the Winchester churches too. He is entered in the New Minster *Liber Vitae* as a benefactor of the monastery, and confirmed it in possession of a Hampshire estate by S 956, as well as giving the cross mentioned earlier. Old Minster (i.e. the cathedral) received a shrine for the relics of St Birinus, a large effigy, a six-branched silver candlestick, two standards,[168] an estate in Somerset (by S 972), and perhaps the confirmation of its privileges.[169] William of Malmesbury comments on the general magnificence of his gifts to Winchester,[170] and he was buried in Old Minster, presumably by his own choice. Now the bishopric of Winchester was second only to Canterbury in wealth, and they were both sees which Cnut wanted for royal priests. Taken together these facts begin to look significant. Cnut's generosity to Christ Church Canterbury and Old Minster Winchester had a great deal to do with their secular importance.

Yet by no means all significant foundations enjoyed his bounty. The bishopric of Worcester, which had considerable power within its own shire, seems to have received nothing. As its archives have survived tolerably well, and as Hemming writes in some detail on this period, argument from silence may here be legitimate, although it is true that Hemming's main

---

[166] Eadmer, *Historia Novorum*, ed. Rule, pp. 107–09, tells how Emma bought this relic for many pounds of silver from the archbishop of Benevento, who was visiting England to raise funds and had to swear to its authenticity. She then gave it to Christ Church on behalf of Cnut and herself.

[167] *Lib. El.*, ii. 79, p. 148, reports Ely's loss of these relics at the battle of *Assandun* and a rumour that Cnut deposited them in Canterbury; but the recipient may have been St Augustine's.

[168] *Annales Monastici,* ed. Luard, ii. 16; *duo signa* could also be translated two bells, or even two pictures.

[169] By S 976, of doubtful authenticity.

[170] *GR* ii. 181, ed. Stubbs, i. 220.

purpose was to record the alienation rather than augmentation of Worcester's lands. Comparative geographical isolation may have been one cause, but it little affected nearby Evesham. Abbot Ælfweard was a relative of the king,[171] one of his leases (S 1423) refers to Ælfgifu the Lady as ruler of the monastery, and Cnut had the relics of St Wigstan transferred there. He is further said to have given a black chasuble with the trappings pertaining to it, and estates in Gloucestershire, Winchcombeshire and Northamptonshire,[172] while also granting Newnham (Northamptonshire) to the monk Ælfric who may have been dean of Evesham.[173] There is additionally a spurious charter, S 957, giving Newnham and Badby to the monastery. Both were later disputed with Crowland. Possibly, as Ann Williams has suggested, Abbot Ælfweard was related to Cnut because he was a kinsman of Ælfgifu of Northampton. If so, the same Ælfgifu, rather than Queen Emma, was perhaps the lady who ruled Evesham.[174]

The bishopric of London did little better than Worcester, which is surprising considering the city's increasing importance at this time,[175] the apparent frequency of Cnut's presence there, and his alleged gift to Westminster Abbey of relics of St Cyriacus[176] and Edward the Martyr, a finger of St Ælfheah, and a finger and other bones of St George.[177] There is S 992, a writ to St Paul's of doubtful authenticity, confirming their judicial and financial rights, but Domesday Book says that Cnut deprived the bishopric of the thirty-hide estate of Southminster, Essex.[178] This would have been a considerable loss, for London was not wealthy. Nor does Bishop Ælfwig, who must have resented the loss of Ælfheah's relics in 1023, sign charters with quite the frequency one might expect, although this may be because many were drafted at some distance from his see.

Another foundation which derived little benefit from Cnut was Glastonbury, even if he did confirm their privileges when he visited Edmund Ironside's tomb, for there is no other evidence of munificence to them, and it seems probable that William of Malmesbury's history of

---

[171] Above, p. 138, n.139.
[172] *Chron. Eve.*, pp.83, 325–26, 75
[173] By S 977. Ælfic, dean of Evesham, died in 1037; *ASC*, i. 160.
[174] Williams, "'Cockles amongst the wheat", 8. However, Emma had taken the English name Ælfgifu after her marriage to Æthelred, and is referred to as Ælfgifu the Lady fairly frequently, for example in S 1386.
[175] Nightingale, 'The Origin of the Court of Husting'.
[176] Above, p.126.
[177] Reported by the fifteenth century Westminster chronicler John Flete, *The History of Westminster Abbey* ed.J.A. Robinson, p.70.
[178] DB, ii. 10–10b.

Glastonbury would have informed us of it had it occurred. Yet no abbey was richer: it had the prestige of being one of the leaders of the tenth-century reformation, and may well have contained members of important West Saxon families. Also, its abbots witnessed royal charters regularly, and usually in a senior position, which ought to mean that they were prominent at court. Maybe it suffered from its close association with the dynasty which Cnut had displaced.

Possibly he did wish to profit by stressing his brotherhood with Edmund Ironside, but too much veneration of the West Saxon monarchy may have been dangerous, considering that Æthelred's sons by Emma were still alive and living in Normandy, where Edward the Confessor seems eventually to have been supported by Duke Robert in taking the title of king.[179] His *Life,* written about thirty years after Cnut's death, tells how Bishop Brihtwold of Ramsbury had a vision in which he saw St Peter consecrate Edward king. This apparently occurred during the period of Danish rule, and, significantly, at Glastonbury.[180] Odd as the tale may be, it hints at what might have been guessed anyway: that within Wessex Æthelred's sons were not totally forgotten, and that they were forgotten least in a house with which their forebears had been closely associated. A nascent cult of Edgar, who was buried there, may have been a part of this picture, although William of Malmesbury's description of the body's translation suggests that it occurred around 1050.[181] It could be argued, of course, that Cnut's visit to Edmund's tomb was intended to nullify Glastonbury's interest in the house of Cerdic by stressing his own links with them. But if so he could have been expected to be rather more generous. Furthermore, it might be necessary to conclude that this was a change of tactic, for on another occasion he seems to have treated the West Saxon dynasty with scant respect.

William of Malmesbury says that when Cnut visited Wilton he insulted St Edith by saying that he could never believe the daughter of such a libidinous man as Edgar to be a saint, and on being contradicted by Archbishop Æthelnoth ordered her tomb to be broken open to discover what signs of sanctity it might contain. When this was done she rose up and attacked him, and he fell to the ground unconscious; he did not like English saints, says William, because he was a foreigner.[182] This final comment is obviously

---

[179] Above, pp.105–06.
[180] *The Life of King Edward,* ed. Barlow, pp.12–15. William of Malmesbury says specifically *tempore regis Cnutonis,* ibid., p.128.
[181] WM *Glaston.,* p.134.
[182] *GP,* ii. 87, p.190.

incorrect, and how much reliance can be placed on the rest of the tale is doubtful. It contrasts somewhat strangely with Goscelin's statement that Cnut showed as much devotion to Edith as if he had been her brother Æthelred, and with the fact that he ordered a probably large gold shrine to be made for her;[183] also, Wilton's standing at the time is suggested by Earl Godwin's selection of it for the education of his daughter Edith, Edward the Confessor's future queen, who was perhaps named after the saint.[184] Quite where this leaves us is unclear. A writer like Goscelin, commissioned to write on Edith by the Wilton nuns, would naturally tend to exaggerate her attractions, and one like William, describing a saint possessed by another house, might wish to denigrate them. Unlike Goscelin, he expresses doubts about the legitimacy of Edith's parentage too.[185] Even so, he may simply be reporting unfavourable traditions about Edith also known to Cnut. Both accounts are therefore open to suspicion, although Goscelin was well informed on Wilton affairs and goes into considerable detail on the new shrine, whose goldsmiths defrauded Cnut by making it of silver-gilt rather than gold. Its existence might therefore reasonably be taken as a fact, and the two stories could be partially reconciled if the shrine was a replacement for the tomb which had been desecrated. If so, either Cnut for some reason radically revised his attitude to Edith and perhaps other of his West Saxon predecessors, which would be interesting, or some of his pious generosity was of a rather casual type, and could embrace lavish giving to a saint whom he was not slow to denigrate in public. Maybe, as his gifts to foreign churches and generosity on the way to Rome also imply, it was sometimes not the direction of the gift that mattered so much as the act of giving, and of being seen to be giving, itself.

Cnut's relations with the English church were an important aspect of his rule, and suggest much about its nature. We cannot know how far he was genuinely pious, although the Letter of 1027 certainly stresses the strength of his desire to visit Rome, as he had vowed some time previously, to seek the favour of St Peter, the keeper of the keys of the heavenly kingdom. He may well have been concerned about his own salvation, for he had seen death often, and at close quarters. What can be known is that religion was politically important to him. Unlike William the Conqueror he was not able, or more likely did not wish, to completely replace the English

---

[183] Goscelin, Vita S. Edithe, ii. 12, ed. Wilmart, pp.278–79.
[184] The Life of King Edward, ed. Barlow, pp.36–37.
[185] See Ridyard, Royal Saints, p.42.

aristocracy with his own followers (see Chapter 5), and therefore had to some extent to reach an accommodation with them. Hence, it was expedient to patronise the church with which they, and previous monarchs, had become closely associated.

But there was more to his behaviour than simply that. He had acquired the throne at the end of a long and bloody series of wars, and whatever the terms he may or may not have made with Edmund Ironside, many Englishmen must have seen him as essentially a usurper. Also, there was almost certainly considerable initial resentment in some quarters against Danish rule. Religion was one of the ways in which such resentment could be expressed. Whatever is made of interest in the saints Ælfheah and Edmund of East Anglia, it is likely that there was at least an element of this in their make-up, connected as the first was, and the second was apparently believed to be, with events in the recent fighting. More than most kings, Cnut needed the Church. 'When we saw the gift that you sent us', wrote Bishop Fulbert of Chartres, 'we were amazed at your knowledge as well as your faith... since you, whom we had heard to be a pagan prince, we now know to be not only a Christian, but also a most generous donor to churches and God's servants'.[186]

This was doubtless much the kind of reaction that he sought, internationally as well as nationally. His gifts abroad may have been much more extensive than can now be proved; he entered into fraternity with the church of Bremen,[187] and is also known to have sent a psalter and sacramentary, both made in Peterborough and beautifully illustrated, to Cologne,[188] and a book written in letters of gold and other royal gifts to Duke William the Great of Aquitaine.[189] The latter volume included St Martial, patron saint of Aquitaine, among the apostles, and Francis Wormald argued that this was because the claim of his church in Limoges that Martial should be regarded as an apostle was supported by Cnut.[190] In Europe, as in England, his religious activities created opportunities, making possible his diplomatic links with the German empire whose rulers he seems to have been eager to emulate, and admitting him, in Sir Frank Stenton's words, to 'the civilised

---

[186] Fulbert, *Letters*, ed. Behrends, pp.66–68.
[187] Adam *Gesta*, scholium 37, p.112.
[188] William of Malmesbury, *Vita Wulfstani*, i. 9, ed, Darlingron, p.16.
[189] *Patrologiæ Cursus Completus*, ed. J.P. Migne, vol. 141, col.122. See also Beech, 'England and Aquitaine in the century before the Norman Conquest'.
[190] Wormald, 'The English Saints in the Litany in Arundel MS. 60', 84–86; also Beech, 'England and Aquitaine', 84–86.

fraternity of Christian kings'.[191] His coronation, his gifts to churches, his pilgrimage to Rome – all partly served the purpose of cloaking a murky past and perhaps a shady present, and giving to his government an aura of legitimacy. They must also have been a useful antidote to expressions of hostility in a religious form. Nevertheless, Cnut's relations with individual churches were sometimes poor, as evidence on Ely, Ramsey, Sherborne and maybe Wilton indicates. Nor, as his association with Ælfgifu of Northampton shows, did he always heed ecclesiastical admonition. However much he needed the support of his churchmen, ultimately Cnut was master, and his reign may have been a difficult time for some churches, troubled by the burden of royal taxation. When he visited Sherborne Cnut gave precious gifts, but Emma contributed twenty pounds of silver for the repair of the roof, through which rain fell upon the tomb of St Wulfsige.[192] No doubt the church of Sherborne knew the weight of his financial exactions, and that what the king gave with one hand he might take back, through his tax collectors, with the other. Did it also know, in common with most of his contemporaries, that Cnut's piety was grounded in this world as much as the next?

[191] Stenton, *Anglo-Saxon England*, p.397.
[192] Goscelin, *De Vita Sancti Wlsini*, xiv, ed. Talbot, p.81.

5

THE DANES, THE ENGLISH AND THE GOVERNMENT OF ENGLAND, 1017–35

Cnut gained the throne of England after about thirty years of intermit-tent but frequently bitter warfare during which the tribulations of its inhabitants must often have been considerable. Hemming comments that Worcestershire was atrociously devastated,[1] and the *Anglo-Saxon Chronicle* speaks repeatedly of the harrying, burning and slaughter which marked the progress of hostile armies. Although exaggeration can always be suspected in such statements, they cannot be wished away entirely. Harrying in this period does often seem to have involved dealing out death and destruction to everything within reach. Thus, the *Chronicle* description of how the Danes spent three months in 1010 burning East Anglia, killing both men and cattle, seems to reflect the same kind of activity as Harthacnut's ravaging of Worcestershire in 1041, when John says that it was the intention to kill every man who could be found.[2] William the Conqueror's Harrying of the North in 1069–70, which had effects still visible to the Domesday commis-sioners seventeen years later,[3] was action of a similar type. Furthermore, the forces faced by Æthelred were ventures with commercial and political pur-poses well-served by ruthlessness: the more raiding they did the more booty they took; the greater the destruction and killing the more the English were likely to pay for peace, and the more inclined they might even be to accept Scandinavian rule. The apparent ease of Swegen's conquest in 1013 indicates not only significant native disillusion with Æthelred, but also the efficiency with which the harriers had carried out their fiery and bloody work. Nor are many of the English likely to have quickly forgotten either the burden

---

[1] Hemming, i. 251.
[2] JW, ii. 532–33.
[3] Darby, *Domesday England*, pp.248–52.

of raising large sums paid to the enemy in tribute, or the loss of relatives
killed in the fighting. Some leading families may have suffered particularly
in this latter respect, and had doubtless supplied many of the hostages muti-
lated by Cnut in 1014 and 1016 too.[4] These men, some of whom lost their
hands, ears and noses, must for the rest of their lives have served as timely
reminders of the realities of the Danish conquest.

At his accession there would have been considerable English resentment
against Cnut and his followers, and for all the ease of Swegen's acceptance in
1013, and the readiness of certain areas to accept his son in 1015–16, this did
not immediately die away, especially in Wessex. The ætheling Eadwig, banished in 1017, returned, and may have been plotting revolt when he was
killed and buried at Tavistock, while Gaimar's tale of a plan to restore the
sons of Edmund Ironside cannot be discounted completely.[5] It may have
been unrest in Wessex, or fear of it, which led Cnut to reserve it for his
immediate control in 1017, and to visit it before his departure for Denmark
in 1019. The banishment of Ealdorman Æthelweard in 1020 shows that
these measures were not a complete success. Even so, we hear nothing of
the kind of revolts which William the Conqueror faced early in his rule, and
although the sources are not good enough for much to be based on arguments from silence (English writers say nothing, after all, of the hostile
relations with Normandy late in the reign),[6] Cnut was eventually able, like
William, to spend longish periods abroad apparently without undue concern. Ultimately, he succeeded in ensuring that the country conquered in
1016 by a fairly narrow margin did not slip from his grasp.

His methods are virtually certain to have involved far more than just the
executions and banishments which marked the first year of the reign. The
use of the hostage was common in this period, and it is likely that Cnut initially held members of important English families in his power. His father
retained English hostages even after Æthelred's flight to Normandy, and
those received by Cnut before his treaty with Edmund in 1016 may have
long remained in his possession, perhaps at first as a guarantee of peace, and
then, after his acquisition of the entire kingdom, at least until the payment
of the great tax of £82,500 in 1018, and Danes and English came to an
agreement at Oxford. The nature of this agreement is unknown, but it may
have been a suitable occasion for the release of hostages. It is also possible

---

4 ASC., i. 145; Thietmar, *Chronicon*, vii. 41, pp.448–49.
5 Above, pp.84–85.
6 Above, pp.105–07.

that Cnut took English forces abroad with him,[7] partly to guarantee the good behaviour of those who remained behind.

SCANDINAVIAN SETTLEMENT IN ENGLAND, 1017–35

Of course, his hold on the country must have been strengthened by the occupation of English land by his followers. A number of them, who appear high in the charter witness lists, seem to have stood at the king's right hand, and probably some or all received estates over a wide area. One was Osgod, maybe always the Osgod Clapa who signs the royal charter S 968. He continued to be important until exiled under the Confessor, and held land in Suffolk, probably in Norfolk,[8] possibly in the Isle of Wight and Oxfordshire,[9] and doubtless elsewhere. In 1042 his daughter's wedding feast was celebrated at Lambeth in Harthacnut's presence, and a dubious writ of the Confessor implies that he had authority in Middlesex. Whether this dated back to Cnut's time is unknown.[10] His daughter (Gytha) married Tofi the Proud, and John of Worcester describes Osgod as a man of great power and Tofi as a Dane and a very mighty man.

Tofi established a church at Waltham in Essex to house the cross found on his Somerset estate of Montacute. It is a striking coincidence that he possessed the Wessex hill later crowned by one of the Conqueror's earliest castles, and not impossible that it had defensive works in the Danish period too. A twelfth-century Waltham tract says that he held lands in Berkshire and many estates in the vicinity of Waltham, including Edmonton, Cheshunt, Mimms, and the barony later owned by William de Mandeville (earl of Essex 1166–89), and that he gave the church property in Essex, Hertfordshire and Surrey.[11] Whatever the substance of these claims, Domesday Book shows that his grandson Esgar later held property in at least ten shires – Berkshire, Middlesex, Hertfordshire, Buckinghamshire, Oxfordshire, Cambridgeshire, Northamptonshire, Essex, Suffolk, Warwickshire

---

[7] Below, p.178.
[8] His Suffolk estate is known from S 1074; ownership of Norfolk land could be inferred from his acting as witness in the shire of the will of Thurstan (S 1531).
[9] S 1391; see Robertson, *Charters*, p.433. Osgod also appears in the *Liber Vitae* of Thorney Abbey.
[10] S 1121; *Writs*, pp. 308–09, 496–99. Nightingale, 'The Origin of the Court of Husting', 565, argues from his appearance in the dubious St Paul's writ S 992 that it did, and included authority in London.
[11] On Tofi, see *FNC*, i. 769–70; Robertson, *Charters*, p.400. Knowledge of his landed possessions comes mainly from the Waltham source, the *De Inventione Sanctae Crucis*, ed. Stubbs, pp.1–12. Possessions in Norfolk could be deduced from his acting as executor of the will of the Norfolk landowner Ælfric Modercope (S 1490).

and probably Surrey.[12] Much of this he may of course have acquired for himself, but if this leaves us somewhat in the dark about the precise extent of his grandfather's possessions, we are at least better informed on Tofi than any of Cnut's other major followers.

They also included Thored, whose known connections are with the south-east. He entered into fraternity with Christ Church Canterbury and granted them a large estate at East Horsley, Surrey by S 1222. His fraternity is listed in a Christ Church gospel book along with those of Cnut and his brother Harald, and one of their later obituaries says that he died on 18 July and gave them Horsley and many other goods.[13] He may well be the Thored nephew of Thorkell who witnesses the Kentish charter S 1465, and the Thored staller who appears in the forged Christ Church grant S 981. A Thored signs Cnut's charters fairly frequently, sometimes high on the list of *ministri*, but two men of the name occur in S 960 and 961, so the single signatures do not all necessarily belong to the same person, and nor need either be identifiable with the *optimate regis nomine Đored* (royal magnate named Thored) who sold (S 1463) Huntingdonshire land to Abbot Ælfsige of Peterborough in London in Cnut's presence. Obviously, the lack of surnames in pre-Conquest England can be a problem, especially when dealing with fairly common names. It must remain an open question whether any of these Thoreds was the one who received land at Ditchampton (Wiltshire) from the Confessor in 1044, which he gave to the nunnery at Wilton along with his two daughters.[14]

If witness lists alone can be infertile ground, other evidence is more fruitful. Late in the eleventh century, at the request of Bishop Wulfstan II of Worcester (1062–95), the monk Hemming compiled an account of lost church estates based on written sources and the testimony of his elders.[15] His statements are obviously likely to be partisan, and do not always accord with other evidence,[16] but he is nevertheless of great value in being the only source to give any real impression of the impact of the Danish conquest

[12] Sawyer, '1066–1086: A Tenurial Revolution?', pp.74, 84. Esgar appears early in the Confessor's reign, and Tofi, if really his grandfather (*De Inventione*, p.13), can have been no youth when he married Gytha (presumably not his first wife) in 1042.
[13] BL MS Royal I. D. ix, f. 43v. I have assumed that *Đord ure broðor* is identical with Thored. The *obit* is in BL MS Cotton Galba E. iii, f. 33r, printed Dart, *The History and Antiquities of the Cathedral Church of Canterbury*, p.xxiv.
[14] S 1010; DB, i. 66b, 68b.
[15] Hemming, i. 248,282–83.
[16] See Round, 'Introduction to the Worcestershire Domesday', p.253, and Ker, 'Hemming's Cartulary', pp.64–65, who comments that 'it is safer to trust to the main facts than to the details of his stories'; also below, p.176.

upon a particular area. He says that in Worcestershire many Englishmen, noble and ignoble, rich and poor, were deprived of their estates;[17] Hakon, who was probably earl of the shire, is accused of having taken lands in western Worcestershire from the monks of Worcester, and Hemming complains that they lost other property in Herefordshire, Worcestershire and Oxfordshire. Herefordshire seems to have been controlled by Earl Hrani, and this together with Earl Eglaf's connection with Gloucestershire and Hakon's with Worcestershire[18] suggests that Cnut's men settled in a greater density in the Welsh border shires than elsewhere. Hemming speaks of soldiers of Hakon and Hrani as occupying English land,[19] and one of the prime objects of this was fairly clearly defence against the Welsh. As some of them had evidently supported Edmund Ironside against Cnut,[20] this may have been particularly important early in the reign, although the area was doubtless a difficult one at the best of times. It contained a fair number of waste and partially-waste estates when visited by the Domesday commissioners fifty years after Cnut's death.

Nevertheless, there are grounds for believing that it did not witness dispossession of English landowners on a substantial scale. Domesday Worcestershire was assessed at some 1,200 hides: roughly 400 were the responsibility of the church of Worcester, and about a third of these were set aside for the upkeep of the monks, and formed Hemming's subject.[21] Such estates as he describes as passing into Danish hands were valued in 1086 at some twenty hides.[22] This was about a sixth of the Domesday holding, although as there had been further alienations by the Normans the relative reduction in Cnut's time may have been rather smaller than this. If hardly catastrophic, neither was it minimal, and no doubt to the monks it seemed serious enough. Their losses in other shires were possibly proportionally greater, as it was no doubt more difficult to keep control of distant lands. Those given up in Oxfordshire, for example, Heythrop and Over Kiddington,

---

[17] Hemming, i. 251.
[18] Below, p. 169.
[19] Hemming, i. 251, 274.
[20] Above, pp. 76–78.
[21] See Round, 'Introduction to the Worcestershire Domesday', p. 245. Hemming, i. 282; see Ker, 'Hemming's Cartulary', pp. 63–64. Hemming's work may not be quite as limited as he says, since he mentions several estates alienated by the Normans which appear in Domesday as belonging to the bishop.
[22] Hemming, i. 251, 255–56. They were Tenbury, Clifton on Teme, Kyre, Ham, Eastham, *Bufawuda* (perhaps Bestewde, which appears with Eastham in Domesday), Astley and Ribbesford. All were in the north-west of the shire and were assessed at twenty hides in 1086, DB, i. 176b–d. This total counts Kyre and Kyre Wyward together, and excludes Ribbesford, which is not separately assessed in Domesday as it was then one of sixteen berewicks of a royal estate rated at twenty hides, DB, i. 172b.

were assessed at ten hides in 1086,[23] and by then the Worcester monks held
nothing in the shire; it should also be remembered that they had further
property confiscated as a result of tax debts.[24]

The effects on Worcestershire's laymen can be established in outline if
not in detail. There is a lease of land in the shire by Bishop Lyfing from 1042
(S 1396) witnessed by three men with Scandinavian names – Atsere, Thuri
and Wigod. Atsere appears again, along with Wagen and 'all the thegns of
Worcestershire, Danish and English', in a lease (S 1406) by Bishop Ealdred
from 1046x53. He may well have been the relative and chamberlain of
Bishop Brihtheah (1033–38) of Worcester mentioned by Hemming,[25] outlawed after 1066, but appearing in Worcestershire Domesday as Azor, a
pre-Conquest tenant of the churches of Worcester, Westminster and Pershore.
Wagen is quite likely the Vagn who was a thegn of Earl Leofric of Mercia,
and according to Domesday held land in Warwickshire and Staffordshire.[26]
Another Scandinavian, recorded in Domesday for Worcestershire and
Warwickshire, was one of Leofric's soldiers, Sigmund, whom Hemming
describes as Danish by birth,[27] and Ann Williams has shown that the Dane
Ocea, connected with a Worcestershire estate by Hemming,[28] married
Ealdgyth, a rich Englishwoman with lands in Gloucestershire. None of these
men was definitely granted English land by Cnut. While Atsere, for exam-
ple, could have been one of his followers, married to an Englishwoman
related to Bishop Brihtheah, the latter was a nephew of Archbishop
Wulfstan of York, who may have come from eastern England,[29] where
Scandinavian names had been common since the ninth-century invasions.
His relative Atsere need therefore have had nothing to do with Cnut.

There are other problems too. Earl Godwin gave his first four sons
Scandinavian names (Swegen, Harold, Tostig, Gyrth), so when recorded
after about 1040 these could refer to Englishmen, just as native ones may
denote men of Scandinavian or mixed descent: Tofi the Proud, for example,
called his son Æthelstan.[30] There is also the possibility of later migration
from Denmark, for men described as Danes by Domesday Book may often

[23] Hemming, i. 280; DB, i. 159a, 160b.
[24] Below, pp. 175, 177.
[25] Hemming, i. 269.
[26] Williams, '"Cockles amongst the wheat": Danes and English in the western midlands in the first half
of the eleventh century', 15.
[27] Hemming, i. 265. I owe these references to Williams, 'Cockles', 13–14.
[28] Hemming, i. 255–56; Williams, 'Cockles', 14.
[29] Sermo Lupi, ed. Whitelock, p. 7.
[30] De Inventione Sanctae Crucis, ed. Stubbs, p. 13.

have been relative newcomers.[31] Furthermore, it is likely that the non-Scandinavian areas of England contained some Scandinavians even before 1016. Æthelred II sold land in Oxfordshire to a Dane by the charter S 943 of 1006xII, and Danes were attacked in Oxford during the massacre of St Brice's Day in 1002, while Scandinavian names appear among the Æthelredian moneyers of Exeter.[32]

But such problems render the evidence difficult, not useless. It is a reasonable assumption that there were few of Scandinavian appellation in Worcestershire before Cnut's time. Bishop Oswald of Worcester's many late tenth-century leases have no examples among their grantees and only a possible one among their ecclesiastical witnesses, and Æthelred's twelve known Worcester moneyers do not include any.[33] Hence, the approximately twenty pre-Conquest landowners with Scandinavian names recorded in Domesday[34] seem likely to be connected in some way with the influx reported by Hemming. Even so, none held much land, and their names are greatly outnumbered by those of the English, which implies that Cnut's men had probably never been much more than a sizeable minority. Similarly, the handful of Scandinavian names in the leases of bishops Lyfing and Ealdred of Worcester mentioned above are far outweighed by a combined total of twenty-three English ones.

Herefordshire evidence gives much the same impression. A record of a law-suit in Cnut's time lists eleven laymen: Earl Hrani and doubtless Thorkell the White were Scandinavian, the rest were English.[35] Leofflœd, Thorkell's English wife, appears in this document, and both are to be found among the pre-Conquest Domesday landholders of Herefordshire. She held some twenty-five hides and her husband just over twenty, although lands totalling another twenty-seven are attributed to a Thorkell who may or may not be the same man. In Herefordshire, as in Worcestershire, there are about twenty pre-Conquest holders with Scandinavian names, but again they are greatly outnumbered by the English.

A pretty much identical picture emerges elsewhere. In parts of southern England the charter evidence for Cnut's reign is at its best. The Dorset

---

[31] For a list of them, Feilitzen, *The Pre-Conquest Personal Names of Domesday Book*, p.23.

[32] S 909, translated *EHD*, pp.590–93; see Williams, 'Cockles', 1. Smart, 'Moneyers of the late Anglo-Saxon coinage', 304.

[33] S 1297–1374. The name of the witness Tuna was possibly Danish, Feilitzen, *Personal Names*, pp.388–89. Smart, 'Moneyers', 246.

[34] Williams, 'Cockles', n.64.

[35] S 1462; Robertson, *Charters*, No. 78. Tofi the Proud, who appears in the document on a royal errand, is excluded from these totals.

estate which the Scandinavian Orc received in 1024 by S 961 he eventually gave to the monastery of Abbotsbury, which he may have founded.[36] If we could assume that most of the abbey's approximately seventy-four hides in Domesday Dorset had been his, then Orc was a landowner of some importance, but he did not receive it all from Cnut: Abbot's Wootton, at least, he got from the Confessor (S 1004). Other Scandinavians granted Dorset estates were Bovi and Agemund. The latter may have been the royal magnate of this name who allegedly took land from the nuns of Wilton,[37] and who is listed among the witnesses of Orc's grant and of two probably-forged Canterbury charters (S 959 and 981). Another Scandinavian known from a Kentish context is Karl, who signs the marriage agreement between Godwin and Brihtric (S 1461) as the king's *cniht*, and was possibly the father of the Domesday Kentish landowners Godric Carlesone and Godwin *filius Carli*.[38] A number of other Scandinavians appear in charters from southern England, and can be reasonably thought to have received land there. Among them are Atsere, Bersi, Brothor, Eglaf, Kartoca, Thurgod, Thurstan, Tofi the Red, Tofi the White and Toki. Their status as witnesses indicates that they were of some consequence, and they may have had followers who were granted estates too. If Toki is the man of that name who came to agreements with archbishops Æthelnoth and Eadsige of Canterbury about land in Buckinghamshire then he was another Scandinavian who married an English wife, Æthelflæd. He may further be the Toki, father of Care, who is mentioned in a Sherborne lease of around 1046, and the powerful and rich royal minister Toki who gave land in Gloucestershire to the bishopric of Worcester. But the name was common, appearing twice, for example, in the Thorney *Liber Vitae*.[39]

   The proportion of Scandinavian to English names in the charters varies considerably. S 961, the grant to Orc from 1024, has thirteen Scandinavian *ministri* and seven English. Some of the former may have belonged to the king's entourage, although there is only one (Thored, discussed above) of whom this is almost certainly so. Of the rest, Bovi and Agemund were definitely Dorset landowners, and others may have been. In other grants the numbers are more or less equally balanced,[40] but in most, and especially

---

[36] On Orc, see *Writs*, pp. 119–22, 425–27, 576.
[37] Goscelin, *Vita S. Edithe*, ii. 14, ed. Wilmart, p. 281. An Agemund appears in Wiltshire Domesday, DB, i. 72b.
[38] See Robertson, *Charters*, p. 398. A Karl also witnesses other grants.
[39] S 1464, 1466, see Brooks, *Early History of the Church of Canterbury*, pp. 301–02; S 1474, 1408.
[40] S 951, 955, 956, 960, 964, 976.

those from the south-west, the English predominate.[41] The number of Scandinavians in Orc's charter may mean that others under-represent them. Perhaps draughtsmen tended to favour the inclusion of Englishmen, or allowed the grantee to instruct them as to who should appear. This might explain both the many Scandinavians in S 961 and why most other grants, mainly to English donees, contain so many native names. However, S 969, like S 961 both in favour of a Scandinavian and probably written by the monks of Sherborne,[42] has fifteen English *ministri* out of twenty. As far as Dorset goes, Domesday Book tends to confirm the impression given by S 969, for the pre-Conquest holders include only about a dozen men with Scandinavian names. As matters stand, it looks as though in southern England, as in the west midlands, Cnut's followers formed a significant minority among the landowning class, but no more than that.

Of what happened in the north we know nothing, and of eastern England little more, for where Scandinavian names were already common the men bearing them were not necessarily newcomers. Those who are numbered among the pre-Conquest moneyers of Chester and in Domesday Cheshire, for example, must often have been descendants of tenth-century settlers in the area. Still, East Anglian casualties in the recent fighting had been heavy, and there was doubtless land to spare there for Cnut's men. The twelfth-century Ramsey chronicle says that a Bedfordshire estate which had belonged to Æthelweard, son of Ealdorman Æthelwine of East Anglia (d. 992), passed into foreign hands after his death at *Assandun* in 1016, and this may have been typical.[43] Certainly, one would expect Thorkell, who was put in charge of East Anglia in 1017, to have received property there, some of which maybe belonged to his English wife Edith, who according to John accompanied him into exile in 1021. Similarly, Earl Eric of Lade must have been given land in Northumbria. All that can be added to this is that the Ramsey chronicle records other grants to Danes in Cambridgeshire, Huntingdonshire and Bedfordshire, all of which eventually came into Ramsey's possession, and that the Thorkell Hoga who witnesses S 961 and appears in the Thorney *Liber Vitae* may well be identifiable with the *Turkilus Hoche* who gave a Nottinghamshire estate and a *monetarium* in Stamford to Peterborough Abbey. He could have been one of Cnut's new men.[44]

[41] S 950, 953–54, 959, 962–63, 969–70, 971, 974.
[42] Below, p.215.
[43] *Chron. Rams.*, p.143.
[44] *Chron. Rams.*, pp.129, 135, 140; Hugh Candidus, *Chronicle*, ed. Mellows, p.70; see also Hart, *The Early Charters of Eastern England*, p.245.

Domesday Book has already been used as evidence for particular shires, but correlation of its information as a whole offers other insights. By 1066, of course, many of those endowed by Cnut are virtually certain to have been dead, or to have disappeared for other reasons; the Confessor may have banished more than Osgod Clapa, and others, who possibly held lands in Scandinavia too (an important matter, about which nothing is known), could well have left of their own free will when Danish rule ended. Even so, Domesday has something to offer. In a number of cases a Norman baron is known to have received the lands of a particular pre-Conquest land-holder (his *antecessor*) in various shires, and thus when Anglo-Saxon owners of the estates of individual Normans have the same name they may well be the same man. Hence the possessions of the Confessor's men of substance can to an extent be reconstructed. Tofi the Proud's grandson Esgar the Staller was mentioned earlier.[45] An Atsere had preceded Earl Aubrey in Wiltshire, Oxfordshire and Northamptonshire, and if all the references to a Wiltshire Atsere (some are *antecessores* of other Normans) are to the same one, he had held nearly seventy hides there; similarly, the Karl who had about 112 hides in Wiltshire owned property in Hampshire, Surrey and Somerset too, making nearly 150 hides in all,[46] and Wigot of Wallingford (of whom more later) held property in at least seven shires, and possibly as many as eleven.[47] These men all have Scandinavian names, and although only Karl may be known from Cnut's reign, and all could have owed much to the Confessor, their existence raises the possibility that some Scandinavians acquired exten-sive lands under Cnut. Others who appear high in the charter witness lists, and whose estates, although unknown, may at one time have been consid-erable, are Aslac, Hakon, Halden, Harold, Hastin, and Thorkell. But this is not certain. The Christ Church fraternity entry which lists Cnut and his brother Harald also includes Kartoca, who witnesses S 961 too. Was he an important English landowner, or, like Harald, simply a visitor from abroad?

The English names which crop up under Cnut are occasionally to be found under Æthelred too, although it is usually impossible to prove that they refer to the same individuals. However, Ælfgeat, Siward and Brihtric the Red had all been significant figures in Dorset: they are mentioned in a

---

[45] Above, p. 151–52.
[46] Darlington, 'Introduction to the Wiltshire Domesday', pp. 65–66; Hooper, 'An Introduction to the Wiltshire Domesday', p. 28.
[47] Sawyer, '1066–1086', p. 75; Darlington, 'Introduction to the Wiltshire Domesday', p. 67; Hooper, 'An Introduction to the Berkshire Domesday', pp. 15–17. See further on *antecessores*, Fleming, *Kings and Lords in Conquest England*, pp. 109–20, who argues that most Anglo-Saxon secular lordships were dispersed after the Conquest.

Sherborne lease from 1014 (S 1422), and sign grants in the south-west under Cnut. Equally, Odda from the same area, who continued to be important under the Confessor, first appears late in Æthelred's reign,[48] while Eadmær, whose only royal charter signature under Æthelred is in S 890, in favour of the bishop of Crediton in 997, may well be the witness of Cnut's Devon grants S 963 and 971. Other cases are more difficult. The Eadwold of Cnut's Dorset charters S 969 and 975 may or may not be the episcopal kinsman Eadwold named in Bishop Ælfwold of Crediton's will,[49] while the Ælfmær, Brihtmær, Leofnoth and Wulfweard who sign south-western charters under Æthelred may also appear in S 953, Cnut's gift to the bishop of Cornwall from 1018; a complicating factor here is that this is possibly a forgery.[50] Finally, the south-western witness Æthelmær is perhaps identifiable with one of those named in Æthelred's charters. Evidence for other areas is less plentiful, and conclusions correspondingly fewer, but Æthelweard, who signs S 956 of 1019, could be one of the at least two Æthelweards known under Æthelred, and it is tempting to link the Ceolric whose only Æthelredian signature is S 934, a Berkshire grant to Abingdon Abbey from 1015, with the Ceolric who witnesses S 964, by which Cnut gave a Berkshire estate to Abingdon in 1032. Likewise, Ælfwig, also in S 964, may be the man of that name listed in one of Æthelred's Berkshire gifts, S 915.[51] The Kentish brothers Siward and Sired seem to have maintained their position too.[52] Many Englishmen make their first appearance in royal charters under Cnut, but this need not mean that he had raised them from nothing. The prominence of the Dorset Ælfgeat, for example, is known from a Sherborne lease, not from royal charters, and others may well have already been important, or have come from established families. In most cases we know too little about them to say either way.[53]

Although much is uncertain, and while it is likely that Cnut's men had possessions in nearly every shire in England, it is clear that there was no replacement of native landowners by foreigners on the scale that followed

[48] For the witnesses of Æthelred's charters, see the tables in Keynes, *Diplomas*.
[49] S 1492, of 1008x12. An Eadwold signs two of Æthelred's charters, S 896 and 911.
[50] Leofnoth also signs S 954, another possible forgery.
[51] He witnesses S 916 too, like S 915 from 1007, and other of Æthelred's charters.
[52] They occur in S 1455, an agreement of 989x1005. Sired may well be the witness of Cnut's Canterbury grants, S 950 and 959, and the Sired ealda of S 1461. Siward's survival is less certain, but he could be the Siword *æt Cilleham* of the forged S 981. S 1461 also mentions an Ælfgar *Syredes sunu*.
[53] This is why charter evidence cannot in my opinion be used to argue that Cnut's reign saw a revolution among English landowners. One would need a far larger number of documents than has actually survived, both in time and (because witnesses are often clearly local) space, to justify such a conclusion. Mack, 'Changing Thegns', offers a different view.

1066. William the Conqueror ruled the country by giving lands to major Norman supporters who proved more trustworthy than the English. Cnut was in a different position. Not all his Scandinavian warlords were reliable, but this was compensated by the willingness of many Englishmen, exasperated by the traumas of Æthelred's time, either to throw in their lot with Danish rule or at least to tolerate it in return for peace; the rest there were other ways of controlling.

CNUT'S HENCHMEN

Cnut's date of birth is unknown, but Ottar the Black's *Knútsdrápa* says that he started his military career unusually young, and mentions an attack on Norwich perhaps identifiable with that by Swegen in 1004. If Cnut was involved in this he could have been born in the early 990s or slightly before. If not, and Ottar's verse refers to an otherwise unknown assault, his earliest campaigns may have been in 1013 and 1014, which might suggest a birth date of around 1000.[54] Whatever his age, he almost certainly owed much of his success in the fighting of 1015–16 to the experienced warlords Earl Eric of Lade and Earl Thorkell.

Eric had long been allied with Swegen, but Thorkell's links with him are less clear. He was one of the leaders of the raiders of 1009–12, with whom Swegen was possibly associated, and John calls him a *Danicus comes* (Danish count) and says that he was joined by forces under Hemming and Eglaf; Hemming may have been his brother.[55] He is the only Scandinavian named in Thietmar of Merseburg's account of Archbishop Ælfheah's martyrdom in 1012, when he entered Æthelred's service with forty-five ships. The Encomiast claims that he was Swegen's military commander, who got permission to take part of the Danish army to England to avenge his brother, became a friend of the English, and remained among them, and has Cnut tell Harald on his return to Denmark in 1014 that Thorkell has deserted them as he did their father. He further alleges that Thorkell then sailed to Denmark with nine ships, swore fidelity, urged Cnut to invade England, and assured him of the goodwill of the thirty ships which remained there. Later, he fought the English at Sherston, not suffering the king to be involved,

---

[54] The thirteenth-century *Knytlinga Saga* 18, ed. Petersons and Olson, p.51, says that he was thirty-seven when he died, but this may be unreliable. It errs in claiming that he had ruled Denmark for twenty-seven years and England for twenty-four.

[55] JW, ii. 462–63; *Encomium*, p.73.

keen as he was, because he was young.[56] The story of Thorkell's visit to Denmark is of doubtful reliability, as he was very likely the leader of the forty ships which according to the *Anglo-Saxon Chronicle* joined Eadric of Mercia in defecting to Cnut late in 1015, but the sources agree that he had been in English service, and like Eadric he was clearly a powerful leader with his own following[57] who knew when to change sides. It is thus hardly surprising that, like Eadric, he was first rewarded and then removed, although by banishment (in 1021) rather than execution, perhaps after a period of good relations. His power in the interim is indicated by his senior position in the charter witness lists, and the way that he is the only earl addressed by name in the Letter of 1019–20.[58] His expulsion must have been an achievement as well as a relief.

If the fortunes of other important Scandinavians under Cnut are less certain, unhappy stories abound. Henry of Huntingdon and William of Malmesbury say that Eric of Lade, earl of Northumbria, was exiled, and John that his son Hakon was too.[59] One is more inclined to take seriously the twelfth-century Roskilde tradition that Cnut had his brother-in-law Ulf murdered in a church there, although as we have seen the belief that Ulf and Earl Eglaf fought against him at the battle of Holy River is unsafe.[60] However, while Thorkell is the only one of Cnut's Scandinavian earls with whom relations definitely broke down, an ambivalent attitude to these powerful figures would have contributed to his undoubted willingness to patronise and use Englishmen. By 1018 he had given an ealdordom in the south-west to Æthelweard. He is not certainly identifiable with the Æthelweard *minister* who witnesses late in Æthelred's reign, as one also occurs in S 956 of 1019, or with the son-in-law of Æthelmær ealdorman in the south-west under Æthelred, and father of the Æthelweard executed in 1017 and perhaps of Archbishop Æthelnoth of Canterbury.[61]

---

[56] *Encomium* i. 2, ii. 1–3, 6, pp. 10, 14–22.

[57] Note also his prominence in the poem *Liðsmannaflokkr*, Poole, 'Skaldic Verse and Anglo-Saxon History', 281–84. For later Scandinavian traditions on Thorkell, some of which name him as leader of the Jomsvikings, a force based somewhere in the Baltic whose historicity has been much disputed, see *Encomium*, pp. 73, 87–91.

[58] If the Letter of 1019–20 was sent from Denmark Cnut had seemingly left him behind as regent; but it could have been written in England.

[59] Henry, *Historia*, vi. 15, pp. 362–63; *GR*, ii. 181, ed. Mynors *et al.*, i. 320–21. Eric's last charter signatures are from 1023. Later Norwegian and Icelandic sources say that he died in England. I agree with Campbell (*Encomium*, p. 72) in rejecting John of Worcester's account of the exile of Hakon, who was put in charge of Norway by Cnut in 1028.

[60] Above, pp. 94–95.

[61] Searle, *Anglo-Saxon Bishops, Kings and Nobles*, p. 435. Æthelred's *minister* and Æthelmær's son-in-law (who signs S 911) may, of course, be the same; for Æthelnoth of Canterbury, see above, p. 137–38.

If Cnut was attempting to use an established family he failed, for Æthelweard was banished in 1020, but other dealings with senior Englishmen were more successful. Like the little-known ealdorman Godric (see below), Leofwine, ealdorman in Mercia, survived from Æthelred's reign. His son Northman was executed in 1017 and the hands of his grandson Æthelwine amputated while he was a Danish hostage.[62] Nevertheless, Leofwine continued in authority, to be eventually followed by another son, Earl Leofric, who according to the Evesham chronicle was given Northman's many estates.[63] Hemming shows us the family profiting from the process of government: Leofric's brother Edwin acquired Worcester church lands by paying the tax due on them.[64]

But the most famous of Cnut's English adherents is Earl Godwin, whose origins have been much discussed.[65] The *Chronicle* C text's reference to Wulfnoth Child, who was accused before King Æthelred in 1009, was altered in Canterbury: D and E call him Wulfnoth the South Saxon, and F adds that he was father of Earl Godwin. A Godwin son of Wulfnoth is mentioned in the will of the ætheling Æthelstan of around 1015 (S 1503), and a Sussex origin may be confirmed by the family's wealth there as revealed by Domesday Book. If Godwin was Wulfnoth's son he looks like a prime example of a nobleman alienated by Æthelred who was willing to serve the new order. He received an earldom no later than 1018, and maybe fought for Cnut in 1016: we do not know.

CNUT'S SOLDIERS:
LITHSMEN, BUTSECARLS AND HOUSECARLS

Yet for all the readiness of some Englishmen to serve him, Cnut was a conqueror who presided over what many doubtless regarded as a harsh regime (see below), and especially at first the trustworthy may not have been readily identifiable. The king therefore needed forces whose loyalty was guaranteed providing that they were regularly rewarded. When the fleet sailed to Denmark in 1018 forty ships remained in England. A payment to

---

[62] Hemming, i. 259; on this family see *FNC*, i. 717–20. I concur with Freeman in dismissing John of Worcester's statement that Northman was an ealdorman in 1017 (he witnesses S 1384 of that year as *minister*) and that Leofric succeeded him. On Leofric and his relatives, see further Keynes, 'Cnut's Earls', p.77.

[63] *Chron. Eve.* p.84

[64] Hemming, i. 278

[65] For example, *FNC*, i. 701–11; Raraty, 'Earl Godwine of Wessex', 4–6; Keynes, 'Cnut's Earls', pp.70–71. On Godwin, see further below, p.172.

Harthacnut's vessels in 1041 was at the rate of eight marks to the *hamele*, and as both the number of ships involved (sixty-two or sixty) and the exact sum paid (£21,099) are known, the crews must have averaged fifty to eighty men a ship if the *hamele* was equivalent to one man, as seems very likely; should it have involved more these figures, and those which follow, would need to be multiplied.[66] Applying these figures to the forty ships of 1018 suggests a force of between 2,000 and 3,200 men, which may have formed the basis for a professional corps used to coerce the English at need. The Danish historians Swegen Aggeson and Saxo Grammaticus told in around 1200 how Cnut created a regularly paid military fraternity of elite troops governed by strict rules, of which he was himself a member. Swegen says that they numbered 3,000, Saxo 6,000 men in sixty ships, paid monthly and housed in barracks during the winter. Both give the regulations, using the *Lex Castrensis* which Swegen claimed to have translated into Latin from a vernacular record written by Absalon, archbishop of Lund, after consultation with Cnut VI (1182–1202), and which allegedly went back to Cnut.[67] However, recent opinion has been sceptical about its value,[68] and we are driven back to the less copious eleventh-century evidence.

In 1012 Æthelred took forty-five Scandinavian ships into his service and instituted a new tax, the *heregeld* (army-payment), to remunerate them. It existed until abolished by Edward the Confessor in 1051, and the *Anglo-Saxon Chronicle* mentions lithsmen paid off the same year.[69] Lithsmen in London also feature in the succession dispute of 1036, when they supported Harold Harefoot and were represented at the Oxford meeting – both signs of their importance. The *Chronicle* E text says that under Harold sixteen ships were paid at eight marks to the *hamele*, as in Cnut's day; perhaps they were crewed by the lithsmen in London. The meaning of the word is uncertain. A derivation from the Anglo-Saxon *lið* (ship), giving 'shipman', would fit the crews of the Confessor's vessels well enough, but a Scandinavian word for ship, *lið*, was also often used to denote a military

---

[66] Whether the mark was worth 10s 8d, 13s 4d, or 16s is unclear. The first gives roughly eighty men a ship, the second about sixty-five, the third about fifty; Lawson, 'The collection of Danegeld and Heregeld', 721–22, 737–38; Lawson, '"Those stories look true"', 386; on the *hamele*, see Rodger, 'Cnut's Geld and the Size of Danish Ships', 397–98, and below, Appendix V.

[67] Swegen, *Lex Castrensis*, ii. ed. Gertz, i. 68–69; Saxo, *Historia*, x, 17–18, ed. Christiansen, pp.36–44.

[68] For revisions of Larson, *The King's Household in England*, pp.152–71, see Hooper, 'The Housecarls in England', 166–69; Hooper, 'Military developments', pp.90–97; Abels, *Lordship and Military Obligation*, pp.161–70; also Eric Christiansen's comments, Saxo, i. 154–55 (including the suggestion that Swegen's attribution of the *Lex Castrensis* to Cnut may have been a product of his own historical imagination) and *The Works of Sven Aggesen*, pp.7–11.

[69] *ASC*, i. 169, 171–72.

force, and appears in this sense on rune stones and in skaldic poems, for example Sighvat's *Knútsdrápa* and the anonymous *Liðsmannaflokkr* (Song of the Lithsmen).[70] Moreover, *lið* is used thus in Anglo-Saxon when the *Chronicle* describes Edward's fleet in 1052 and Harold's army in 1066.[71] The lithsmen of London may therefore have served by land as well as sea, especially as Scandinavian troops seldom confined themselves to one or the other. In so far as they are to be identified with the ships' crews, they look like professional soldiers whose main and possibly only form of remuneration was their presumably annual and distinctly generous eight marks each.

Butsecarls (boatmen) definitely served at sea, and could have been mercenaries of a similar type to lithsmen, stationed on the south coast. Those of Hastings and from the vicinity of Sandwich joined Earl Godwin during his illicit return from exile in 1052, and Tostig took butsecarls from Sandwich in 1066, while John mentions butsecarls in London who wished to elect the ætheling Edgar king late in 1066.[72] However, Dover, Sandwich and Romney are known to have owed naval service to the king before the Conquest, and Dr Hooper has contended that butsecarls were simply the relevant inhabitants of these towns.[73] This may be so, although it would then be very surprising that Malmesbury in Wiltshire was expected to pay twenty shillings to feed them when the king went on a military expedition, or to send a man itself. Indeed, this makes them look very like mercenaries to be employed in preference to the national levy if the king wished.[74] Royal mercenaries or not, there is no evidence of their existence earlier than 1052, even though the deployment of these men, with a name[75] so like that of the Scandinavian housecarls (see below), may well date from the period of Danish rule.

Housecarls are the third category of troops who appear in England at this time. It would be unwise to insist on their absolute differentiation from lithsmen, for words are seldom used with the precision that historians find convenient, but they do appear in a wider range of contexts. One was essentially military: almost all Harthacnut's housecarls accompanied the forces which ravaged Worcestershire in 1041, and those of Edward the

---

[70] Lund, 'The armies of Swein Forkbeard and Cnut', 110–12; Lund, 'The Danish Perspective', pp.119–30. Note Poole's comment on *Liðsmannaflokkr* that the text 'suggests an *esprit de corps*, combined with a capacity to criticize and evaluate', *Viking Poems*, p.113.
[71] *ASC*, i. (E) 178, (C) 197. *Lidman* is also used for the viking raiders in *The Battle of Maldon*, lines 99, 164, ed. Scragg, pp.60, 62.
[72] *ASC*, i. 178; JW, ii. 606–07.
[73] Hooper, 'Some Observations on the Navy', pp.206–07.
[74] DB, i. 64c. See Plummer's comments, *ASC*, ii. 239–40.
[75] Butsecarl may be derived from the Scandinavian *buza*, a type of merchant ship or warship, but in the twelfth century the word also appears in medieval Latin.

Confessor and Earl Siward of Northumbria took part in the Scottish expedition of 1054.[76] But Harthacnut used his housecarls to collect tax too: it was the murder of the pair sent to Worcester which triggered the harrying of its shire. Furthermore, unlike lithsmen as far as we know, housecarls were sometimes given land. The English rubric to Bovi's Dorset grant (S 969) says that he was Cnut's housecarl; Orc also received an estate there and is addressed in a writ of the Confessor as 'my housecarl',[77] and such men are listed as landholders in Domesday Book, where the formula 'housecarl of King Edward' or of one of his earls appears twenty-five times, while men are described simply as housecarls on forty-one occasions.[78] The Domesday use of the word presents difficulties. A man denoted a housecarl in one place may be called a thegn elsewhere, and as the majority are recorded in the shires visited by one particular set of Domesday commissioners[79] this suggests that they used the term when others did not, and that the number of housecarls owning estates may thus have been much greater than Domesday Book tends to imply. But if some lived on the land, not all did so all the time. The Domesday entry for Wallingford says that King Edward possessed there fifteen acres where housecarls stayed (*manebant*), and that by 1086 this area belonged to Miles Crispin, the Domesday jurors knew not how. This is most likely to refer to a housecarl garrison,[80] and it is worth noting that Miles Crispin had elsewhere succeeded to estates of Wigot of Wallingford. The town was an important one, and it is tempting to believe that Wigot's prosperity owed something to a connection with this garrison, which perhaps not only controlled and protected Wallingford itself, but also enforced the authority of royal officials in the surrounding area. Of course, this does not necessarily prove anything about Cnut's reign, but Wigot had a Scandinavian name, so did twenty-eight of the thirty-two known eleventh-century housecarls of kings or earls,[81] and the arrangements which they represent seem very likely to date from the period of Danish rule.

If we set aside Swegen Aggeson and Saxo, evidence on the housecarls in Cnut's reign itself is scanty.[82] Only once are they glimpsed in action, in

---

[76] JW, ii. 532–33; *ASC*, i. 185.

[77] S 1063; *Writs*, pp.120–21.

[78] I owe these statistics to the kindness of Nick Hooper.

[79] A point made by Hooper, 'The Housecarls in England', 173.

[80] DB, i. 56b. Stenton, *Anglo-Saxon England*, p.582, and Campbell, *The Anglo-Saxon State*, p.205, seem to me more convincing here than Hooper, 'The Housecarls', 171, and Hooper, 'Military developments', pp.92–93.

[81] Again, I am grateful to Nick Hooper for providing these figures.

[82] It should perhaps be pointed out that the word housecarl appears in the translation of verse 5 of Thorarin's *Tøgdrápa*, in *EHD*, p.340, but is not in the original.

Osbern's description, written in Christ Church Canterbury in the late eleventh century, of the translation of the relics of St Ælfheah from London to Canterbury in 1023. Another account of this event, probably also composed in Christ Church and possibly at a considerably earlier date,[83] is in the D version of the *Anglo-Saxon Chronicle*. This has circumstantial details which encourage belief in its reliability,[84] but also a tone of considerable religious fervour, and in presenting the affair as a dignified and popular occasion may reveal rather less than the truth, at least as far as the attitude of the people of London is concerned. Osbern claims to have heard the story as a boy from a monk who was involved, and gives details of considerable interest. He says that Cnut organised the event as a military operation because of fear of hostile intervention by the citizens of London, sending some of the soldiers of his household (*familia*), in the Danish tongue called housecarls, to distant parts of the city to create disturbances intended to distract attention from the business in hand, while others occupied London bridge and the banks of the Thames lest the people hinder those leaving with the body. This was accompanied by a strong force of housecarls, and Archbishop Æthelnoth later followed on with yet more troops. Those with the saint, seeing behind them the cloud of dust raised by the archbishop's men, thought them the citizens emerging from the city, and prepared for battle at Plumstead, only to meet friends where they had expected enemies.[85]

Osbern is clearly making the most of a good story, which features the fairly common hagiographical theme of the theft of relics, in which remains are acquired surreptitiously and at the risk of violence.[86] It was also common for hagiographers to cite witnesses as evidence, and for both reasons Osbern's account is much less straightforward than it seems. Even so, his comments on housecarls can be fitted into a credible historical context. London had fought long and hard against the raiders in Æthelred's time; by 1016, when its inhabitants were partly responsible for the election of Edmund Ironside as king, their dislike of the enemy was no doubt considerable. Nor need it have been much diminished by the £10,500 taken from them in taxation two years later, and married with it may have been a

---

[83] Above, p.56.
[84] It names two of the bishops who assisted Æthelnoth of Canterbury as Ælfsige and Brihtwine. The former was from Winchester, the latter possibly represented Wells (above, p.139 n.143). This makes sense, as Ælfheah had been bishop of Winchester himself, and previously abbot of Bath, within the diocese of Wells.
[85] Osbern, *Translatio Sancti Ælfegi*, ed. Rumble, pp.300–11.
[86] For other examples from this period, see Rollason, *Saints and Relics*, pp.180–81. Osbern's work has a certain amount in common with Goscelin's account of the translation of St Mildred's relics in 1030 (above, p.99), also written in Canterbury in the late eleventh century.

definite military potential, for the civic militia system based on the wards (subdivisions of the city) known from later sources could already have existed. At any rate, it had never been taken by assault, despite the attempts made on it in 994, 1009, 1013 and 1016. Moreover, the cult of the archbishop so brutally murdered by Scandinavians in 1012 seems to have been popular, and was arguably partly an expression of hostility to Danish rule.[87] Hence the removal of his relics might well have been expected to provoke resistance, although none apparently occurred. Osbern may therefore be correct in saying that housecarls were present to prevent trouble, and the account in the *Chronicle* D text, although different in tone, does not preclude this. If so, the event is a striking instance of how the existence of housecarls gave Cnut the option of coercing the English when necessary; that the one known instance of such action involved the citizens of London is particularly interesting in view of their difficult relations with twelfth- and thirteenth-century kings over royal taxation, which was almost certainly an issue in Cnut's time too. It is worth remembering that William the Conqueror built the Tower to control them: the belief that Cnut maintained a garrison in the city apart from the lithsmen and their ships is unprovable but plausible.[88] The possibility that other important towns, in addition to Wallingford, had garrisons too cannot be excluded.

The housecarls were remunerated with the proceeds of taxation, as well as land. The Domesday entry for Dorchester (Dorset) says that it was assessed at ten hides and so (*scilicet*) paid one mark of silver for the needs of the housecarls (*ad opus huscarlium*). Wareham did the same, while Bridport gave half a mark as it answered for five hides, and Shaftesbury's twenty hides produced two marks.[89] These sums are too low to have supported town garrisons, but it is conceivable that Domesday is preserving here a memory of a national housecarl levy of one silver mark on every ten hides, perhaps in the Confessor's reign. If so, a country assessed at about 70,000–80,000 hides should have produced some 7,000–8,000 marks, which would have funded about 875–1,000 housecarls at the 1040 naval rate of eight marks each. If Cnut paid the forty ships of 1018 at eight marks a man, they would have cost nearly £14,000 a year, while the sixteen vessels of the professional navy late in the reign must have received over £5,000 a year.[90] Such figures may be small compared with those paid in Æthelred's time, but they are

[87] Above, p. 130–32.
[88] The case is elaborated by Nightingale, 'The Origin of the Court of Husting', 566–68.
[89] DB, i. 75a.
[90] Lawson, 'The collection of Danegeld and Heregeld', 721–22.

minimum totals to which the wages of unknown numbers of housecarls, who need not have been drawn exclusively from the 1018 crews, may have had to be added, and they were presumably levied as routine taxation, not as irregular payments at intervals of several years intended to rid the country of enemies. £14,000 a year was a large amount compared with later taxation (see below), and the *Chronicle* D text's statement that the *heregeld* oppressed men in various ways may be near the mark.

Such imposts are likely to have been unpopular, as can be seen from the riot at Worcester during the raising of £21,099 to pay Harthacnut's fleet. It reveals much about the political opportunities available to Cnut and his son that housecarls collected this sum. They had taken over a thoroughly administered country whose considerable wealth could be tapped through taxation. This would in turn pay for troops who safeguarded the king's position, increased his administrative power even further, and acted as a counter-balance to the influence of the great nobles. It need be no accident that only nine ships accompanied Cnut to Denmark in the winter of 1019–20; the presence of the remaining thirty-one was presumably thought necessary in England.[91] That earlier and later rulers probably had within their households military men equivalent to housecarls and lithsmen[92] does not diminish their importance. They were one reason among several why Cnut did not need to replace the English landholding class. He simply made sure that the administrative network was under control, by patronising major Englishmen, by giving housecarls estates in the localities, and perhaps by establishing garrisons in towns like London and Wallingford. His servants' self-interest would then do much of the rest.

CNUT'S EARLS

At the head of the administration stood the king and his earls, although knowledge of the latter is patchy. Cnut is sometimes credited with creating three great earldoms in 1017, but it is not clear that he did anything of the sort. The *Chronicle* says that he divided the country into four, keeping Wessex for himself and giving East Anglia to Thorkell, Mercia to Eadric and Northumbria to Eric. Even so, it does not call these areas earldoms, nor (here) their recipients earls, and the act is more likely to have been intended to provide an interim military government than a basis for future

[91] A point made by Larson, 'The Political Policies of Cnut', 733.
[92] Hooper, 'The Housecarls', 170–71; Campbell, *The Anglo-Saxon State*, pp.204–05.

administration. Eadric was in any case dead by the end of the year, and it is doubtful how far Eric's authority as earl of Northumbria, which the *Chronicle* suggests he received in 1016, extended into Bernicia (now Northumberland), where the family of earls based on Bamburgh seems to have continued to rule (see below). Still, the arrangements of 1017 did endure in that Earl Thorkell retained a position in eastern England, although little is known of his activities there. He is entered in the *Liber Vitae* of Thorney Abbey, witnessed a gift to Ramsey, and monks are said to have been introduced into Bury St Edmunds with his authority.[93]

More can be said about the earls appointed by Cnut in the west mid-lands. Hemming states that Herefordshire was given to Hrani, and an account of a lawsuit records his presence with Bishop Æthelstan of Hereford, Ealdorman Leofwine's son Edwin, the shire-reeve Bryning and others at a shire meeting at Aylton which was visited on the king's business by Tofi the Proud.[94] Earl Eglaf seems to have been connected with Gloucestershire. He witnesses a lease (S 1424) by a Gloucester abbot of around 1022, and the *Annales Cambriæ* record his devastation of Dyfed in south Wales in the same year. Later Welsh chronicles say that he fled to *Germania* (possibly Scandinavia) after Cnut's death.[95] Hakon was probably earl of Worcestershire: Hemming complains that he and his soldiers took church estates there,[96] and he is addressed with Bishop Leofsige of Worcester, the shire-reeve Leofric, and all the thegns of the shire in a royal writ (S 991) of uncertain authenticity. He also appears at shire meetings in two other documents, selling land with Leofric in an Evesham lease (S 1423), and judging a lawsuit with Ealdorman Leofwine and Leofric (S 1460). Leofwine's presence in S 1460 may or may not indicate that Hakon was under his authority.

Indeed, although such evidence shows Scandinavian and English earls administering the country in familiar ways, little is really known about them or their powers. Many are thoroughly obscure. Halfdan, for example, is possibly the *Haldanus* whose brief and shadowy intervention in the Danish history of Cnut's early years was discussed in Chapter 3.[97] Haram, Harold, Regnold, Thrim, and Wrytsleof appear once each, the first in a

[93] *Chron. Rams.*, p.147; above, p.32 n.108.
[94] Hemming, i. 274; S 1462; see also JW, ii. 532–33, and Keynes, 'Cnut's earls', pp.60–61.
[95] *Brut y Tywysogyon, Red Book of Hergest version*, ed. Jones, pp. 22–23; *Peniarth Ms. 20 version*, trans. Jones, p.13. See *Encomium*, pp.86–87.
[96] Hemming, i. 251.
[97] Above, p.89.

doubtful and the second in a forged charter,[98] while the third may not have been an earl at all;[99] if they ever held authority in England no record of it has survived, and at least some of these men, like Bishop Gerbrand of Roskilde who occurs in S 958, were probably visitors from abroad; Professor Keynes has suggested that Wrytsleof was 'perhaps a visiting Slavic prince' [100] An earl Sihtric signs three south-western grants, two of them from 1031. Maybe he had power thereabouts, although Professor Keynes has shown that he also possessed estates in Hertfordshire. [101] Eglaf's brother Ulf is mentioned three times in charters of doubtful reliability, and although Adam of Bremen calls him Duke Ulf of England, in the Thorney *Liber Vitae* he is simply Ulf, brother of Earl Eglaf, and to John he was Ulf the Danish count.[102] It is thus not certain that he held an earldom here; if he did, its location is unknown. Some undoubtedly English earls are little more familiar. Æthelred features only twice, in grants of 1019: S 954, possibly a forgery, has him interceding with Cnut about the oppression of the church of St Mary in Exeter, and his existence in the area may be confirmed by his presence in the witness list of the Dorset charter S 955.[103] Another south-western figure was Æthelweard, banished in 1020. He signs as ealdorman in 1018, when he gave a copy of Bede's work on the Apocalypse to the *monasterium* of St Mary (probably in either Crediton or Exeter) and was involved with Cnut in the foundation of Buckfast Abbey.[104] Archbishop Æthelnoth bought land in Kent from Earl Sired (S 1389), who is presumably the Syrhod of S 954 and the Siræd of S 960; his earldom doubtless lay somewhere in southern England. Earl Ælfwine witnesses from 1033, and is identifiable with the Ælfwine who had earlier occupied a senior position among the *ministri*,[105] but the area of his jurisdiction is obscure, like that of

[98] S 954, 981. Keynes, 'Cnut's earls', p.66, suggests that the Harold of S 981 is the Earl Harold who witnesses S 1396 of 1042 and 'is presumably the person of that name who was apparently a son of Earl Thorkell' and who left England after Harthacnut's death in 1042.

[99] He is listed as such only in some copies of the dubious S 959, whereas others call him *minister*, along with S 958 and S 980; see Robertson, *Charters*, p.410; Keynes, 'Cnut's earls', p.64.

[100] On Gerbrand, see above, pp.92–93; Keynes, 'Cnut's earls', p.65.

[101] S 962, 963, 971. I withdraw the suggestion, made in the earlier version of this book, that these references may be to Sihtric Silkbeard, the Scandinavian king of Dublin; Keynes, 'Cnut's earls', p.65.

[102] S 980, 981, 984; Adam, *Gesta*, ii. 54, p.114; Gerchow, *Die Gedenküberlieferung*, p.327; JW, ii. 548–49. Alistair Campbell noted (*Encomium*, p.86) that Ulf's three charter signatures may imply that his name occurred more frequently than extant documents reveal.

[103] Larson, 'The Political Policies of Cnut', p.727, suggested that the name might in both cases be a scribal error for Ealdorman Æthelweard; similarly, Keynes, 'Cnut's earls', p.75.

[104] *Exeter Book*, ed. Chambers *et al.*, pp.85–87; on Buckfast, above, p.67, n.26; see further on Æthelweard, Keynes, 'Cnut's earls', pp.67–70.

[105] Ælfwine is listed in S 976 of 1035 as first of the *ministri*, but this text is of doubtful authenticity, and insufficient warrant for accepting Robertson's contention (*Charters*, p.409) that his signatures as earl are errors.

Godric, who occurs late in Æthelred's reign and again in the witness lists of the doubtful S 980 and 984.

Leofwine and Leofric of Mercia are better-known figures, although whether the former replaced Eadric as ruler of all Mercia in 1017 is not clear. He disappears from the charters in the early 1020s, and while Leofric signs as earl in S 979 of around 1023, this witness list has some suspicious features,[106] and he does not occur again until S 964 of 1032. It may thus be dangerous to assume that he succeeded his father immediately. He led the supporters of Harold Harefoot in 1036, and was obviously then a significant figure, but there were probably still at least two other earls, Eglaf and Hrani, within Mercia when Cnut died.

In Æthelred's later years the whole of Northumbria had been ruled by Earl Uhtred of Bamburgh, who evidently took over authority in Yorkshire after the murder of Ealdorman Ælfhelm in 1006. When Uhtred was himself put to death on Cnut's orders in 1016 the *Chronicle* says that Eric (of Lade) was appointed earl of Northumbria just as Uhtred had been. This ought to mean that he had authority in Northumberland too, but if so may be incorrect, as two works apparently composed in Durham, the late eleventh-century *De Obsessione Dunelmi* and the slightly younger *De Primo Saxonum Adventu*, allege that Uhtred was succeeded in Northumberland by his brother Eadwulf Cudel, who was in turn followed by Uhtred's son Ealdred.[107] It would therefore seem that Eric of Lade received the southern Northumbrian earldom based on York. Apart from helping to execute Eadric Streona, he is a shadowy figure after 1016, although he witnesses charters fairly regularly until his final appearance, in S 960 of 1023.

What happened to the York earldom in the next ten years is obscure, but in 1033, in Cnut's grant (S 968) to the archbishop of York, we get the first signature of Earl Siward. Nothing worthwhile is known of his origins: according to twelfth-century legend his Danish father had furry ears because he was descended from a white bear and a noblewoman.[108] He is not the Siward minister who witnesses Cnut's four Dorset grants, as the last of them, S 975, is from 1035, and his name could actually be the English Sigeweard; but that he was a Dane is implied by the *Life* of Edward the Confessor, which states that he was called in the Danish tongue *Digara*, that is, 'The Strong'.[109]

[106] See Robertson, *Charters*, pp.412–13.
[107] Symeon, *Opera Omnia*, ed. Arnold, i. 218–19, ii. 383. Kapelle, *The Norman Conquest of the North*, pp.20–26, tries to take things further, implausibly in my opinion.
[108] See Mr Christiansen's note, Saxo, i. 190. Steenstrup, *Normannerne*, iii. 437–40, attempted to link him with the family of the earls Ulf and Eglaf.
[109] *Life of King Edward*, ed. Barlow, pp.34–35.

Godwin was undoubtedly the most important of Cnut's English earls. He was married to Ulf's sister Gytha, received his office no later than 1018, and after 1023 always witnesses charters as the first of the earls; the *Life* of the Confessor says that after he had served Cnut well abroad he was appointed earl and office-bearer (*dux et baiulus*) of almost the whole kingdom.[110] Although he may have come from an established family (see above), he was obviously much indebted to Cnut: precisely how much we would dearly like to know, and never will. Domesday Book shows that in 1066 the possessions of the Godwin family exceeded in value those of the king, but this probably owed a great deal to events after the Confessor's accession in 1042.[111] He must have been powerful in Cnut's reign, for he would otherwise have been less use, but there is reason to doubt whether he was the colossus of later years. In 1036, for example, although initially a supporter of Harthacnut in the succession dispute which followed Cnut's death, he switched sides to Harold Harefoot when Harthacnut remained in Denmark, and was then involved in the capture of the ætheling Alfred, who had just arrived from Normandy and later died after being blinded. When his half-brother Harthacnut eventually became king, Godwin gave him 'for his friendship' a magnificently equipped ship crewed by eighty picked men, and swore that he had acted on Harold Harefoot's orders in dealing with Alfred.[112] These look like the actions of a man concerned to conciliate royal power, and given Cnut's readiness to destroy over-mighty subjects such as Eadric Streona and Thorkell it seems improbable that he saw Godwin in this light. How much territory his earldom comprised is not known: doubtless a great deal, although the likely existence of other earls in southern England has been noted above and should not be forgotten. No surviving document records Godwin's activities in the shire courts, or anywhere else in England, during Cnut's reign, but we do hear of expeditions abroad: he allegedly accompanied the king to Denmark in 1019, and William of Malmesbury connects him with the battle of Holy River of around 1025.[113]

[110] *Life of King Edward*, ed. Barlow, pp.10–11.
[111] Fleming, *Kings and Lords in Conquest England*, pp.55–103. Fleming, 'Domesday Estates of the King and the Godwines', (998–99, elaborated *Kings and Lords*, pp.92–96) argues that Cnut gave Godwin estates in Hampshire and Sussex to improve south coast defences, and also comments (1007) that the 'meteoric rise of the family did not occur in Cnut's reign but in Edward's'. The statement that Cnut 'created the earldom of Wessex in 1017, and within a year he appointed Godwine as the district's earl' (*Kings and Lords*, p.92) goes some way beyond the evidence.
[112] JW, ii. 530–33.
[113] Henry, *Historia*, vi. 15, pp. 362–65; *Life of King Edward*, ed. Barlow, pp.8–11; *GR*, ii. 181, ed. Mynors *et al.*, i. 322–25. There is no reason to suppose him the Godwin of S 1461, a Kentish marriage agreement, but he may be the one referred to in S 1220 who owned swine-pasture in Kent; see Robertson, *Charters*, pp.394, 397. The name was common: five Godwins are mentioned in S 1461.

ROYAL TAXATION

The administration over which these men presided is best known for its taxation. In 1018 the *Anglo-Saxon Chronicle* says that the English paid £82,500 to Cnut and his forces. This was basically a tribute similar to those levied under Æthelred: agreed in 1016, it was intended to remunerate the army which had fought hard for Cnut, although how much was given to the men and how much retained by him and other leaders is unknown. If we add up the payments recorded by the *Chronicle* between 991 and 1018 the total is £240,500[114] Of them all, the 1018 figure is much the biggest, and it can hardly be over-emphasised that it and some of Æthelred's tributes are very large indeed. They far exceed the most sizeable recorded sum paid to Scandinavian raiders in ninth-century Francia (£12,000) and other known English taxation of the eleventh and twelfth centuries. William the Conqueror's levy of six shillings on the hide in 1084, for example, is described by the *Chronicle* as heavy; yet if the 1018 payment was raised purely as a land tax the rate for a country assessed at roughly 70,000–80,000 hides would have been about £1 on the hide – more than three times as much. Small wonder that a century later Henry of Huntingdon thought it astonishing.[115]

Even so, is it credible? Some of the *Chronicle* figures escalate too neatly for comfort: £24,000 was given in 1002, £36,000 in 1007, £48,000 in 1012, and £72,000 (plus £10,500 from London) in 1018. This is clearly suspicious, and there is a danger that some of these totals represent guesses by an annalist who wanted to show how the sums progressively increased in size. But that this does not render their order of magnitude implausible is clear from the £21,099 paid to Harthacnut's sixty (or sixty-two) ships in 1041. Not only does the *Chronicle* E text give a very precise total here, but by specifying the rate of pay of eight marks to the *hamele* (confirmed by C) it allows the calculation of crew sizes which are entirely convincing.[116] In other words, all the 1041 statistics work. These vessels had been intended to assist an invasion which the death of Harold Harefoot rendered unnecessary, and it would have been unwise to rouse the ire of their crews with

---

[114] And the list may not be complete, Lawson, 'The collection of Danegeld and Heregeld', 737. For the debate on the reliability of these figures, see (sceptically) Gillingham, '"The Most Precious Jewel in the English Crown"' and 'Chronicles and Coins as Evidence for Levels of Tribute and Taxation', opposed by Lawson, '"Those stories look true"' and 'Danegeld and Heregeld Once More'.

[115] Henry, *Historia*, vi. 15, pp.362–63.

[116] Lawson, 'The collection of Danegeld and Heregeld', 737–38; above, p.163, n.66.

insufficient reward; on the other hand, they had not spent years plundering the country, as had some of the forces bought off by Æthelred. It is therefore likely that the sums handed over late in his reign, when there seems to have been no other means of defence, greatly exceeded the £21,099 paid in the relative calm of 1041.

One can arrive at the same conclusion from a different direction. The treaty which Æthelred made probably with the raiders of 994 records a payment of £22,000 in gold and silver,[117] which is actually higher than the *Chronicle* figure for that year of £16,000. Although this force had attacked London unsuccessfully, its position hardly rivalled that of its successors in 1007 and 1012, whose bargaining position must have been strengthened by the obvious failure of the English resistance. Equally, the *Chronicle* says that £21,000 was given to Scandinavian ships in Æthelred's service in 1014, a total which is the more credible because it does not fit the regular duodecimal pattern discussed above, and which again suggests that other payments were fairly definitely considerably bigger. Indeed, the 1018 sum was handed over in circumstances unparalleled in English history: the country had been defeated by men whose prime purposes included the taking of wealth, led by a king no doubt eager both to pay them off and to fill his own treasure chests. The fact that it took over a year to collect, and that special minting arrangements were apparently made to accommodate it,[118] both indicate that it was an exceptional levy.

It is also unlikely to be coincidence that the coin types in circulation when the 1012 and 1018 imposts were made, *Last Small Cross* and *Quatrefoil*, seemingly achieved a volume well in excess of most others of the period.[119] Current estimates of coinage volume may eventually need revision, but at the moment the idea that many of these pennies were struck specifically for the payments is very plausible; so is a level well in excess of £20,000, and perhaps as high as £80,000, for that of 1018.

Naturally, taxation on such a scale is well reflected in the sources. Domesday Book gives an instance of an estate confiscated by the shire-reeve because its owner had not met the tax on it,[120] and it is virtually

[117] *Gesetze*, i. 224.
[118] Below, pp.181–82.
[119] Metcalf, 'Continuity and Change in English Monetary History *c*.973–1086. Part 2.', 63, estimates *Last Small Cross* at 30 million and *Quatrefoil* at 47 million. Only the *Crux* type of the 990s, at 40 million apparently the largest of the period *c*.973–1016 (not *c*.973–1066 as stated Lawson, '"Those stories look true"', 402) compares. It should be noted, however, that an unknown proportion of each tribute would have been paid in objects of gold and silver.
[120] DB 141a.

certain that this was Cnut's practice too. Hemming says that in his reign those who had not paid the shire-reeve by the appointed time forfeited their land to whoever gave the money due, and the twelfth-century Peterborough chronicler Hugh Candidus says that those who did not have the necessary money lost their lands and possessions irrevocably, with many churches suffering badly in this way.[121] William of Malmesbury states that Glastonbury gave up its estates in Wiltshire in the time of the Danes, when the country was burdened by insupportable taxes; they were added to the royal fisc or elsewhere as a pledge, and were eventually redeemed by Bishop Brihtwold of Ramsbury, who would give his ring to the creditors if so much as a halfpenny was lacking.[122] Claiming 'English writings' as his source, he also describes how the abbot of Malmesbury, Brihtwold, was oppressed by a heavy tax and forced to alienate church lands, either by mortgaging them or selling for a small price.[123] Laymen were affected too: when the Scandinavian Bovi received a Dorset estate in 1033 by S 969 it was judged wise to record in Anglo-Saxon that he had defended the land with his money in payment of tax due on it, with the shire's witness.[124]

Not all were so fortunate. There is no reason to doubt Hemming's evidence that his church was deprived of property in Warwickshire worth at least seventeen hides, and that Earl Leofric's brother Edwin acquired their lands at Bickmarsh in Warwickshire and Wychbold in Worcestershire, together valued at sixteen hides, and others in Shropshire. Hemming also attributes losses in Herefordshire to Earl Hrani and his men partly to taxation.[125] Hugh Candidus says that Peterborough forfeited many estates, but names only Howden in Yorkshire and Barrow-upon-Humber in Lincolnshire. This is consistent with other evidence: the Peterborough monks had received (S 782) Barrow from their patron Bishop Æthelwold of Winchester, who paid King Edgar £40 in silver and a gold cross for it in 971, while Edgar had granted Howden to the *matrona* Quen, who probably gave it to Peterborough, as her charter (S 681) survives only in their cartularies; both were valuable: the one belonged to Earl Morcar in 1066 and was

---

[121] Hemming, i. 278, and for a Domesday example, DB, i. 216c; Hugh, *Chronicle*, ed. Mellows, p.65.

[122] WM *Glaston.*, p.140.

[123] *GP*, v. 258, ed. Hamilton, p.411. Brihtwold seems to have been abbot under Æthelred, see Knowles *et al.* (ed.) 1972, p.54. Even so, his problems with *magno illo geldo, qui tunc Danis dabatur* look as though they refer to the 1018 tax.

[124] *Charters of Sherborne*, ed. O'Donovan, pp.68, 72. I have followed Dr O'Donovan's translation of this difficult passage.

[125] Hemming, i. 274, 277-78; see Lawson, 'The collection of Danegeld and Heregeld', 729.

worth £32, the other was royal and worth £40.[126] Presumably many went to great lengths to raise the necessary money rather than face the permanent drop in revenue which a reduction in their landed holdings would entail. Thus, early in Cnut's reign the Gloucester abbot Eadric, in great necessity, leased out lands for life to one *Stamarcotus* in return for a payment of £15 which he used to redeem the monastery's other estates from a great *heregeld* (army tax) – surely that of 1018.[127] At much the same time Bishop Eadnoth of Crediton intended to redeem lands by borrowing thirty mancuses of gold from Brihtnoth, who was leased an estate in return. Why they needed redeeming is not stated, but that it was to be done with money may imply a link with tax.[128] The same could be suspected of the six marks of gold which Abbot Ælfweard of Evesham gave Cnut to redeem Broadwell, Gloucestershire.[129] Also, Luddington (Warwickshire) is one estate which Hemming says his church lost through taxation, and a lease survives in which the community at Worcester gives it for three years to Fulder in return for a payment of three pounds. Although undated, the term was very short, and the document may come from around 1018, and show one expedient which the monks adopted to get ready cash to pay their dues. The land was eventually alienated from the church, perhaps because Fulder, whose name may be Scandinavian, simply kept it. There was clearly rather more to some of the matters described by Hemming than he says.[130]

Other evidence is less precise but no less compelling. William of Malmesbury's statement that Abbot Brihtwold was only able to mortgage for a small price suggests that land values had fallen, possibly because many needed credit and little was available. The resultant impression of widespread difficulties, among laymen as well as ecclesiastics, is perhaps confirmed by his assertion that Brihtwold of Ramsbury redeemed all Glastonbury's estates in Wiltshire. Of course, this could be exaggeration, for they had nearly 260 hides there in 1066, but equally the country's richest abbey presumably faced one of the biggest tax bills, and William's evidence may indicate that they were in serious trouble. Nor was land the sole commodity expended. Late in Æthelred's reign Archbishop Wulfstan complained not only that the people had been greatly afflicted by taxation, but also that the

---

[126] DB, i. 360b, 304c; see further Lawson, 'The collection of Danegeld and Heregeld', 730.

[127] S 1424, dated about 1022; see Lawson, 'The collection of Danegeld and Heregeld', 724.

[128] S 1387; see the discussion and translation, *Crawford Collection*, pp.76–77. A gold mancus was worth thirty silver pennies.

[129] *Chron. Eve.*, p.83.

[130] S 1421, in a hand which Dr Ker thought Hemming's own. I owe this reference to Williams, 'Cockles', 13; see also Robertson, *Charters*, p. 402.

churches had been stripped inside of all that was seemly;[131] the likely reason is not far to seek. Sacrificing precious objects was an obvious way to satisfy the tax collector, and Hemming describes how the Worcester monks broke up ornaments to meet a tribute forced upon the country by Swegen, although they eventually had to sell estates too.[132] The drawing of extra bullion into the mints in this way must partially explain where the extra silver for the voluminous *Last Small Cross* and *Quatrefoil* coin types came from.

The 1018 levy, in addition to being very large, was paid when the devastation caused by the recent fighting would have been at its worst, and when reserves had already been depleted by the earlier tributes. This goes a long way to provide a context for the evidence mentioned above, but even so the sources are not full enough to allow a precise assessment of its effects. England was a wealthy country, and how much of its bullion resources were absorbed by the payments there is no way of knowing. Some churches clearly felt the pinch, but not necessarily all. The twelfth-century monastic histories of Ely and Ramsey, the *Liber Eliensis* and the Ramsey chronicle, say nothing of tax losses, and the argument from silence is of some weight here as both are fairly detailed on this period. Not only may some foundations have survived with their possessions intact, but others prospered from the general misfortune. Indeed, that this taxation system must have produced winners as well as losers makes it more comprehensible as an act of government. Some of those who gained, naturally, were Scandinavians. Beneficiaries of previous tributes must often have had ready cash, and were well-positioned to profit from a system granting land to those paying the tax due and producing landowners eager to sell or lease on easy terms. This was maybe a major means by which Cnut's followers acquired English estates, for it need be no coincidence that the recipients of the Gloucester and Worcester leases had possibly Scandinavian names, and that Hrani and his men gained possessions in Herefordshire by this method. Other winners would have included natives with the resources to do the same, like Earl Leofric's brother Edwin, who acquired lands belonging to the Worcester monks, and his deserts, Hemming thought, when killed by the Welsh.[133]

Royal officials no doubt profited too, often illicitly. In William the Conqueror's day it is known that tax collectors in some shires were allowed to keep a small portion of the proceeds,[134] but Hemming accuses Ælfric,

[131] *Sermo Lupi*, ed. Whitelock pp. 50, 54.
[132] Hemming, i. 248–49.
[133] Hemming, i. 278.
[134] Lawson, 'The collection of Danegeld and Heregeld', 731-32.

shire-reeve of Staffordshire, of taking three estates which rightly belonged
to his church in the confusion following Æthelred's death, and claims that
in Worcestershire lands were sometimes granted away to those eager for
them even when the tax due had been paid on time.[135] If so, it looks as
though it was collected twice, from the old owner and the new, in which
case some probably found its way into the shire-reeve's pocket. There are
hints of irregularity in other sources. Wulfstan included in his legal texts the
provision that all who have defended their land (i.e. discharged public burdens, almost certainly including tax) before the shire are to have undisputed
possession of it,[136] and the 1027 Letter instructs Cnut's reeves not to infringe
the right of just possession to collect money for him, which strongly implies
that they had been doing. It looks as though the seizure of estates to meet
Cnut's tax demands often went some way beyond what was strictly legal,
harsh as what could be judged legal in the eleventh century undoubtedly
was. The 1027 Letter, and the efforts of Christ Church Canterbury to protect itself from the attentions of the Kentish reeve,[137] show that extortion by
royal officials did not cease with the collection of the great payment of
1018; it would have been remarkable if it had. As stated earlier, the forty
ships retained in 1018 would, at eight marks to the *hamele*, have cost nearly
£14,000 a year, and sixteen ships later in the reign just over £5,000. Cnut
allegedly took fifty vessels with him to Norway in 1028, and if all were
crewed by mercenaries they would have absorbed over £17,000 a year; but
it is unlikely that they were, for the stories about Godwin's activities abroad
and English casualties at Holy River imply that the English ship-levy
system was used in Cnut's Scandinavian campaigns. Yet if this reduced his
need to pay for soldiers it was not necessarily cheaper for his subjects. Like
Æthelred, Cnut would have wanted ships crewed by men equipped with
helmet and byrnie, and we saw in Chapter 1 that such items were expensive. Of course, while the fleet which sailed against Norway may have been
a formidable force, bribery had already done much to achieve his ends, and
here again the English may well have footed much of the bill. But how big
that bill was in the years after 1018 there is no way of knowing; nor was the
tax system Cnut's only source of English revenue. His wealth was further
increased by the produce of royal estates, which the system of confiscating
defaulters' land would have made rather more numerous, and by the

[135] Hemming, i.,276–78 Compare DB,i., 141a,where land confiscated by the shire-reeve for non-pay of
      tax had according to the men of the shire been exempt from it.
[136] II Cnut 79; *Gesetze*, i. 366.
[137] Above, p.120.
[138] *ASC*, i. 194-95.

coinage system and other royal perquisites, such as the fines produced by the judicial system (see below). All may have been pressed hard, and pressed his subjects. When the author of the eulogy of Edward the Confessor in the *Chronicle* C and D texts under 1065[138] characterised the period of Danish rule in England by saying that riches were distributed he was not being complimentary.

THE COINAGE

The coinage is a subject in itself, and a fascinating one. Late in Edgar's reign the Anglo-Saxon monetary system was reformed. Thereafter, coin types were changed frequently, maybe (although this has been seriously questioned) at regular intervals of six or seven, later (i.e. after 1035) two or three, years. Each reissue may have involved the recall of all pennies of the previous type, or they were possibly just made invalid for certain purposes, such as the payment of royal dues. Coins of different issues were struck at different weights, and some individual types are known to have had a series of weight standards, which were gradually lowered as the period of currency progressed; thus the early coins of the type are the heaviest. The reasons for these variations are not yet fully understood, and may never be, but they look like the product of conscious fiscal policies, and there can be little doubt that the system as a whole was designed essentially for the king's profit.

New issues were lucrative. They necessitated new dies, for which Domesday Book shows that the moneyers sometimes paid £1, and the (probably variable) rate at which old coins were exchanged for new at the mints may have favoured the authorities: for every ten coins handed in, for example, perhaps only nine of the next type would be given in return. The sophistication of this system has emerged in the last forty years through intensive study of the tens of thousands of English pennies found in Scandinavian hoards. It is now possible to estimate both the total volume of the various issues and the output of individual mints,[139] and the fact that all pennies bore the name of moneyer and mint means that individual careers

---

[139] The crucial literature is Mossop, *The Lincoln Mint*; Metcalf, 'The Ranking of the Boroughs'; Metcalf, 'Continuity and Change in English Monetary History *c*.973–1086. Part 1.'; Metcalf, 'Continuity and Change in English Monetary History *c*.973–1086. Part 2.' It must be stressed that these figures are estimates, involve complex calculations (those whose understanding of mathematics is superior to my own may care to consult Lyon's 'Die Estimation'), assume an average output of 10,000 coins per reverse die, and may eventually be revised; Lyon has recently commented ('Anglo-Saxon Numismatics', 75) that they 'must be treated with extreme caution'.

can often be traced. Moreover, each of the hand-engraved iron dies was unique, as can obviously be seen from the coins they struck, and stylistic similarities and dissimilarities in the output of different mints show that dies were sometimes produced centrally, sometimes at different regional centres. Together with the variations in weight within and between different issues, such phenomena must reflect changes of policy motivated by political and economic considerations. The work of numismatists presents the historian with an increasingly fruitful field of study.[140]

Cnut issued three types, *Quatrefoil, Pointed Helmet* and *Short Cross*. Their sequence is known, their dates are not, although the theory which assigns six- or seven-year periods to every issue before 1035 (and which not all numismatists accept) might give 1017–23, 1023–9, and 1029–36.[141] *Quatrefoil* has been the subject of a detailed study by Mark Blackburn and Stewart Lyon. In the mid-tenth century dies were issued from about eight regional centres, but Edgar's first reformed type from only one. This new policy of centralisation was soon abandoned, and by the start of Æthelred's reign, perhaps because of the troubles after Edgar's death, at least six centres were issuing dies. Even so, the four types culminating in *Helmet* (withdrawn ?1009) were struck from dies made in only one or two places, probably London and Winchester, supplemented later in each type by additions and replacements from regional centres; but Æthelred's final *Last Small Cross* issue was decentralised from the beginning, with dies supplied by Winchester, Exeter, ?Gloucester and York, but not, at first, London. The latter then began operating, and was joined by Lincoln, Canterbury, Ipswich, an East Anglian centre, one in Sussex, and possibly Chester. It is tempting to see in this decentralisation, which previous policy implies was thought undesirable, a reflection of the political problems of the period 1009–16. In *Quatrefoil* the process went further still; eight major die-cutting centres were active throughout: London, Winchester, Lincoln, York, Chester, Gloucester, Exeter and Thetford. Five minor ones, Lewes (or Hastings), Chichester, Bath, Worcester and Norwich, also began the

---

[140] Other major work includes Dolley and Metcalf, 'The Reform of the English Coinage'; Lyon, 'Variations in Currency'; Lyon, 'Some problems in interpreting Anglo-Saxon Coinage'; Lyon, 'Anglo-Saxon Numismatics'; Petersson, *Anglo-Saxon Currency*; Petersson, 'Coins and weights'. Stewart, 'Coinage and recoinage after Edgar's reform', is an important summary and critique; see also Blackburn, 'Æthelred's Coinage'.

[141] See Blackburn and Lyon, 'Regional die-production in Cnut's *Quatrefoil* issue'. What follows is drawn from this article. There is also comment on the centres which cut dies for Æthelred's final *Last Small Cross* type in Lyon, 'Die-Cutting in the *Last Small Cross* Type of Æthelred II', 21–22, and at 35–36 he raises the possibility that '*Last Small Cross* continued to be struck in Æthelred's name until well into 1017'. For Cnut's coinage generally, see Jonsson, 'The coinage of Cnut'.

issue, but Norwich closed during it, and six more opened later: Oxford, Taunton (or Ilchester), Shrewsbury, Stamford, Bedford and Northampton (or Huntingdon).

The unusually large number of centres producing *Quatrefoil* dies is very likely to be linked to its exceptional volume. The type was half as big again as *Last Small Cross*, and the patterns of minting throw up some interesting features. Professor Metcalf has shown that output in the less important mints seems to have increased much more dramatically than the general rise of a third over *Last Small Cross* requires, while that of the major mints on the whole did not.[142] Of the latter, London and York did go up by about a third, while Winchester and Lincoln apparently saw no significant increase. The generally less prolific Southampton mint, on the other hand, is estimated to have used thirty-five reverse dies in *Quatrefoil* compared with five in *Last Small Cross* and none in *Pointed Helmet*. Many small mints in the west, south-west and midlands follow this general pattern. One of the most remarkable is Ilchester (Somerset), where 120 reverse dies are thought to have been used in *Quatrefoil* compared with none in *Last Small Cross* and ten in *Pointed Helmet*. From the west there is the important mint of Chester, with seventy-six, 242 and sixty-nine respectively, and in the east midlands Cambridge, with fifty-one, 150 and eighteen. These are extreme cases, but represent a trend from which only the smaller south-eastern mints appear exempt: in Canterbury, Dover, Lewes and Rochester output of *Quatrefoil* seemingly did not equal that of *Last Small Cross*.

Obviously, one is tempted to connect this remarkable activity with the period preceding the remarkably large payment of £82,500 to Cnut's army in 1018, during which smaller mints may have been far busier than usual because of a widespread need for coin. Unfortunately, there is a problem, apart from our ignorance of the percentage of the sum handed over in gold and silver bullion rather than currency. At some of the mints which saw great increases in activity – Southampton, Bristol and Ilchester, for example – striking was to the lighter weight standards, and as these were usually lowered as issues progressed, this ought to have been relatively late in the type's life. In other words, assuming that minting was spread reasonably evenly

---

[142] This paragraph is based on Metcalf, 'Can we believe the very large figure of £72,000 for the geld levied by Cnut in 1018?'. The estimates are in reverse dies because it was the die which struck the reverse of the coin which bore the name of mint and moneyer. Much depends on the assumption that surviving coins of the *Quatrefoil* type and adjacent issues are a representative sample of the whole. A used iron reverse die of Cnut's *Short Cross* type with the name of the mint of Norwich has been found in London, see O'Hara, 'An iron reverse die of the reign of Cnut'; Archibald, *et al.*, 'Four early medieval coin dies', espec. 181–87.

over a six- or seven-year span, the increased activity associated with the lighter coins should have occurred after 1018. But this would be historically incomprehensible, and there is another explanation. Even if *Quatrefoil* lasted six years (which is far from certain), it is quite likely, given the excessive nature of the 1018 tax, that the bulk of it, including many of the lighter coins, was struck before the payment was made, and that the amount issued thereafter was small because the demand for coin from people who had been taxed hard was also small. This argument seems historically convincing; whether it will prove numismatically so remains to be seen.[143]

Blackburn and Lyon's analysis of *Quatrefoil* has cast light on the weight standards used at the major mints too. In London, Lincoln, York and Chester it began at around 1.40g and fell four times (or possibly three in York) to end at around 1.00g, while at Winchester it concluded there after beginning at around 1.50g, and some south-western mints struck many coins as low as around 0.90g. About thirty per cent of the type is believed to have been minted to the first three standards, forty per cent to the fourth, and thirty per cent to the fifth.[144] *Pointed Helmet* and *Short Cross* have so far received less attention. Their volume is estimated at 22 million and 14 million respectively, the number of moneyers fell, and the number of die-cutting centres was reduced to six or fewer.[145] This return to more centralised die-issue hints at a tightening of royal authority after the stresses of Cnut's early years, and the volume of *Short Cross*, broadly similar to Edgar's and some of Æthelred's issues, might imply that the economic life of the country was returning to normal. Even so, all Cnut's types were struck very light: *Pointed Helmet* shares with one of the Confessor's types the dubious distinction of having the lowest weight of any produced between about 973 and 1066. It and *Short Cross* were also minted within much narrower weight ranges than

---

[143] It is favoured by Professor Metcalf. See further on this problem, Eaglen and Grayburn, 'Gouged Reverse Dies', 28–31.

[144] Blackburn and Lyon, 'Regional die-production', pp.254–56. More recent work utilising electron-probe micro-analysis (Eaglen and Grayburn, 'Gouged Reverse Dies', 23–26) has shown that a degree of debasement with brass or brass and copper is to be found in coins of the *Last Small Cross* type minted in Stamford and in *Quatrefoil* issues from Huntingdon and Stamford, the lightest coins apparently also being likely to be the most debased. Further work of this type may extend the picture to other mints and provide further evidence of the stresses experienced by the coinage system late in the reign of Æthelred and early in that of Cnut. When this book went to press I had not been able to see Metcalf and Northover, 'Sporadic debasement in the English coinage *c.*1009–1052'.

[145] Dolley and Ingold, 'Some thoughts on the Engraving of the Dies for the English Coinage *c.*1025'; Blackburn and Lyon, 'Regional die-production', p.225; Jonsson, 'The coinage of Cnut', pp.204–05; Archibald *et al.*, 'Four early medieval coin dies', 194, n.61, suggest that even in *Short Cross* 'die-cutting was not yet fully centralized', but point out that the finding in London of the Norwich die 'shows that some progress towards the centralisation of die-cutting... had been made in Cnut's reign'.

earlier issues, although multiple weight standards within types are still believed to have been in use.[146] This almost certainly reflects a deliberate change of policy, and indicates that minting was being closely controlled. Together with their lightness, it could be broadly attributed to a shortage of silver. However, a more sophisticated explanation is available.

Dr Nightingale believes that the weight of Cnut's coins was intended to bring English and Scandinavian currency units into line, and that during *Quatrefoil* the penny which had begun at a standard of around 1.40g was lowered to around 1.02g so that twenty-four would match the weight of a Scandinavian ora of 24.5g; and just as eight oras equalled a Scandinavian mark of 196g, ten would now equal an English pound of 240 pence. Some sort of regular relationship was thus established between mark and pound. She has further argued that around 1026 Cnut established a weight standard of around 1.14g for coins minted in Skåne and the Danish islands, and that his English *Short Cross* type was then struck to around 1.12g to create an ora of 27g and a mark of 216g in both England and Denmark, because 27g was the weight of the Roman and Byzantine ounce, and he wished to establish a link between English and Scandinavian weight standards and those of the Byzantine gold coinage, as it suited his political or commercial policies in Europe. Hence, he introduced a weight standard of 27g for both gold and silver, and dropped the existing measure for gold, the mancus.[147]

This is a brief sketch of part of a brilliantly conceived and elaborate theory on eleventh-century English weights which it would be impossible to discuss properly here, even if the present writer were competent, which he is not. But it is appropriate to make one or two observations. With *Quatrefoil* for example, even though it is true that the median weight of the numismatist H.B.A. Petersson's sample of 5,590 coins of this type is 1.02g,[148] it is uncertain how far a new standard of around 1.02g[149] can reasonably be identified in a type struck at various levels between around 1.50g and around 0.95g, and when Æthelred's *Last Small Cross* issue too had

[146] Petersson, *Anglo-Saxon Currency*, pp.185–86; Blackburn and Lyon, 'Regional die-production', p.253.

[147] See Nightingale, 'The Evolution of Weight-Standards', and both parts of her 'The Ora, the Mark, and the Mancus'; also, Lyon, 'Historical Problems of Anglo-Saxon Coinage'.

[148] Petersson, 'Coins and weights', p.347. The median weight is that 'which would divide the coins so that no more than half were heavier than it and no more than half were lighter'; Lyon, 'Some problems in interpreting Anglo-Saxon Coinage', 199; Petersson, 'Coins and weights', pp.216–17. On all matters involving weight standards it is necessary to bear in mind the fact that the Scandinavian hoards from which the pennies mainly come may be deceiving us if they include predominantly pennies minted only at a certain stage of an issue struck at varying weights; Lyon, 'Variations in Currency in Late Anglo-Saxon England', p.111.

[149] Nightingale, 'The Ora, the Mark, and the Mancus... Part II', 242.

fallen to this weight and lower. *Pointed Helmet* is more firmly centred on this point, but it is less clear that *Short Cross* and succeeding types were increased to around 1.12g. Much depends which statistics one stresses. Petersson's 3,325 *Short Cross* coins give an average weight of 1.08g, which yields an ora of under 26g and a mark some way below the 216g suggested by Dr Nightingale; the *Jewel Cross* and *Fleur-de-lis* types of Harold Harefoot's and Harthacnut's time are similar. However, the median weights of *Short Cross* and *Jewel Cross* are 1.12g, while that of *Fleur-de-lis* is slightly lower at 1.08g.[150] Furthermore, Cnut's East Scandinavian standard now seems to have been around 1.0g, not around 1.14g, while in Jutland it was around 0.75g.[151] The around 1.0g weight is close enough to the English weight to hint at a connection, although if Cnut was really seeking Anglo-Scandinavian uniformity it is difficult to see why the standard in Jutland was so much lighter. Indeed, this suggests that Scandinavian weights were a Scandinavian affair. On the other hand, the mancus does seem to disappear after the early eleventh century, and the mark of gold to crop up more frequently, although mancuses are mentioned in II Cnut 71a on heriots (payable to the king on a man's death).[152] The mark was known in England before Cnut's time, but it may well have been more widely used under Scandinavian rule. The lithsmen were paid in them, and the Domesday entry on the Dorset boroughs implies that the housecarls were too.

THE IMPORTANCE OF ENGLISH WEALTH

Whatever the truth of these matters, Cnut's administration clearly kept careful control of the coinage system because this was, and had long been, a world where wealth was power, and where it derived not only from exploitation of the land, but of trade and industry too. At least as far back as the eighth century, when Offa of Mercia strove to conquer Kent, the great trading centre of the day, kings appreciated the importance of taxing commerce. By the tenth century the West Saxon rulers had founded towns and greatly expanded the coinage system partly to facilitate this, for tolls from markets and rents from burgesses went into the royal purse. The concern of

[150] Ibid; Petersson, 'Coins and weights', p.347.

[151] Becker, 'The Coinages of Harthacnut and Magnus the Good at Lund', p.120; the discussion of Cnut's Danish coinage by Jonsson ('The coinage of Cnut', pp.223–27) stresses 'the development of different weight standards in Denmark'.

[152] But this is not an objection to Dr Nightingale's theory, as II Cnut's heriot rates had existed under Æthelred (Brooks, 'Arms, Status and Warfare', p.89) and could have been copied by Wulfstan from an older document.

the laws that trading should take place in towns was partly concern for the payment of toll.[153] Kings, or their servants, interested themselves in industry too. They profited from the salt-works at Droitwich (Worcestershire) and in Cheshire, and Dr Maddicott has argued that royal exploitation of the tin trade was also important in this period, and that the prosperity of Exeter and Lydford was partly based on tin; he thinks that kings profited from the mining of silver-bearing lead in the Mendips too.[154]

The Scandinavians who raided England were well aware of its commercial attributes. They sacked Lydford in 997 and attacked Exeter unsuccessfully in 1001, but captured it in 1003. The plundering of other towns – including Norwich, Wallingford, Oxford, Thetford, Cambridge, Northampton and Canterbury – shows an appreciation of their wealth, and especially that of London, where a quarter of the national coinage was struck, and which was assaulted repeatedly but in vain. Cnut, in addition to taxing it heavily in 1018, must have known it to be in his interest to maintain its commercial prosperity and that of other towns. His awareness of the importance of trade is demonstrated by his negotiations with Emperor Conrad II, Rudolf of Burgundy and the Pope to reduce the barriers and unjust tolls which were troubling English merchants and pilgrims journeying to Rome, and the 1027 Letter's stress on their success; nor is the Letter the only evidence. A document which describes the dues paid to the royal treasury at Pavia at this time refers to Englishmen who were wont to visit it with their wares, and recalls how their anger at having their baggage examined by treasury officials often led to verbal abuse and violence; but then the king of the Angles and Saxons agreed with the king of the Lombards (i.e. the German emperor) that in return for his subjects being given exemption from the ten per cent tax known as the *decima* (payable, among other commodities, on wool, tin and slaves) he would send to the treasury every third year fifty pounds of silver, two fine greyhounds with collars bearing the royal arms, two shields, two lances and two swords, together with two pounds of silver and two coats of miniver for the treasury-master.[155] The English and Lombard kings involved are not named, but the agreement seems very likely to be that described in the 1027 Letter, and if so Cnut clearly went to some trouble to please a trading lobby. The introduction of a royal coinage into Denmark points in the same direction, although it seems to have

[153] Maitland, *Domesday Book and Beyond*, pp. 192–95.
[154] Maddicott, 'Trade, industry and the wealth of King Alfred'.
[155] Translated *Medieval Trade in the Mediterranean World*, ed. Lopez and Raymond, pp. 56–60. I owe this reference to Dr Ben Hudson.

occurred fairly late in the reign, with the establishment of mints at Lund, Roskilde, Slagelse, Ålborg, Viborg, Ørbœk, Århus, Ribe and probably Hedeby, each of which struck their own type of penny.[156]

In this context the uncertainty whether Seebohm and Kinsey were correct in arguing that the text known as IV Æthelred really comes from Cnut's reign is particularly unfortunate.[157] Its initial provisions are statements about tolls payable by foreign merchants in London, and look like the results of an inquest into the king's rights in the city.[158] Then come chapters on crime, including the minting and use of false coin, and the instruction that royal officials are to be on the watch for coiners of base money among both Danes and English. The penultimate one says that every weight is to be stamped according to the weight at which my (i.e. royal) money is received, and each of them is to indicate that fifteen oras make a pound. The only real evidence for connecting this document, which bears no royal name, with Æthelred is its survival among other of his codes in the twelfth-century legal compilation *Quadripartitus*, although Patrick Wormald has pointed out that III Æthelred 16, decreeing death for moneyers who work in woods, also appears in IV Æthelred 5.4, and suggested that the death penalty in III Æthelred 8 against those striking false coin since it was forbidden is a reference to the prohibition which appears in IV Æthelred 5.3[159]

This may be so, but there are arguments for assigning IV Æthelred to Cnut. It decrees the loss of a hand for false moneyers, but in III Æthelred the penalty is death. However, II Cnut 8 states that 'after this' false moneyers are to lose their hand, and the reeve too if he can be shown to have given his permission. The first provision mirrors IV Æthelred, and while it is quite possible that III Æthelred increased IV Æthelred's penalty of mutilation to death and that Cnut altered it back the similarity between IV Æthelred and II Cnut 8 may equally be because the former is from Cnut's reign. That Cnut may have reduced the punishment (and thus returned to the practice given by II Æthelstan 14) is perhaps hinted by the 'after this' which introduces II Cnut 8.1,[160] and may explain why Wulfstan was happy to include it

[156] Becker, 'The Coinages of Harthacnut and Magnus the Good at Lund', pp.154–55.

[157] Seebohm, *Tribal Custom in Anglo-Saxon Law*, pp.340–43; Kinsey, 'Anglo-Saxon Law and Practice relating to Mints and Moneyers', 19–21. Edited, *Gesetze*, i. 232–36.

[158] Richardson and Sayles, *Law and Legislation from Æthelberht to Magna Carta*, p.28.

[159] Wormald, 'Æthelred the Lawmaker', p.62; see also Wormald, *The Making of English Law*, pp.322–27. The numbers by which these texts are known today implies nothing about their original order.

[160] A point made by Kinsey. There is also a link between IV Æthelred 4 and II Cnut 62 on housebreaking: both specify that £5 is payable to the king.

in his work, for he approved of the replacement of capital punishment by mutilation.[161] More striking is that the mention of Danes and English in IV Æthelred 8, as Kinsey said, seems an odd order of precedence for Æthelred's reign in a measure not confined to the Danelaw. But it is the order used in the ninth chapter of the Letter of 1019–20, the prologue of the 1018 code, and II Cnut 83, and also in the *Chronicle* for 1018 and 1025 and two Worcestershire leases of the Confessor's time (S 1406, 1409), although another (S 1394) reverses it, as does chapter 6 of the Letter of 1027. Finally, the statement that a pound is to consist of fifteen oras might be most intelligible in a context where increasing use of this subdivision of the mark had resulted from the Danish conquest, and clarification was needed.[162] All this is inconclusive, but if IV Æthelred is from Cnut's time it shows him conducting an inquest into London trade and the royal tolls which it produced – six shillings on a large ship belonging to Normans from Rouen, for example, and a twentieth of their cargo of fish – and his concern to stop false coining, and thus the desire of his government to safeguard its fiscal rights. Also, an inquest in London would imply that, like William the Conqueror with Domesday Book, he was a king eager to know the value of what he had conquered, and that he may have conducted inquests elsewhere too.

Dr Nightingale has discussed the increasing importance of London at this time,[163] and that Cnut is known to have been present there on several occasions is what one might expect of a king whose Scandinavian interests made a major port on the east coast very useful. Nevertheless, his reign did not have much discernible impact on the city The number of known London moneyers with Scandinavian names actually dropped, from the six of Æthelred's reign to four,[164] and the suggestion that the civil and commercial court, the husting, received its Scandinavian name in his time is rendered difficult by its appearance in a late tenth-century will and doubts whether the word is a Scandinavian loan at all: Professor Sawyer has noted

[161] Another possibility, of course, is that the change is Wulfstan's, not Cnut's. Although the first part of II Cnut 8 is from VI Æthelred, the rest is not from any known text. The statement, IV Æthelred 9, that the number of moneyers is to be reduced, could fit Æthelred (Wormald, 'Æthelred the Lawmaker', p.63), but would also tie in with Cnut's reduction in *Pointed Helmet*.
[162] See, on this clause, Lyon, 'Historical Problems of Anglo-Saxon Coinage', 214. A fifteenth of a pound of 240 pence is 16 pence, which is the reckoning often found in Domesday and other sources, Nightingale, 'The Ora, the Mark, and the Mancus... Part I', 248–49. As we have seen, Dr Nightingale believes that the ora was the equivalent of 24 pence in Cnut's time.
[163] Nightingale, 'The Origin of the Court of Husting'.
[164] Smart, 'Moneyers of the late Anglo-Saxon coinage', 279. The number of moneyers fell generally: 100 men with Anglo-Saxon names struck for Æthelred, but only eighty-four for Cnut.

that both the elements *hus* and *thing* appear in Anglo-Saxon.[165] Moreover, the dedications of six city churches to St Olaf (killed 1030) cannot be shown to be early, although as his cult certainly entered England before 1066 some may be from Cnut's reign. John says that the Danes had a cemetery in London, where Harold Harefoot's body was eventually buried,[166] but there is little to add to this; Scandinavian traders are not listed among those frequenting London in IV Æthelred, but a set of twelfth-century London customs allows Danes to stay in the city a year and (unlike Norwegians) to visit markets anywhere in England, and it is conceivable that this privilege was granted under Cnut.[167] Physical evidence comprises two apparently eleventh-century stone slabs decorated with scenes in the Scandinavian Ringerike style, one part of a sarcophagus from St Paul's churchyard showing a quadruped resembling that on the greater of the Jelling rune stones, and with an incomplete runic inscription, 'Ginna and Toki had this stone set up'.[168] Such a monument cannot have been cheap: maybe Ginna and Toki were lithsmen.

CNUT'S LAW

The crown also profited, and fulfilled one of its most important functions, by implementing the law and maintaining public order. England must have been in a disturbed state after the traumas of Æthelred's later years, and in so far as disorder disrupted the royal administration and interfered with its revenue, and its suppression produced fines and confiscations which increased that revenue, Cnut would have had other than altruistic reasons for taking action. Unfortunately, for reasons discussed in Chapter 2, Wulfstan's legal texts are likely to contain only measures which the archbishop found acceptable, such as mutilation for false moneyers, and to frame provisions so that they make the best of matters of which he disapproved; thus we are told that landholders who have discharged public burdens on their estates are to have undisputed possession of them, not that they are otherwise likely to be confiscated. Elsewhere, the archbishop is clearly trying to control abuse.

---

[165] Nightingale, 'The Origin of the Court of Husting', 559–63, argues that the reference to the husting has been interpolated into the will, which exists only in a twelfth-century Latin translation (*Chron. Rams.*, p.58); Sawyer, 'Anglo-Scandinavian trade', p.192.
[166] JW, ii. 530–31.
[167] Sawyer, 'Anglo-Scandinavian trade', pp.186–87.
[168] A number of spearheads and axeheads of likely Scandinavian origin, some decorated in the Ringerike style, have also been found in the Thames and near London Bridge; Roesdahl *et al.*, *The Vikings in England*, pp.161–64.

II Cnut 70, 71 and 73.4 on heriots (money and military equipment given to a lord, often the king, on a man's death), stipulate that they are to be according to rank, that a widow shall not be fined if she pays within twelve months, and that a lord is to take no more than his due heriot from the property of one who has died intestate. Similarly, II Cnut 72 protects wife and children from claims on their property only advanced after the husband's death.

There is the further problem that all Wulfstan's provisions may be from older legislation. Even so, some could be products of Cnut's government. II Cnut 77 punishes those who flee from a military expedition by land and sea with death and forfeiture, which is slightly stronger than Wulfstan's earlier statements on the matter,[169] and II Cnut 78, remitting the heriot of a man killed before his lord at home or abroad, may reflect the use of English forces in Scandinavia.[170] II Cnut 75, dealing with what should happen to those who innocently lay aside weapons which are then put to criminal use by others, could have resulted from a particular case. II Cnut 23 and 24, on vouching to warranty and the purchase of goods (nobody is to buy anything worth more than four pence without four trustworthy witnesses), may also be instructions issued by him. II Cnut 30.4 sentences those convicted of wrongdoing by the ordeal for a second time to lose hands or feet or both, and II Cnut 30.5 those guilty of still greater crime to forfeit eyes, nose, ears and upper lip or scalp, whatever was judged most appropriate. I Æthelred, from which Wulfstan drew II Cnut 30, had imposed capital punishment. The archbishop certainly approved of the substitution of mutilation, and so this may not reflect Cnut's methods; or perhaps it did, or Wulfstan found the king open to persuasion, for mutilation was not only part of previous English practice (Edgar is said to have introduced comprehensive mutilation for all sorts of crimes)[171] but the sort which Wulfstan specifies echoes Cnut's treatment in 1014 of English hostages who were deprived of their hands, ears and noses.

Away from the dilemmas posed by the texts I and II Cnut, a little more can be said on confiscation. When Cnut (and possibly Æthelred) took the lands of tax-defaulters he acted in an English tradition, as forfeiture of all a man's possessions, presumably including his lands, is a penalty which appears

---

[169] VI Æthelred 35 threatens deserters of armies led by the king with the loss of property, V Æthelred 28 with that of life and possessions (or wergeld).
[170] But, of course, Æthelred had allegedly attacked Normandy, above, p.42.
[171] Keynes, 'Crime and Punishment', pp.72–73. See also Ine 18, 37, and III Edmund 4, edited in *Gesetze*.

in a number of earlier law-codes.[172] Tenth-century documents mention
confiscations for various reasons, such as theft, witchcraft and piracy, and
under Æthelred charters give about twenty examples of forfeiture for
crime, including fornication and adultery, theft, killing, defiance of royal
authority and treachery.[173] The evidence is thinner under Cnut. The
Ramsey chronicle says that he gave the inheritance of certain English
nobles, proscribed and killed by his judgement for treachery to his royal
predecessors, to Danish companions, one of whom received Ellesworth,
Cambridgeshire. We are then regaled with a rousing tale of witchcraft and
murder, which ends with the donation of Ellesworth to Bishop Æthelric of
Dorchester, who presented it to Ramsey.[174] The monks clearly had traditions of some sort about these events, and elsewhere their chronicle simply
lists lands given by Æthelred and says that they knew not how he acquired
them,[175] which makes one slightly more inclined to trust the suggestion
that the executions and forfeitures, which may be identifiable with those
of 1017, followed a proper legal process, and show Cnut using the charge of
treachery to seize land according to English precedent. S 1229, a record
of the gift by Emma of Newington (Oxfordshire) to Christ Church
Canterbury in Cnut's time, says that it had been forfeited to the king by the
thegn Ælfric, and the writ S 991 claims that he granted Bengeworth
(Worcestershire) to Brihtwine after it was forfeited. But in these two cases
the reasons for confiscation are not given, and the tendency of Æthelred's
charters to describe how the lands concerned came into the king's hands
disappears under Cnut. This may itself be significant. It was noted in
Chapter 1 that Æthelred's grants perhaps stress the legality of his possession
because some of his ways of acquiring land were not thought legal. Of
course, other explanations are possible: Professor Keynes suggests that the
practice was simply a fashion among charter draughtsmen.[176] This may be
so, but that it apparently did not continue in the new reign [177] is the sort of
striking coincidence that invites explanation, and possibly more than a trick
of the evidence, even though Cnut's charters are a smaller and maybe less
representative sample than Æthelred's.

---

[172] For example, Ine 6, 51; Alfred 1.4; II Edward 5.1; II Æthelstan 3.1, 25.2; II Edmund 1.3, 6; I Edgar
3.1; II Edgar 4.3.
[173] Keynes, 'Crime and Punishment', pp.77, n.67, and 77–78.
[174] *Chron. Rams.*, pp.129–34.
[175] *Chron. Rams.*, p.144.
[176] Keynes, 'Crime and Punishment', p.77.
[177] S 949, 956 and 960 describe something of the circumstances of the grants, but not how the king
came to own the land.

It could well be that he did exercise greater control over his officials, and that the worst abuses prevalent under his predecessor were rectified. The promises of good government which appear in the Letters of 1019–20 and 1027 and Wulfstan's law codes may have been framed by churchmen, but it is likely that Cnut was happy enough to be associated with them, and may have been involved in their initiation, even if one guesses, and repeated statements on reeves suggest, that fair words were occasionally followed by foul deeds. Nor need this have resulted solely from a cosmetic wish to appear the good, law-giving Christian king. An administration which allowed excessive freedom to its officials and let order decline was likely to face political opposition, as Æthelred no doubt discovered, and the Northumbrian revolt against Earl Tostig in 1065 also shows, and Cnut may have reflected that, providing his own needs were met, his henchmen's profits might prudently be limited to what sufficed to keep them loyal. Of course, it could be argued that his periods of absence from the country can have seen little royal control, that he may well have had sufficient support and resources (not least the housecarls) to stifle opposition fairly easily, and that what harmed Æthelred need not have worried a ruler who was eventually in a much stronger position. He undoubtedly provided the English with protection from foreign invasion, and thus fulfilled at least one of the requirements of a Christian king. Whether he supplied another – justice – there is in the end insufficient evidence to say. We do not know whether Archbishop Wulfstan's legal texts are a true reflection of the young ruler in whose name they were written, or have simply grossly deceived posterity.

CONCLUSION

T he Danish conquest of England was a product of its time in bringing to fruition long-standing links between England and Scandinavia (see the Introduction), but a harbinger of things to come, or a phenomenon of long-term importance, it was not. In 1041 Harthacnut, who allegedly suffered from frequent illness,[1] invited Edward the Confessor to return from exile in Normandy. The following year he died, Edward became sole king, and the Anglo-Saxon royal house regained the position it had lost in 1016. Less than a quarter of a century later, the Viking Age in England effectively ended forever when, on 25 September 1066, the last great victory of Old English arms secured the defeat and death of King Harald Hardraada of Norway in the fields of Stamford Bridge in Yorkshire. Twenty-four ships sufficed to carry home the survivors of an army which is said to have arrived in 300, but shortly afterwards Duke William of Normandy landed at Pevensey, and there followed a conquest far more celebrated than that of 1016, and undeniably important, however much historians may argue over its details.

Much of this is attributable to chance. None of Cnut's sons reached the age of thirty, with consequences which can hardly be exaggerated in a period when a great deal depended on a ruler's longevity as well as his ability. Had their father lived to sixty like William the Conqueror, and Harthacnut to the same age as Henry I (d.1135), events would have been different,[2] and probably neither the Confessor nor William would ever have occupied the English throne. But that in reality the country's future did not lie in closer political links with Scandinavia may seem more inevitable to us

[1] William of Poitiers, *Gesta Guillelmi*, i. 5, ed. Davis and Chibnall, pp.6–7.
[2] As Patrick Wormald observed to me.

than it did to contemporaries, and was not immediately apparent. Part of England wanted Harthacnut, then ruling Denmark, as king in 1035, and all of it, as far as we can tell, in 1040. The expeditions launched by Æthelred's sons in 1036 gained no known support. Indeed, Edward was violently opposed, and even after his accession the threat of Scandinavian invasion remained. Harald Hardraada presumably envisaged a northern empire like those created by Swegen and Cnut, and Swegen Estrithsson of Denmark, Cnut's nephew, eventually turned his attention across the North Sea too. William of Poitiers thought that Danes fought alongside the English at the battle of Hastings,[3] and in 1069 a Danish fleet sailed into the Humber to assist rebels against the Normans, to be joined the following year by Swegen himself, who was met by people expecting him to conquer the whole country. His appearance in the Danelaw recalls that of Cnut's father in 1013, but had a different result. William bought him off, and Swegen, who for all that doubtless realised that he was dealing with no Æthelred, returned to Denmark. Another fleet, under his son Cnut, arrived to support a further rebellion in 1075, but, says the *Chronicle*, they dared not join battle with King William, and went home. He took them seriously, even so, and in 1085 made careful preparations to meet an invasion by Cnut which never sailed.

It is true that little commitment to Anglo-Danish union can be discerned in the crisis of 1035–36, but information on it is scanty. Harold Harefoot's support in the midlands and north might suggest a desire for a king who was half English, but that the lithsmen in London favoured him too hints at other factors which cannot now be recovered. One reason why England and Normandy remained under the same ruler for most of the century and a half after 1066 was that major families long held lands in both. Nothing is known of the Scandinavian possessions of Cnut's men, and they probably received far less in England than the Conqueror's followers had by his death in 1087, but even so one would have thought that a similar force might have been felt after 1035. Also, although Cnut's intentions about the succession are unclear, there is no difficulty in believing that he did want Harthacnut to take both England and Denmark, for in his lifetime he retained a strong commitment to Scandinavian politics, and the continued existence of a North Sea empire based on naval power may not have seemed unrealistic.

Moreover, despite the brevity of his reign, links were forming between its component countries which might eventually have contributed to that empire's continuance. English missionaries and moneyers worked in

[3] William of Poitiers, *Gesta Guillelmi*, ii. 16, ed. Davis and Chibnall, pp. 126–27.

Scandinavia, and Englishmen perhaps helped to build the church of St
Clement at Roskilde in around 1040, one of the first in Denmark constructed of stone,[4] while an apparently eleventh-century comb bearing the
name *Eadrinc* (Eadric) found at Lund in Skåne implies that either an
Englishman was living there or that English names were in use.[5] More
striking, because it hints at administrative influence which given time could
have been very important in creating more permanent links, is the
(undated) appearance of the English word thegn (indicating a royal agent)
on memorial rune stones not only in Jutland and Skåne, but also in
Västergötland and eastern Sweden.[6]

In England itself the Danish conquest naturally increased the impact of
Scandinavian culture. The slab from the St Paul's sarcophagus, with its beast
in the Scandinavian Ringerike style, itself possibly influenced by the ten-
drils found in the contemporary English Winchester style, can be set beside
the stone from Old Minster Winchester showing the story of Sigmund.
Even more noteworthy is the presence of a Ringerike-style snake with a
head similar to that on the St Paul's stone in a manuscript, the Winchcombe
Psalter, which may have been produced in Gloucestershire, and the existence of Scandinavian features in a number of other English drawings of the
period.[7] Anglo-Scandinavian contacts developed further during Cnut's
reign, and might have helped perpetuate political union had that union
lasted longer than it did.

But in fact the last of his sons died in 1042, the future lay elsewhere, and
the value of speculating on what might have been has its limits. Identifying
what was is difficult enough. The Danish conquest is relatively forgotten
today not only because it was short-lived and without significant consequences, but because a scarcity of sources makes elucidation of its nature,
and not least that of its main figure, arduous and frequently inconclusive.
The early medievalist, accustomed to being faced by puzzles with few
remaining pieces, often feels that they can be fitted into a number of varying and sometimes mutually contradictory pictures, all of which may seem
equally valid; it is no accident that books on the reigns of individual Anglo-
Saxon kings are rare, and that more general surveys frequently concern
themselves with institutions as much as with politics or individuals, who are

[4] Olsen, 'St Jørgensbjærg kirke'.
[5] Roesdahl *et al.*, *The Vikings in England*, p.179.
[6] Above, p.97.
[7] Graham-Campbell, *The Viking World*, p.152; Backhouse *et al., The Golden Age of Anglo-Saxon Art*, No.
64; Temple, *Anglo-Saxon Manuscripts*, No. 80; Wormald, *English Drawings of the Tenth and Eleventh
Centuries*, pp.38–42. On evidence of the Scandinavian presence in Winchester, see above, p.122, n.58.

easily regarded as beyond the limits of our perception. But as far as Cnut is concerned such pessimism is not fully justified, for while there is a great deal that will either never be known or remain no more than guesswork (hence the expressions of doubt and reservation with which parts of this book are heavily laced), there is also a by no means negligible amount that can be either established beyond reasonable doubt or estimated with a fair degree of probability.

It is sufficiently clear, for example, that Cnut was, by the standards of his day, the most successful of all pre-Conquest rulers in Britain. There had never been a king of such greatness in England before, says Henry of Huntingdon, for he was lord of all Denmark and of all England and of all Norway and also of *Scotia*, and he did three particularly magnificent things: he married his daughter to the Roman emperor, he secured the diminution of tolls on the way to Rome, and when the tide refused his command not to rise he proclaimed the vanity and frivolity of the power of earthly rulers compared with that of Him who commands heaven, earth and sea. Such comment must be allowed its due. The only previous Anglo-Saxon monarch to marry a female relative to a future emperor (Otto I) was Æthelstan. None had attended an imperial coronation in Rome, or ruled Denmark, Norway and part of Sweden too, as well as probably having some sort of overlordship over other parts of the British Isles. If it is true that Norway had been lost before Cnut's death, and that his empire did not survive him, that may dim his success, but does not destroy it or its significance.

Above all, it signifies a man skilled in the complex art of rulership. In 1016 he had many rivals: potentially dangerous Englishmen like Eadric Streona, Æthelweard of Wessex and the royal æthelings, great Scandinavian warlords such as Thorkell, hostile foreign potentates like Olaf of Norway and Malcolm of Scotland; maybe even his own brother, Harald. None prevailed. Cnut, like virtually all successful medieval kings, was ruthless at need. His enemies were banished, killed, bought or brought to terms. Much territory was subdued, and it is a reasonable assumption that Norway would have been recovered had he lived. Moreover, if the extent of his dominions is not sufficient testimony to his skill in managing men and political opportunities, this is further illustrated by his dealings with the English.

He was fortunate in succeeding to a country exhausted by war, and by a ruler who almost certainly lacked many of his own qualities, but possessing a powerful and elaborate administrative system able to exploit its great wealth, and magnates in some cases prepared to make the most of a new government. That he did not completely replace the native aristocracy with his own men, or build numerous castles, or destroy the north of England, may make Cnut seem less of a conqueror than William; arguably the reverse is true, even allowing for the possibility that he was luckier with a few important individuals. Perhaps the expedients adopted by William the Conqueror were unnecessary because Cnut transcended him in his understanding of the English political system, those who ran it, and the considerable opportunities it offered to an able and ruthless politician. Maybe he saw that neither it nor most of its operators had to be replaced, providing they were secured: so he executed, banished and took hostages, and some of his followers received English land; and he taxed; and the fruits of his taxation paid for troops who could enforce his will and his taxes, garrison and control recalcitrant areas, give him a power base which eased his reliance on warlords Scandinavian or English, and make the administration stronger still, so that it contributed to his control of Denmark and eventually Norway and part of Sweden too.

There is against him, of course, the possible charge of political irresponsibility and short-sightedness in allowing three of his earls – Godwin, Leofric and Siward – a position which developed into the rivalries and crises of Edward the Confessor's time. There is no denying that the power of the Godwin family eventually waxed very great indeed, but in the absence of convincing evidence about its extent before 1042 Cnut's role in establishing it cannot be ascertained, and nor can he be blamed for failing to foresee the early deaths of his own sons, which placed Edward on the throne which his father Æthelred had occupied so inauspiciously. It may be that his activities in Scandinavia and elsewhere in Britain and Europe led him to delegate a considerable amount of authority to others, and that he did so to an extent that was imprudent. However, in England he possessed a country with an elaborately organised and well-staffed administrative system which one can be fairly confident could operate without constant supervision from above, and it is not at all clear why simply handing over the reins to Earl Godwin, or endowing him with more wealth than was necessary to secure his loyalty, would have been more effective than allowing it to do so. There are also good grounds to doubt whether a king who early in his career had been obliged to deal with men such as Earl Thorkell and Eadric Streona, and had done so harshly and successfully, would have knowingly bequeathed a similar figure to his own sons, and Harthacnut, at least, seems to have had Godwin well under control, if John of Worcester's story of the latter's eagerness to appease his wrath over the death of the ætheling Alfred can be relied upon.[8] The idea that Cnut allowed his earls to wax too great cannot be dismissed absolutely, but it is not proven.

Whatever the politics of his reign, they were certainly complex, because they took place within an intricate social and political framework. Perceptions of the late Anglo-Saxon state have been deeply and irreversibly influenced in the last thirty years by the work of James Campbell. He sees the English kingdom of the tenth and eleventh centuries as densely populated, economically advanced, thoroughly governed, and ruled by kings whose ability to coerce should never be underestimated; yet at the same time, power did not lie exclusively with kings and nobles, but extended at least as far down society as the hundred courts and maybe beyond, and into the hands of other influential pressure-groups such as the churches, townsmen and merchants. Cnut can be seen attempting to please the former in his negotiations with the Pope in 1027 about the money exacted from English archbishops when they went for the pallium, for Archbishop Wulfstan had earlier written to Rome complaining about the necessity for this journey. It must have pleased merchants that their king at the same time concerned himself with securing a reduction in the tolls levied upon them in Italy. It is one of the more rewarding aspects of studying Cnut's reign that the sources are just good enough for the intricacies of English politics to surface elsewhere too, so that we are able to go beyond institutions and into the political events which occurred within and around them. His dealings with the aristocracy and probably shrewd use of the country's administrative resources and economic wealth have already been mentioned, but it is in his relations with the church that we come nearest to understanding the texture of his time, in which ecclesiastics struggled to impose their conceptions of kingship as God-given and God-related office upon a monarch whose followers had earlier been reviled as the precursors of Anti-Christ, who kept two consorts, whose regime was certainly in some respects oppressive, and who had to learn how to court and patronise English saints and churches so that he could acquire for himself a badly-needed aura of legitimacy and at the same time ensure that the hostile exploitation of figures such as Archbishop Ælfheah and Edmund of East Anglia was not able to add indefinitely to his political problems.

In so far as his rule contained elements displeasing to many of his subjects, much of it was forgotten in later years, as his name tended to become enveloped in a benevolent haze. Writers in churches which had benefited

[8] Above, p.172.

from his generosity, for example Hermann of Bury St Edmunds, Symeon of Durham and the author of the Ramsey chronicle,[9] were naturally inclined to speak well of him, and this favourable tradition was possibly facilitated by the survival of Wulfstan's legal works, whose pious and homiletic tone must have seemed to confirm the general picture. To the Ramsey chronicler Cnut was a most Christian king, inferior to none of his royal predecessors in virtue (*virtus*) and the practice of war, who began most eagerly to honour holy church and defend religious men, to pour forth alms, and both to establish new just laws and to observe old ones. He ruled not only England but also Denmark and Norway, and yet was humble in disposition, inclined to mercy, a most faithful lover of lovers of peace, but a most severe punisher of those who either by robbery or rapaciousness violated the laws of the kingdom. Others, too, believed in Cnut's just laws. The twelfth century, a period of great interest in law, saw the production of the texts now known as the *Instituta Cnuti*, which drew not only on Wulfstan's legal material but also on the codes of Ine, Alfred and Edgar, the similar *Consiliati Cnuti*, and a tract on forest law which was attributed to Cnut.[10]

Even so, not all twelfth-century legal compilations flattered him: the *Leges Edwardi Confessoris* says that Edward's law had originally been formulated by Edgar, but had lapsed in the years between his death and the accession of his grandson,[11] and there are less favourable comments elsewhere too. The eleventh-century authors of the *Life* of Edward the Confessor and the poem commemorating him in the *Anglo-Saxon Chronicle* praise their subject by referring to Cnut's reign disparagingly.[12] The Worcester monk Hemming and the Peterborough chronicler Hugh Candidus, who both record losses of church possessions, have nothing good to say about him. Popular tradition may have retained unpleasant memories. Although the Ramsey chronicle speaks well of Cnut himself, it also tells a story which throws some unusual and not entirely pleasing light on his reign. A rich Dane in Hertfordshire oppressed his peasants and made them guard his house at night because of fear of English hostility. Eventually hearing them plotting to kill him, he sold the estate to Bishop Æthelric of Dorchester, who gave it to Ramsey; he believed that the English hated the

---

[9] Hermann, *De Miraculis Sancti Eadmundi*, xvi–xvii, ed. Arnold, i. 46–47; Symeon, *Libellvs de exordio*, iii. 8, ed. Rollason, pp. 166–69; *Chron. Rams.*, pp. 125–26.
[10] *Gesetze*, i. 612–26; see Hudson, 'Administration, Family and Perceptions of the Past', pp.94–98; Wormald, *The Making of English Law*, pp.350–52.
[11] *Gesetze*, i. 663.
[12] *Life of King Edward*, ed. Barlow, pp.14–15; *ASC* C and D texts under 1065, i. 192–95.

Danes because they had invaded their country.[13] Similarly, Gaimar may be
reflecting a view of the period of Danish rule prevalent among some of his
twelfth-century contemporaries in saying that the English did not love the.
Danes and were pleased at the deaths of Cnut's sons, as their countrymen
held the natives cheap and insulted them.[14]

Whether or not such statements do reflect authentic memories, their gist
cannot be entirely false. Although Cnut's actions after he became king may
have been less drastic than William the Conqueror's, the conquest itself, the
culmination of fighting extending back over more than thirty years, was
longer and bloodier than that of 1066, and characterised by a level of taxation possibly without parallel either before or since. Many Englishmen, and
not only those who lost land, treasure and relatives, must have been aware
that the regime which followed was the price of defeat. Cnut himself may
have stressed his brotherhood with Edmund Ironside when he visited
Glastonbury, but at other times and places he was less careful about offend-
ing English sensibilities. Ottar the Black's *Knútsdrápa* celebrates his victories
over them in no uncertain terms, and Sighvat's *Knútsdrápa* (which was not,
however, certainly composed at Cnut's request) credits him with killing or
driving out each and every one of Æthelred's sons.[15]

At times, as we know from the Letters of 1019–20 and 1027, and from his
promulgation of Wulfstan's legal work, Cnut wanted to appear solicitous for
the welfare of his people, but how far such statements were mirrored in his
government there is no way of knowing. He was generous to some English
churches when it came to offering precious gifts, and made full use of the
considerable opportunities which religion offered for enhancing and legit-
imising his own position, but whether his reign was generally beneficial to
the church is far from clear. Some foundations are known to have been
pressed by taxation and the royal servants who levied it, and this may have
been one factor leading to an apparent recession in church building.

In other areas too, what did not happen may be just as significant as what
did. Major scholars were active in Æthelred's reign, in continuance of the
activities of the tenth-century monastic reformation. Brihtferth of Ramsey
wrote lives of two bishops of Worcester, St Ecgwine (d.717) and Ramsey's
patron St Oswald (d.992), and produced the *Historia regum*, a chronicle of
Northumbrian history to 888, and the *Manual*, a guide to the church

[13] *Chron. Rams.*, pp.140–43.
[14] Gaimar, *L'Estoire*, ed. Bell, pp.140, 151; translated Hardy and Martin, ii. 143, 151.
[15] It is unlikely that Englishmen could have understood such poems unless they had become bilingual,
    but many of Cnut's court may have done so.

calendar in Latin and English which has been described as the most important scientific treatise to appear in England since the time of Bede.[16] Ælfric
was another product of the reformers, having been taught by Bishop
Æthelwold of Winchester. He adapted existing Latin lives of Æthelwold and
King Edmund of East Anglia (turning the latter into English), as well as
writing a *Grammar* and a *Colloquy* to help boys learning Latin, translating
parts of the Old Testament into English, and producing an extensive series
of sermons and saints' lives also in the vernacular.[17] The sermons were
intended to be used by priests, including the rural clergy, and Archbishop
Wulfstan, who received guidance from Ælfric, wrote English homilies too,
as well as legal material for Æthelred and Cnut, and a range of other works,
such as the *Institutes of Polity*, which is concerned with status and the correct
ordering and government of society. Wulfstan, like Ælfric, was a learned
man,[18] but they and Brihtferth were not the only authors active in
Æthelred's time. Wulfstan the Cantor wrote his *Narratio metrica* on St
Swithun and a Latin life of St Æthelwold later adapted by Ælfric, and
Shaftesbury Abbey may shortly after 1000 have provided itself with a biography of Edward the Martyr, whose relics it possessed, while accounts of
Archbishop Dunstan were the work of an English cleric known as B (possibly signifying Brihthelm) and a monk of Ghent, Adelard.

Cnut's reign has little to set beside all this, apart from Wulfstan's later
writings. The narrative of the Danish conquest in the *Anglo-Saxon Chronicle*
was produced in his time, but (the later brief *Chronicle* entries apart) no
contemporary Englishman celebrated Cnut's achievements as far as we
know. This was left to the Icelandic skalds and the foreign cleric who later
wrote the *Encomium Emmae*. Despite the popularity of the cult of St
Ælfheah, Christ Church Canterbury possessed no life of him until the century's end. English scribes continued to copy earlier works in the
vernacular, especially those of Ælfric, which were sometimes modified,[19]
and the *Chronicle* A text was transcribed in Canterbury to form G (largely
destroyed by fire in 1731). The reign also saw the manufacture of some lavishly illustrated Latin gospel books. But there seems to have been more
rewriting than new writing. It could be that Cnut has been exceptionally
unfortunate in the survival of sources, and clearly the burst of activity
generated by the tenth-century monastic reform movement may have

---

[16] Stenton, *Anglo-Saxon England*, pp. 450–51.
[17] For the Ælfric canon, see *Homilies of Ælfric*, ed. Pope, i. 136–45.
[18] On Wulfstan's works and learning, *Sermo Lupi*, ed. Whitelock, pp. 17–37.
[19] As, for example, in BL MS Cotton Vitellius C. v. See *Homilies of Ælfric*, ed. Pope, i. 27–28.

expended itself anyway by around 1020; at the least, the Danish conquest did little to reverse this decline, and may have contributed to it.

If there is scant evidence that Cnut had much interest in stimulating Latin learning, he gave his Icelandic poets little cause for complaint. Thorarin Praise-Tongue was paid fifty marks, a very considerable sum, for his *Tøgdrápa* and such verses bring us as near as we shall ever get to identifying the ways in which Cnut wanted to be seen, by himself and others. He was the friend of monks and a pilgrim to Rome, but above all he was the successful warrior, concerned to have his victories put on record and celebrated in his court: for all his piety, he may well have agreed with the *Beowulf* poet that fame after death is a man's best memorial. If so, that fame was not to be quite as he envisaged. The poets of the ancient north occasionally exhibited a pessimism which has endeared them to modern audiences, some of whom need little convincing that Time washes away our victories. Yet even they could not have foretold that the achievements of one of the most successful of all early medieval kings would not only be largely forgotten, but replaced by a story in which he demonstrated his folly by attempting to turn back the tide. Whether or not this tale was rooted in a misunderstanding of a genuine act of extravagant piety, where he used his failure to demonstrate the insignificance of his power compared with that of the king of heaven, the Christianity which Cnut cultivated so assiduously, and which was so much a part of the political world in which he operated, cost him rather more than he knew.

APPENDICES I-V
SELECT BIBLIOGRAPHY
GENEALOGICAL TABLES
INDEX

APPENDIX I

THE *ANGLO-SAXON CHRONICLE* C, D AND E TEXTS 1017–35

C

1017 In this year King Cnut succeeded to all the kingdom of the English, and divided it in four, to himself Wessex, and Thorkell East Anglia, and Eadric Mercia, and Eric Northumbria. And in this year Ealdorman Eadric was killed, and Northman son of Ealdorman Leofwine, and Æthelweard son of Æthelmær the Stout and Brihtric son of Ælfheah of Devonshire. And King Cnut drove out the ætheling Eadwig and afterwards had him killed. And then before 1 August the king ordered to be fetched to him the widow of King Æthelred, Richard's daughter, to be his wife.

1018 In this year was that tribute paid over all England. That was in all £72,000, in addition to what the citizens of London paid, £10,500. And some of the army then went to Denmark and forty ships remained with King Cnut, and Danes and English came to an agreement at Oxford.

1019 In this year King Cnut went to Denmark and stayed there all winter.

D

1017 In this year King Cnut succeeded to all the kingdom of England, and divided it in four, to himself Wessex, and Thorkell East Anglia, and Eadric Mercia, and Eric Northumbria. In this year was also Ealdorman Eadric killed, and Northman son of Ealdorman Leofwine, and Æthelweard son of Æthelmær the Stout and Brihtric son of Ælfheah of Devonshire. And King Cnut drove out the ætheling Eadwig and Eadwig king of the ceorls. And then before 1 August the king ordered to be fetched to him the widow of the other king, Æthelred, Richard's daughter, to be his wife.

1018 In this year was that tribute paid over all England. That was in all £72,000, in addition to what the citizens of London paid, that was £10,500. And some of the army then went to Denmark and forty ships remained with King Cnut, and Danes and English came to an agreement at Oxford to Edgar's law.

1019 In this year King Cnut went with nine ships to Denmark and stayed there all winter. And in this year Archbishop Ælfstan died, who was named Lyfing, and he was a man very firm in counsel, whether in matters of church or state.

E

1017 In this year King Cnut succeeded to all the kingdom of the English, and divided it in four, to himself Wessex, and Thorkell East Anglia, and Eadric Mercia, and Eric Northumbria. And in this year Ealdorman Eadric was killed, and Northman son of Ealdorman Leofwine, and Æthelweard son of Æthelmær the Stout and Brihtric son of Ælfgeat of Devonshire. And King Cnut drove out the ætheling Eadwig and Eadwig king of the ceorls. And then before 1 August the king ordered to be fetched to him the widow of Æthelred the other king, Richard's daughter, to be his queen.

1018 In this year was that tribute paid over all England. That was in all £72,000, in addition to what the citizens of London paid, £11,000.[1] And some of the army then went to Denmark and forty ships remained with King Cnut, and Danes and English came to an agreement at Oxford. And in this year Abbot Æthelsige died at Abingdon and Æthelwine succeeded thereto.

1019 In this year King Cnut went to Denmark and stayed there all winter.

C

1020 In this year Archbishop Lyfing died and King Cnut came back to England, and then at Easter there was a great meeting at Cirencester. Then Ealdorman Æthelweard was outlawed and Eadwig king of the ceorls. And in this year the king went to *Assandun* and Archbishop Wulfstan and Earl Thorkell and many bishops with him and hallowed the minster at *Assandun*.

1021 In this year at Martinmas King Cnut outlawed Earl Thorkell.

1022 In this year King Cnut went out with his ships to *wiht* and Archbishop Æthelnoth went to Rome.

D

1020 In this year King Cnut came back to England, and at Easter there was a great meeting at Cirencester. Then Ealdorman Æthelweard was outlawed. And in this year the king and Earl Thorkell went to *Assandun* and Archbishop Wulfstan and other bishops and also abbots and many monks and hallowed that minster at *Assandun*. And the monk Æthelnoth, he who was dean at Christ Church, was in the same year, on 13 November, consecrated as bishop of Christ Church.

1021 In this year at Martinmas King Cnut outlawed Earl Thorkell, and Bishop Ælfgar the charitable died in the early morning of Christmas (Day).

1022 In this year King Cnut went out with his ships to *Wihtland* and Archbishop Æthelnoth went to Rome, and was there received with much honour by Benedict the reverend pope, and he placed the pallium on him with his own hands, and consecrated and blessed him with great reverence on 7 October. And the archbishop immediately sang Mass on the same day and soon thereafter dined in state with the pope himself. And also he himself took the pallium from St Peter's altar, and then afterwards journeyed happily home to his country.

1023 In this year King Cnut in London in St

E

1020 In this year King Cnut came to England. And then at Easter there was a great meeting at Cirencester. Then Ealdorman Æthelweard was outlawed. And in this year the king went to *Assandun* and Archbishop Lyfing died. And Æthelnoth, monk and dean at Christ Church, was the same year consecrated as bishop thereto.

1021 In this year King Cnut at Martinmas outlawed Earl Thorkell.

1022 In this year King Cnut went out with his ships to *Wiht*, and Bishop Æthelnoth went to Rome, and was there received by Benedict the pope with much honour, and he placed the pallium on him with his own hands, and with reverence consecrated him archbishop. And he afterwards said Mass with the pallium as the pope ordered him, and he dined after that with the pope and afterwards returned home with his full blessing. And Abbot Leofwine, he who was unlawfully driven out of Ely, was his companion, and he there cleared himself of each thing that had been said against him, as the pope directed, in the witness of the archbishop and of all the company which was with him.

1023 In this year King Cnut came back to England and Thorkell and he were reconciled, and he entrusted Denmark and his son to Thorkell, and the king took Thorkell's son with him to England. And he afterwards had St Ælfheah's relics transferred from London to Canterbury.

1024 [no entry]

Paul's minster gave full leave to Archbishop Æthelnoth and Bishop Brihtwine and all the servants of God who were with them that they might take up from the tomb the archbishop St Ælfheah. And they did so on 8 June, and the glorious king and the archbishop and the diocesan bishops and the earls and very many ecclesiastical and also lay people conveyed his holy body by ship over the Thames to Southwark and there entrusted the holy martyr to the archbishop and his company, and they then with a distinguished crowd and pleasant joy took him to Rochester. Then on the third day Emma the Lady came with her kingly child Harthacnut, and they then all with great pomp and joy and songs of praise conveyed the holy archbishop to Canterbury, and thus brought him worthily into Christ Church on 11 June. Afterwards, on the eighth day, on 15 June, Archbishop Æthelnoth and Bishop Ælfsige and Bishop Brihtwine and all who were with them placed St Ælfheah's holy body on the north side of Christ's altar, to the praise of God and the honour of the holy archbishop, and to the eternal salvation of all those who daily seek his holy body there with devoted hearts and with all humility. May God Almighty have mercy on all Christian men through the holy merits of St Ælfheah.

1024 [no entry]

1023 In this year Archbishop Wulfstan died and Ælfric succeeded him. And the same year Archbishop Æthelnoth transferred the relics of St Ælfheah the archbishop to Canterbury from London.

1024 Hic Ricardus Secundus obiit; Ricardus filius eius regnauit prope uno anno, et post eum regnauit frater eius viii annis.[2]

C	D	E
1025 [no entry]	**1025** [no entry]	**1025** In this year King Cnut went with ships to Denmark to the Holme, at the Holy River, and there came against him Ulf and Eglaf and a very great army, both a land army and a naval army, of Swedes. And there were very many men killed on King Cnut's side, both Danes and English, and the Swedes had possession of the field.
1026 [no entry]	**1026** In this year Bishop Ælfric went to Rome and received the pallium from Pope John on 12 November.	**1026** [no entry]
1027 [no entry]	**1027** [no entry]	**1027** [no entry]
1028 In this year King Cnut went to Norway with fifty ships.	**1028** In this year King Cnut went from England with fifty ships to Norway and drove King Olaf from that land and appropriated all that land.	**1028** In this year King Cnut went from England with fifty ships to Norway and drove King Olaf from that land and appropriated that land.
1029 [no entry] [annal no. squeezed in]	**1029** In this year King Cnut came back home to England.	**1029** In this year King Cnut came back home to England.
1030 In this year King Olaf was killed in Norway by his own people and was afterwards holy. And before that in this year the brave Earl Hakon died at sea.	**1030** In this year King Olaf came back to Norway and that people gathered themselves together and fought him. And he was there killed.	**1030** In this year King Olaf came back to Norway and that people gathered themselves together and fought him. And he was there killed.
1031 [no entry]	**1031** In this year King Cnut went to Rome, and as soon as he came home he then went to Scotland, and the king of the Scots surrendered	**1031** In this year King Cnut went to Rome, and the same year he went to Scotland and the king of the Scots submitted to him, Malcolm and two

to him and became his man, but held to it for a little while.

1032 [no entry]

1033 [no entry]

1034 In this year Bishop Æthelric died, and he lies at Ramsey.

1035 In this year King Cnut died on 12 November at Shaftesbury, and he was taken from there to Winchester, and there buried, and Ælfgifu the Lady then stayed there...

other kings, Mælbæth and Iehmarc. Rodbertus comes obiit in peregrinatione; et successit Rex Willelmu in puerili ætate.

1032 In this year there appeared the wildfire such as no man ever remembered before, and also it everywhere did damage in many places. And in the same year Ælfsige bishop of Winchester died, and Ælfwine the king's priest succeeded thereto.

1033 In this year died Bishop Merehwit of Somerset, and he is buried at Glastonbury.

1034 In this year Bishop Æthelric died.

1035 [no entry]

1032 [no entry]

1033 In this year Bishop Leofsige died, and his body rests at Worcester. And Brihtheah was raised to his see.

1034 In this year Bishop Ælfric (?Æthelric) died, and lies at Ramsey. And the same year Malcolm king of Scotland died.

1035 In this year King Cnut died and his son Harold succeeded to the kingdom. He died at Shaftesbury on 12 November, and was taken to Winchester and buried there, and Ælfgifu the Lady then stayed there...

1036 In this year King Cnut died at Shaftesbury and he is buried in Winchester in the Old Minster, and he was king over all England very nearly twenty winters....

¹ See *ASC*, ii 201–02.
² The Latin entries in E were added from a set of Norman annals probably after 1066.

APPENDIX II

BRIEF LIST OF ROYAL CHARTERS AND WRITS 1017–35

SAWYER DATE DETAILS
NO.

949 N/d Cnut to Fécamp Abbey, land at *Rammesleah*, Sussex, with its port. See also S 982.

950 1018 Cnut to Archbishop Ælfstan (i.e. Lyfing) of Canterbury, grant of land at Hazelhurst, Sussex.

951 1018 Cnut to Bishop Brihtwold (called Burhwold) of Cornwall, confirmation of grant by King Edmund exchanging land in Cornwall for land in Devon. Authenticity uncertain.

952 1018 Cnut to Christ Church Canterbury, confirmation of privileges. Authenticity uncertain.

953 1018 Cnut to St German's minster Cornwall, grant of freedom from royal taxation and secular burdens. Authenticity uncertain.

None 1018 Foundation charter of Buckfast Abbey, granted by Cnut at the request of Ealdorman Æthelweard. Text lost. See above, p.67, n.26.

954 1019 Cnut to Abbot Æthelwold and the brethren of St Mary's Exeter, grant of freedom from royal and secular burdens. Authenticity uncertain.

955 1019 Cnut to Agemund, grant of land at Cheselbourne, Dorset.

956 1019 Cnut to New Minster Winchester, restoration of land at Drayton, Hampshire.

957 1020 Cnut to Evesham Abbey, grant of land at Badby and Newnham, Northamptonshire. Probable forgery.

958 1022 Cnut to Abbot Leofric of Ely, grant of land at Wood Ditton in exchange for land at Cheveley, Cambridgeshire. Probable forgery.

959 1023 Cnut to Christ Church Canterbury, grant of the port of Sandwich, Kent. Probable forgery.

960 1023 Cnut to Leofwine, confirmation of land at Hannington, Hampshire.

961 1024 Cnut to Orc, grant of land at Portisham, Dorset.

962 1026 Cnut to Bishop Lyfing, grant of land at Abbots Worthy, Hampshire. Authenticity uncertain.

963 1031 Cnut to Æthelric, grant of land at Meavy, Devon.

971 1031 Cnut to Hunuwine, grant of land at Stoke Canon, Devon.

964 1032 Cnut to Abingdon Abbey, grant of land at Lyford, Berkshire, and the *monasteriolium* of St Martin in Oxford.

SAWYER NO.	DATE	DETAILS
965	1032	Cnut to Crowland Abbey, confirmation of lands and privileges. Forgery.
966	1032	Cnut to Glastonbury Abbey, grant and confirmation of privileges. Authenticity uncertain.
967	1033	Cnut to Abbot Siward and the brethren of Abingdon Abbey, grant of land at Myton, Warwickshire.
968	1033	Cnut to Archbishop Ælfric of York, grant of land at Patrington, Yorkshire.
969	1033	Cnut to Bovi, grant of land at Horton, Dorset.
970	1033	Cnut to Earl Godwin, grant of land at Polhampton, Hampshire.
971		See above, after S 963.
972	1033	Cnut to Old Minster Winchester, grant of land at Bishop's Hull, Somerset.
973	1034	Cnut to Abingdon Abbey, grant of land at Myton, Warwickshire.
974	1035	Cnut to Bishop Eadsige, grant of land at Berwick, Kent.
975	1035	Cnut to the monks of Sherborne, grant of land at Corscombe, Dorset.
976	1035	Cnut to Old Minster Winchester, grant of freedom from secular service. Authenticity uncertain.
977	N/d	Cnut to the monk Æfic, grant of land at Newnham, Northamptonshire
978	N/d	Cnut to Bishop Ælfwine, confirmation of the lands owned by St Paul's in London.
979	N/d	Cnut to Abbot Æthelwine and the brethren of Athelney, grant of land at Seavington, Somerset.
980	N/d	Cnut to Bury St Edmunds Abbey, grant of privileges, and of renders of fish and eels. Probable forgery.
981	N/d	Cnut to Christ Church Canterbury, reversionary grant of land at Folkestone, Kent. Probable forgery. See also S 1643.
982	N/d	Cnut to Fécamp Abbey, grant of land at *Rammesleah* and Brede, Sussex, with two parts of the toll of Winchelsea. Authenticity uncertain. See also S 949.
983	N/d	Cnut to Godwin, grant of land at *Lytlacotan* (unidentified).
984	N/d	Cnut to St Benet of Holme Abbey, grant of land at Horning, Norfolk. Authenticity uncertain.
985	N/d	Writ of Cnut confirming the liberties of Christ Church Canterbury. Authenticity uncertain.
986	N/d	Writ of Cnut granting judicial and financial rights to Archbishop Æthelnoth of Canterbury. Authenticity uncertain.
987	N/d	Writ of Cnut in favour of Archbishop Æthelnoth. Authenticity uncertain.
988	N/d	Writ of Cnut granting to Archbishop Æthelnoth all the property which Ælfmær had. Authenticity uncertain.
989	N/d	Writ of Cnut granting judicial and financial rights to the brethren of St Augustine's Canterbury. Probable forgery.
990	N/d	Writ of Cnut granting St Augustine's Canterbury the body of St Mildred, all her land, and all the customs belonging to her church. Authenticity uncertain.

SAWYER NO.	DATE	DETAILS
991	N/d	Writ of Cnut granting Brihtwine land at Bengeworth, Worcestershire, with reversion to Evesham Abbey. Authenticity uncertain.
992	N/d	Writ of Cnut confirming the judicial and financial rights of the priests of St Paul's, London. Authenticity uncertain.
1642	1035	Cnut to Bishop Eadsige, grant of the church of St Martin, Canterbury, and land at Appledore and Wittersham, Kent. Text incomplete.
1643	dated 1038	Cnut to Christ Church Canterbury, grant of land at Folkestone, Kent. Text incomplete. Probable forgery.

APPENDIX III

THE PRODUCTION
OF ROYAL CHARTERS AND WRITS
1017–35

There are basically two ways of tracing the origin of a document. Some survive on single sheets of parchment in what is apparently their original form, and comparison of the script with others of the period can occasionally place the scribe in a particular church. Otherwise, there is the text itself, which contains a number of distinct elements, or formulae (see Appendix IV). Pictorial and verbal invocations (for example, a cross, and words such as 'In the name of the Lord') are often followed by a proem stating why the grant is being made. The royal name and title then precede a dispositive clause which actually makes the transfer of ownership, whether of land or privileges, perhaps with certain reservations, and a sanction threatens those ignoring it with divine wrath. If an estate is involved a boundary clause in Old English often describes its location, and there is usually a dating clause and a witness list headed by the king. Charter draughtsmen had various options. They could copy an earlier document in full, making only such essential changes as the names of donor, donee, grant and witnesses; or they could employ a proem from one existing text, a dispositive clause from another, a sanction from a third, and so on; or they could formulate an original. Hence, some formulae are unique, while others occur fairly frequently. The appearance of all or part of a text's formulae in other charters can offer clues about its origin, and this method can be used with all charters (including those only extant in later cartularies — books into which charters were copied). But it is hazardous, because many documents have not survived, while those which have are sometimes either outright forgeries or originals altered to meet the forger's purpose. Using formulae to trace a charter's origin is therefore akin to doing a jigsaw with unknown numbers of genuine pieces missing and spurious ones present What, for all that, happens when Cnut's charters are examined?

Their script suggests that S 950 and 974, both connected with Christ Church Canterbury and surviving in the original, were written by its scribes. S 950, a grant to Archbishop Lyfing, has been attributed to Eadui Basan, probably a Christ Church monk, and responsible for several fine gospel books,[1] while S 974, to the future archbishop Eadsige, is also in a Canterbury hand, and parallels in wording hint that its draughtsman had before him S 447 and 464, tenth-century charters in the cathedral archives. Its invocation reappears with additions in S 959, Cnut's grant of Sandwich to

---

[1] Backhouse *et al., The Golden Age of Anglo-Saxon Art*, No. 169; for S 974, Bishop, *English Caroline Minuscule*, p.xxiii. S 950 is translated in Appendix IV.

them. This exists in Old English and Latin versions which may represent alterations made to an original text in the 1070s or 1080s. S 981, giving Folkestone, is almost certainly a late-eleventh-century forgery, while S 952, confirming the privileges of Christ Church, is also dubious, having come down to us in an irregular form in later copies. The four writs in favour of Christ Church, S 985–8, are extant as copies in two of its gospel books, and even if genuine it is uncertain whether they reached Canterbury in anything more than an oral form, which entry into holy texts was intended to strengthen and preserve.[2]

There are links between S 970, a grant to Earl Godwin in Hampshire, and S 972, to the Old Minster Winchester. Godwin is said to have made them gifts, and part of the land he received by S 970 was in their possession in the Confessor's time. The bulk of its text is also found in S 1001, a charter to the bishop of Winchester from 1044, and there are links with S 1008, 1009 and 1012, further gifts by Edward to the bishop, Godwin, and Old Minster respectively. There are some complex possibilities here, but one is that S 970 and 972 were drawn up in the Old Minster. Maybe S 970 was only drafted when Godwin gave them the land concerned – i.e. later than its date of 1033.

S 951, 953, 954, 962, 963 and 971 can be connected with the sees of Crediton and Cornwall, united when Lyfing of Crediton annexed the latter on the death of Bishop Brihtwold, his uncle, perhaps late in Cnut's reign.[3] S 963 and 971 (see also, above, pp.68–69) give Devon estates to laymen. Their formulae and witness-lists have much in common, while the sanction of S 963 is similar to that of S 890, an Æthelredian charter in favour of the bishop of Crediton, and the royal styles of both, and the sanction of S 971, are close to those of S 880, from Æthelred to the bishop of Cornwall. Both also share the phrase by which Cnut signs with S 953 and 962, and with S 880, and Emma's signature with S 951, 953 and 962. S 951, Cnut's confirmation of a gift to Brihtwold of Cornwall, survives in a somewhat later manuscript, and may not be completely authentic. Its witness list is very similar to that of S 953, and it shares its proem and royal title, and part of its dispositive clause, with S 962. S 953 and 954 both appear to be partially modelled on S 880, and may be forgeries. S 962, to Lyfing of Crediton, has elements in common with other members of the group, but is dated 1026, although Lyfing probably did not receive his see until at least 1027. Either it is a forgery or Lyfing had it written some time after receiving the land. On the whole, it looks as though these charters were drafted by churchmen connected with the sees of Crediton, Cornwall and Exeter (to which Crediton was moved in 1050) and that they produced S 963 and 971 for local laymen.[4]

[2] On S 952, *Writs*, p.169; S 959 and 981, Brooks, *The Early History of the Church of Canterbury*, pp.292–94, 300–01; S 985–88, *Writs*, pp.168–72; S 985, Brooks, *Early History*, pp.288–90. It is not in favour of the writ S 987 that it permits Archbishop Æthelnoth to discharge the obligations on his land as he did before Æthelric was reeve, for if Æthelric is the *prefectus* whose name is smudged in the witness list of S 950 of 1018 (see Appendix IV) he was reeve of Kent before Æthelnoth became archbishop.

[3] This group is discussed in *Encomium*, pp.59–60, and also includes S 998. What follows owes much to Chaplais, 'The Authenticity of the Royal Anglo-Saxon Diplomas of Exeter'. A note in the episcopal lists given by John of Worcester says that Lyfing took Cornwall in the Confessor's time, but this may be mistaken. William of Malmesbury (*GP*, ii. 94, p.200) implies that it occurred under Cnut, and Brihtwold's last charter signature is S 979 of *c.*1023x32. Understanding of these charters will doubtless be clarified further by the publication of *Charters of Exeter, Crediton and St Germans*, edited by Charles Insley.

[4] S 963 survived in the archives of Christ Church Canterbury, and Bishop, *English Caroline Minuscule*, p. xxiii, attributed it to a Canterbury scribe. However (ibid.), the scripts used in Canterbury and Crediton/Exeter in the middle of the eleventh century closely resembled each other.

Their neighbours in Sherborne were acting likewise. Two Dorset laymen, Orc and Bovi, received charters (S 961, 969) with similarities in the dispositive clauses and disqualifications of older grants in almost identical terms, while Bovi's charter has links with S 933, a grant by Æthelred to Sherborne from 1014. Cnut's Sherborne charter, S 975, has a phrase introducing the bounds very similar to that of S 1004, a later gift to Orc by the Confessor, which is itself linked to S 933 and 961. A further connection between S 961, 969 and 975 is that all include royal priests among the witnesses, whereas only four of Cnut's other charters do,[5] and one of them, S 979, is related to S 975 (see below). Other churches too seemingly drafted their own charters. Two of Cnut's Abingdon grants, S 964 and 967, have parallel material and use formulae found in other Abingdon documents, but this is not true of a third, S 973, which concerns the same land as S 967.[6] Similarly, S 968, giving Patrington to the archbishop of York, was possibly based on S 679 and 712, tenth-century charters from the York archives, while S 966, to Glastonbury, has links with other of their documents, and was probably either drafted or forged there. There are serious doubts, too, about the authenticity of the Bury St Edmunds charter, S 980, apparently concocted during a dispute sixty years later.[7] It has a witness-list closely akin to that of the St Benet of Holme grant, S 984. One was perhaps drawn up partly on the basis of the other. Cnut's Ely charter, S 958, may be spurious too. A phrase referring to the 'decree of Peter, prince of the apostles' in the signature of Archbishop Æthelnoth of Canterbury implies that he had got back from his visit to Rome in October 1022, while the appearance of Bishop Gerbrand of Roskilde, known to have been consecrated by Æthelnoth in England, could be connected with Cnut's return from Denmark early in 1023. Unfortunately, S 958's elaborate dating clause is correct for 23 June 1022, and this raises the possibility that it was fabricated during later litigation over the estate, Wood Ditton in Cambridgeshire, which Ely leased to Archbishop Stigand of Canterbury under the Confessor and subsequently lost.[8] However, the witness list could have come from a genuine charter, as Gerbrand's presence is unusual, and not the likely invention of a forger. S 957 is almost definitely an Evesham forgery based on S 977, for both deal with land later in dispute between Evesham and Crowland. S 977 itself seems to be genuine. The grantee, the monk Æfic, may have been dean of Evesham,[9] and the document was possibly drawn up there. It has some wording in common with S 911, Æthelred's charter for Evesham. Even so, the signature of Æthelric of Dorchester implies that he was connected with the drafting, and the land concerned was within his diocese.[10]

S 977 is interesting because it has a passage in common with S 969, of the Sherborne group, and Cnut, Emma and Wulfstan of York's signatures match those of S 910, a Devon grant of Æthelred which has survived in the Sherborne cartulary. Also, there are extensive parallels between the wording of another of the Sherborne group, S 975, and Cnut's

[5] S 962, 964, 967, 979.
[6] Keynes, *Diplomas*, p.11, is sceptical about the authenticity of many Abingdon charters of this period; they have been discussed more recently in the edition (*Charters of Abingdon Abbey*) by Kelly, who edits and comments on those attributed to Cnut in *Part 2*, pp.540–49.
[7] *Writs*, pp.433–34; Gransden, *Historical Writing in England*, pp.10–11.
[8] *Lib. El.*, p.417; Fleming, *Kings and Lords*, p.82. Keynes, 'Cnut's earls', p.49, treats S 958 as authentic, and suggests that Gerbrand was consecrated before Æthelnoth left for Rome.
[9] *ASC*, i. 160, reports the death of dean Æfic of Evesham in 1037.
[10] I have not discussed the Fécamp grants S 949 and 982 (see Haskins, 'A Charter of Canute for Fécamp'), S 965, 976, 978, 983 and the writs S 989–992 (see *Writs*). On S 955, 956 and 960, see below.

grant to Athelney, S 979.[11] These similarities could be attributed to the production of charters not by local ecclesiastics, as argued above, but by a royal secretariat. Professor Keynes believes that such an office existed from at least the reign of Æthelstan (d.939) onwards, while Dr Chaplais has denied its existence.[12] A further point, stressed by Keynes in his analysis of Æthelred's charters, is that there are regularities in the witness lists. Emma's signature, for example, appears after those of the archbishops in charters of 1018 and 1019, but thereafter almost always before,[13] except in texts of the Crediton group. Also, the bishops of Winchester and London practically invariably witness high in the order, as does Brihtwold of Ramsbury. Of the abbots, those of New Minster Winchester and Glastonbury are usually given pride of place, and it is noticeable that Brihtwig of Glastonbury very often signs higher than Brihtmær of New Minster, but his successor Æthelweard does not. The earls' signatures are much the same: Thorkell of East Anglia appears first if at all; later, Godwin of Wessex signs first and Leofric of Mercia usually second: even in the gift to the archbishop of York (S 968), witnessed by many northern thegns, Siward of Northumbria is third.

Something must lie behind such regularities, if not necessarily the drafting of documents by a royal secretariat. Ecclesiastics attending national meetings probably often had scribes with them. Archbishop Wulfstan of York instructed that ink and parchment were to be taken to synods so that their instructions could be recorded, and we have seen that synods and meetings of the national council, the *witan*, could be broadly the same thing.[14] Also, Æthelred's confirmation (S 939) of the will of Æthelric of Bocking says that it was written down immediately and read out to king and *witan*. Its tenor suggests that this was done by a scribe from Christ Church Canterbury, yet the meeting had assembled at Cookham in Berkshire. Unless Archbishop Ælfric wrote it himself, he must have had a scribe with him. If various scribes drew up various charters at various meetings, with witness lists following a fixed order of seating or ranking, or if they compiled memoranda of those present for future use on the same basis, it would not be surprising if lists produced by different agencies showed similarities. Although no direct evidence survives on seating arrangements, it is interesting that a London council in 1075 asked English elders about past episcopal seating practice, and was told that Canterbury ought to sit with York on the right and London on the left, with Winchester next to York.[15] This indicates that the English had followed rules of precedence, and may partially explain

---

[11] See further on this, n.16 below. Other links between charters apparently of different groups include the similar immunity clauses of S 955, 968, 969 and 973, and the sanctions of S955 and 968; but these are common formulae, like the phrase *Discedite a me maledicti in ignem aeternum,* used in the sanctions of S951, 955 and 968. The royal styles of S 966 and 969 are identical, but again are common, and S 960, 968 and 973 all begin with an invocation and a dating clause, while the archbishop of Canterbury's signature in S 956 is the same as Emma's in S 977. S 949, 956 and 960 briefly describe the circumstances of the donation, like some of Æthelred's charters. S 956 and 960 are also linked by both being grants in Hampshire, and are alone among Cnut's charters in having a second sanction after the witness list. Their invocations have words in common too; maybe they were produced by the same agency. See further the discussion in *Charters of the New Minster, Winchester,* ed. Miller, p.162.
[12] Keynes, *Diplomas* and Keynes, 'Royal government and the written word in late Anglo-Saxon England', p.256; Chaplais, 'The Anglo-Saxon Chancery: from the Diploma to the Writ'; Chaplais, 'The Royal Anglo-Saxon "Chancery" of the Tenth Century Revisited'. For a recent discussion, see *Charters of Abingdon Abbey Part 1,* ed. Kelly, pp.lxxiii ff.
[13] An exception is S 983.
[14] *Canons of Edgar,* ed. Fowler, p.2; above, pp.59–63.
[15] Lanfranc, *Letters,* ed. Clover and Gibson, pp.74–75.

why London and Winchester witness so high. Furthermore, if they also observed the provision of the fourth council of Toledo of 633, renewed in 1075, that bishops ought to sit according to the date of their ordination, this might account for the prominence of Brihtwold of Ramsbury, the most senior of Cnut's bishops. Equally, the alteration in the position of the abbots of New Minster and Glastonbury may reflect Æthelweard of Glastonbury taking a lower seat than his predecessor. There is no certainty that laymen too had their formal positions, but it is by no means impossible that they had.

Parallels in charter formulae could be explained in much the same way. If, as is probable, scribes from various churches associated together at meetings, documents with parallel wording may sometimes have resulted. Also, of course, ecclesiastics sometimes moved from one church to another, and must have taken their knowledge of charter formulae with them. It would not be totally implausible, for example, to connect the similarity of texts apparently produced in Sherborne and Evesham (see above) with the period of control of the latter by Bishop Æthelsige of Sherborne in Æthelred's reign.[16] All the same, Æthelred is known to have had a scribe,[17] Cnut may have done too, and some charters could have been drawn up by them. Indeed, it might be argued that important churches like Canterbury, York and Winchester drafted their own texts, that many of Cnut's other ecclesiastical grants are forgeries, and that parallels between such charters as remain, and links with those of Æthelred, are attributable to common origin in a central writing office. S 955 and 956 were both issued in 1019, although dissimilarities in their witness lists suggest not on the same occasion.[18] However, both have elaborate introductions possibly drafted by the same person. If so, this individual, apparently in attendance upon the king, may have been a royal scribe; but equally, he could have been associated with a major churchman. The likely ability of such people to perform extensive royal commissions on an ad hoc basis has been strikingly demonstrated by the discovery that the nearly 400 folios of Great Domesday were probably largely the work of a scribe connected with the bishop of Durham.[19] Such of Cnut's surviving writs as were originally issued, possibly with a two-sided seal attached, by the royal entourage may have been produced similarly.

Given that the links which there are between different texts can be explained in other ways, a royal writing office under Cnut is not conspicuous by its presence. Even so, the evidence is unsatisfactory, and it would be unwise to base too much upon it. The technique of tracing documents by comparing their wording is obviously rendered hazardous by the unknown number which have not survived, and might have spoken differently if they had. Indeed, the whole problem is one of such complexity as to seem incapable of final resolution. Still, there is a final point. The titles assigned to Cnut match those of his predecessors in referring to him as king of England, or of Britain, and sometimes of the surrounding islands. No undoubtedly genuine text includes his

---

[16] *Chron. Eve.*, p.80; above, p.118, n.34. Moreover, Æthelwine, bishop of Wells early in Cnut's reign, had previously been abbot of Evesham, and if the grant to Athelney (S 979), within the diocese of Wells, was drawn up by its diocesan bishop, one could (by postulating lost texts) thus explain the links between S 975 and 979. Such a theory can hardly be pressed, but does illustrate the complexities with which we are struggling.

[17] Keynes, *Diplomas*, pp.135–36.

[18] Identification of the scribe of S 956, which exists as an original, might take the matter further.

[19] Chaplais, 'William of Saint-Calais and the Domesday Survey'. I therefore differ from the judgement that 'while kings might on occasion have relied on others to produce the written records of government, it is simply inconceivable that they could have done so as a matter of normal course', Keynes, 'Royal government and the written word', p. 256.

Scandinavian territories,[20] although the introduction[21] of the Letter of 1027 does. It would be surprising if a royal secretariat, drafting formal Latin charters for a king ambitious enough and sufficiently conscious of his own status to eventually adopt a crown modelled on that of the German emperors,[22] ignored such an obvious way of demonstrating his authority.[23]

[20] S 976 mentions his rule over the Danes, and the Crowland forgery (S 965) Denmark, Norway and Sweden.
[21] This exists only in a later copy and the title may not be authentic. Above, p.97, n.66.
[22] Above, pp.127–28.
[23] Dr Chaplais tells me that he hopes to publish a paper which will argue that the physical appearance of surviving originals renders it unlikely that they were produced by a single agency.

A CHARTER OF CNUT
FROM 1018

S 950. Cnut grants land in Sussex to Archbishop Ælfstan (i.e. Lyfing) of Canterbury. This charter survives in a contemporary manuscript, and has been identified as the work of the Christ Church scribe Eadui Basan. There is a facsimile in Backhouse *et al*. The *Golden Age of Anglo-Saxon Art*, 'Sussex Anglo-Saxon Charters', p.166. This translation is based on that of Barker 1949, pp. 110–11. The boundary clause is in Anglo-Saxon. Part of the name of the fifth witness in the second column is smudged.

All things which are seen by human eyes in this present world quickly disappear, but the things which are located on the mountains above flourish in continual amenity, remaining fixed in eternity under the rule of the great thunderer; and therefore it is for us children of a dying age to devote ourselves, so that by good works we may earn enjoyment of the good things of heaven, to live forever with the holy angels. Whence, I, Cnut, king of the English, at the request of my wife and queen Ælfgifu, grant to the venerable Archbishop Ælfstan a certain grove of woodland commonly called Hazelhurst in the famous forest of Andredesweald, that he may have it for his lifetime with all the things rightly pertaining to it, free from all earthly service, and after his death may leave it to whatever heir he pleases in perpetual inheritance. If any man, as we do not wish, ever attempts to alter or infringe this our gift, may he be cursed forever by Christ and all his saints, unless before his death he makes amends with appropriate recompense for his breach of our royal decree. The aforesaid grove is surrounded by these bounds:

These are the forest boundaries of Hazelhurst. Firstly along the stream of the fern-clearing to the boundary of Rowley, from Rowley boundary along Holbeanwood boundary, from Holbeanwood boundary direct to Whiligh, above the smithy to the gate, from the gate into the ditch, along the ditch into the broad stream, down along the broad stream by the archbishop's boundary again into the fern-clearing stream. This charter was written in the eighteenth year when a thousand had passed, with the agreement of those witnesses whose names are written below.

> †I, CNUT, king, hand this gift over in perpetuity to the venerable archbishop ÆLFSTAN.
> †I, WULFSTAN, archbishop, corroborate this gift of the king.
> †I, ÆLFGIFU, queen, sought the gift for the aforementioned archbishop from my lord the king.

†I, GODWIN, bishop, confirmed.
†I, ÆLFWIG, bishop, assented.
†I, ÆLFMÆR bishop, agreed.
†I, ÆLFSIGE, bishop, corroborated
†I, BRIHTWOLD, bishop, handed over
†I, BRIHTWINE, bishop, concluded
†I, ÆLFMÆR abbot
†I, ÆLFWIG, abbot
†I, ÆLFRIC, abbot
†I, THURKIL, dux, witness

†I, GODWIN, dux, witness
†I, SIGERYD, minister, witness
†I, BRIHTRIC, minister, witness
†I, ÆTH [?ELRIC], prefect, witness
†I, ÆTHELRIC, faithful witness
†I, GODWIN, faithful witness
†I, ÆLFSIGE, faithful witness
†I, ÆLFRIC, faithful witness

APPENDIX V

THE SIZE OF DANISH SHIPS

In 1995, in the course of an article on the size of Danish ships which non-specialists are likely to find an extremely valuable contribution to the study of a complex subject, the naval historian Dr N.A.M. Rodger examined my calculations of the average size of crews to be deduced from the details given in the *Anglo-Saxon Chronicle* for the payments made to Harthacnut's fleet in 1041. After considering many possibilities, he judged them more likely to be right than wrong, in arriving at a figure of about eighty men a ship, 'which would fit a longship of twenty rooms or somewhat more'. However, he also made statements about and criticisms of my work which are not justified by what I actually wrote. My interest in the Harthacnut figures has always centred on them as evidence of taxation, of the kinds of sums paid to troops in Cnut's time, and of the numbers of men involved. Nowhere have I deduced the size of Danish ships, as distinct from that of their crews, from these figures, and hence Rodger's statements that I had 'calculated the size of the Danish ships' and proposed 'ships of eighty oars, or forty rooms' are completely incorrect.[1] It is true that I followed Dorothy Whitelock in translating the Anglo-Saxon word *hamele* as rowlock, when Rodger suggests that it in fact referred to oars rowed by means of tholes (rowlocks not being in use at this date), although he points out that as ships of this period in fact utilised oarports the *Anglo-Saxon Chronicle* is not in any case using the word here 'in its literal sense'. It is also true that I referred to the men paid at eight marks to the *hamele* as 'rowers'; as a non-specialist this still seems to me reasonable enough, given that *hamele* certainly has something to do with rowing, and that John of Worcester Latinised the word as *remex* (rower) early in the twelfth century.[2] However, as I was not concerned about the size of the ships I nowhere stated explicitly that I thought the number of rowers equivalent to the number of the vessels' oars, much less proposed 'ships of eighty oars, or forty rooms'; instead, I repeatedly used phrases referring to crew size: of crews which 'averaged eighty men a ship', of 'the average number of rowers to a ship', of 'average sizes for the ships' crews', and of crews which 'averaged fifty to eighty men

---

[1] Rodger, 'Cnut's Geld', 392, 401. Other historians criticised by Rodger on the same grounds could make the same defence. Neither Professor Campbell nor Dr Hooper, for example, have 'calculated the size of the Danish ships', the former (*The Anglo-Saxon State*, p.203) speaking not of ships but of 'ship's companies', and the latter ('Some Observations on the Navy in Late Anglo-Saxon England', p.205) of 'some eighty men to each of these ships'.

[2] JW, ii. 530–31.

a ship'.[3] It is true that the equivalence of rower and oar might have been inferred from the use of the term 'rowlock', but I also commented that Ole Crumlin-Pedersen had told me that the ship known as Skuldelev 2 (found in Roskilde Fjord in Denmark, but now believed to have been built in Ireland) might have had a crew of eighty men, and as this ship probably had between forty and fifty oar-ports there was in fact a rather stronger inference that I did not think the number of 'rowers' and oar-ports necessarily identical.[4] Furthermore, this sentence on Skuldelev 2 and my consistent (and deliberate) use of phrases like 'ship's crews' might also have suggested to Rodger that I had considered both the possibility that the term *hamele* was not being used 'in its literal sense' and that vessels could often have contained more men than rowing positions, both considerations which according to him I ignored. At the very least, there is a significant difference between a reader's inference and an author's explicit statement, a difference of which Rodger's article, and his attribution to me of views that I have never expressed, takes insufficient account.

[3] Lawson, 'The collection of Danegeld and Heregeld', 721–22, 738; '"Those stories look true"', 386; *Cnut*, p.177.
[4] Not being concerned with the size of ships, I did not comment on the number of rowing positions in Skuldelev 2.

SELECT BIBLIOGRAPHY

PRIMARY SOURCES

Adam of Bremen, *Gesta Hammaburgensis Ecclesiae Pontificum*, ed. B. Schmeidler (3rd edn., Hannover, 1917); trans. F.J. Tschan, *History of the Archbishops of Hamburg-Bremen* (New York, 1959).

Adémar of Chabannes, *Chronique*, ed. J. Chavanon (Paris, 1897).

Ælfric, *Catholic Homilies*, in *The homilies of the Anglo-Saxon Church*, ed. B. Thorpe (London, 1844–46).

Ælfric, *Homilies of Ælfric: A Supplementary Collection*, ed. J.C. Pope (Early English Text Society, 1967–68).

Ælfric, *Lives of Saints*, ed. W. Skeat (Early English Text Society, 1881–85).

Anglo-Saxon Charters, ed. A.J. Robertson (2nd edn., Cambridge, 1956).

Anglo-Saxon Chronicle, in *Two of the Saxon Chronicles Parallel*, ed. C. Plummer (2 vols, Oxford, 1892–99); the 'C' text is also in *The C-Text of the Old English Chronicles*, ed. H.A. Rositzke, *Beiträge zur englischen Philologie* (xxxiv 1940); the 'D' text is also in *The Anglo-Saxon Chronicle: a collaborative edition. Volume 6. MS D*, ed. G.P. Cubbin (Cambridge, 1996); there is a facsimile of E, *The Peterborough Chronicle*, ed. D. Whitelock (Early English Manuscripts in Facsimile IV, Copenhagen, 1954). The best translation of the *Chronicle* is in *EHD*; also trans. in *The Anglo-Saxon Chronicle*, ed. M.J. Swanton (London, 1996). See Appendix 1.

Anglo-Saxon Prose, ed. M.J. Swanton (London, 1975).

Anglo-Saxon Wills, ed. D. Whitelock (Cambridge, 1930).

Anglo-Saxon Writs, ed. F.E. Harmer (2nd edn., Stamford, 1989).

Annales Cambriæ, ed. J. Williams ab Ithel (RS 20, 1860).

Annales Danici Medii Ævi, ed. J. Jørgensen (Copenhagen, 1920).

Annales Monastici, ed. H.R. Luard (RS 36, 1864–69).

Annals of Tigernach, ed. W. Stokes, *Revue Celtique*, xvii (1896), 337–420.

Annals of Ulster, ed. S. Mac Airt and G. Mac Niocaill (Dublin, 1983).

The Battle of Maldon, ed. and trans. D. Scragg, in *The Battle of Maldon AD991*, ed. Scragg, pp. 18–31; also trans. *EHD*, No. 10.

Brut Y Tywysogyon, Peniarth Ms. 20 version, trans. T. Jones (Cardiff, 1952); *Red Book of Hergest version*, ed. T. Jones (Cardiff, 1955).

Carmen de Hastingae Proelio, ed. and trans. F. Barlow (Oxford, 1999).

Carmen de Hastingae Proelio, ed. and trans. C. Morton and H. Munz (Oxford, 1972).

Cartularium Saxonicum, ed. W. de G. Birch (London, 1885–93).

Charters of Abingdon Abbey Part 1, ed. S.E. Kelly (Oxford, 2000).

Charters of Abingdon Abbey Part 2, ed. S.E. Kelly (Oxford, 2001).

Charters of Burton Abbey, ed. P.H. Sawyer (London, 1979).

Charters of Exeter, Crediton and St Germans, ed. C. Insley (Oxford, forthcoming).

Charters of the New Minster, Winchester, ed. S. Miller (Oxford, 2001).

Charters of Rochester, ed. A. Campbell (London, 1973).

Charters of St Augustine's Abbey Canterbury and Minster-in-Thanet, ed. S.E. Kelly
   (Oxford, 1995).

Charters of Shaftesbury Abbey, ed. S.E. Kelly (Oxford, 1996).

Charters of Sherborne, ed. M.A. O'Donovan (Oxford, 1988).

Chronicon Abbatiæ de Evesham, ed. W.D. Macray (RS 29, 1863).

Chronicon Abbatiæ Rameseiensis, ed. W.D. Macray (RS 83, 1886).

Chronicon Monasterii de Abingdon, ed. J. Stevenson (RS 2, 1858).

Chronicon Roskildense, in *Scriptores Minores*, ed. Gertz, i. 3–33.

'Cnut's law code of 1018', ed. A.G. Kennedy, *ASE*, 11 (1983), 57–81.

Codex Diplomaticus Aevi Saxonici, ed. J. Kemble (London, 1839–48).

Corpus Poeticum Boreale, ed. G. Vigfússon and F.Y. Powell (Oxford, 1883).

The Crawford Collection of Early Charters and Documents, ed. A.S. Napier and W.H.
   Stevenson (Oxford, 1895).

Danmarks Runeindskrifter, ed. L. Jacobsen and E. Moltke (Copenhagen, 1942).

De Inventione Sanctae Crucis, ed. W. Stubbs (Oxford, 1861).

De Obsessione Dunelmi, in *Symeonis Monachi Opera Omnia*, ed. T. Arnold (RS 75,
   1882–5); translated Morris, *Marriage and Murder*, pp. 1–5.

De Primo Saxonum Adventu, in *Symeonis Monachi Opera Omnia*, ed. T. Arnold (RS 75,
   1882–85).

Diplomatarium Danicum, ii. ed. L. Weibull (Copenhagen, 1963).

Domesday Book, ed. A. Farley and H. Ellis (London, 1783–1816); and published by
   the Phillimore Press in county volumes.

Dudo of St Quentin, *De Moribus et Actis primorum Normanniæ Ducum*, ed. J. Lair
   (Société des Antiquaires de Normandie, Caen, 1865); trans. E. Christiansen as *Dudo
   of St Quentin, History of the Normans* (Woodbridge, 1998).

Eadmer, *Historia Novorum in Anglia*, ed. M. Rule (RS 81, 1884); trans. G. Bosanquet,
   Eadmer's History of Recent Events in England (London, 1964).

The Earliest English Poems, ed. M. Alexander (Harmondsworth, 1966).

Encomium Emmae Reginae, ed. and trans. A. Campbell, with a supplementary
   introduction by Simon Keynes (Cambridge, 1998); first published as Camden Third
   Series, lxxii, 1949.

English Historical Documents c.500–1042, ed. D. Whitelock (2nd edn., London, 1979).

English Kalendars before A.D. 1100, ed. F. Wormald (Henry Bradshaw Society, 1934).

The Exeter Book, ed. R.W. Chambers *et al.* (London, 1933).

Facsimiles of Ancient Charters in the British Museum, ed. E.A. Bond (London, 1873–78).

Förster, M. ed., 'Die Altenglische Glossenhandschrift Plantinus 32 (Antwerpen) und
   Additional 32246 (London)', *Anglia*, xli (1917), 153–54. Prints a copy of a letter to
   a priest *Ælf* preserved in Antwerp, Plantin-Moretus Museum, MS 47, f. 48v. There
   is a facsimile in Bodley, MS Facs. d. 76.

Fulbert, *The Letters and Poems of Fulbert of Chartres*, ed. F. Behrends (Oxford, 1976).

Gaimar, G., *L'Estoire des Engleis*, ed. A. Bell (Oxford, 1960); ed. and trans. Sir T.D.
   Hardy and C.T. Martin (RS 91, 1888–89).

Gervase of Canterbury, *Gesta Regum*, ed. W. Stubbs, *The Historical Works of Gervase of Canterbury* (RS 73, 1879–80).

Die Gesetze der Angelsachsen, ed. F. Liebermann (Halle, 1898–1916).

Goscelin, *De Vita Sancti Wlsini*, ed. C.H. Talbot, *Revue Bénédictine*, lxix (1959), 73–85.

Goscelin, *Liber de Miraculis S. Augustinis*, *Acta Sanctorum Maii*, vi (Antwerp, 1688), 397–411.

Goscelin, *Translatio Sancte Mildrethe Virginis*, ed. D.W. Rollason, *Mediaeval Studies*, 48 (1986), 139–210.

Goscelin, *Vita S. Edithe*, ed. A. Wilmart, *Analecta Bollandiana*, lvi (1938), 34–101, 265–302.

Gunnlaug Serpent's Tongue, *Drápa* on Æthelred (only the refrain survives), ed. Jónsson AI, 194; BI (with Danish translation), 184; Kock, i. 98; *Gunnlaug's Saga Ormstungu*, ed. Foote and Quirk (with English translation), pp. 14–15; English translation, *END*, pp. 190–91.

Gunnlaug's Saga Ormstungu, ed. P.G. Foote and R. Quirk (London, 1957).

Hallvard Háreksblesi, *Knútsdrápa*, ed. Jónsson AI, 317–18; BI (with Danish translation), 293–94; Kock, i. 149; text and English translation in Frank, 'Cnut and his skalds', pp. 119–21.

Harek Eyvindarson, *Lausavísur* (Verses), ed. Jónsson, AI, 308–09; BI (with Danish translation), 286; Kock, i. 146.

Helgaud, *Epitoma Vitae Regis Rotberti Pii*, ed. R.H. Bautier and G. Labory (Paris, 1965)

Hemming, *Chartularium Ecclesiae Wigorniensis*, ed. T. Hearne (Oxford, 1723).

Henry of Huntingdon, *Historia Anglorum*, ed. D. Greenway (Oxford, 1996).

Hermann, *De Miraculis Sancti Eadmundi*, in *Memorials of St Edmund's Abbey*, ed. Arnold.

Historia de Sancto Cuthberto, in *Symeonis Monachi Opera Omnia*, ed. Arnold.

Historiola de Primordiis Episcopatus Somersetensis, ed. J. Hunter, *Ecclesiastical Documents*, (Camden Society, Old Series, viii, 1840).

The Homilies of the Anglo-Saxon Church, ed. B. Thorpe (London, 1844–46).

Hugh Candidus, *Chronicle*, ed. W.T. Mellows (London, 1949).

John of Wallingford, *The Chronicle attributed to John of Wallingford*, ed. R. Vaughan (Camden Society, Third Series, xc, 1958).

John of Worcester, *The Chronicle of John of Worcester. Volume II. The Annals from 450 to 1066*, ed. and trans. R.R. Darlington and P. McGurk (Oxford, 1995); the entries for Cnut's reign are translated (under the name Florence of Worcester) in *EHD*, pp. 310–15.

Knytlinga Saga, ed. C.J.F. Petersons and E. Olson (Copenhagen, 1919).

Lanfranc, *Letters*, ed. H. Clover and M. Gibson (Oxford, 1979).

The Laws of the Kings of England from Edmund to Henry I, ed. A.J. Robertson (Cambridge, 1925).

Liber Eliensis, ed. E.O. Blake (Camden Society, Third Series, xcii, 1962).

The Liber Vitae of the New Minster and Hyde Abbey Winchester British Library Stowe 944, ed. S. Keynes, Early English Manuscripts in Facsimile xxvi (Copenhagen, 1996); printed text, *Liber Vitae: Register and Martyrology of New Minster and Hyde Abbey Winchester*, ed. W.G. de Birch (London, 1892).

The Life of King Edward who rests at Westminster, attributed to a monk of Saint-Bertin, ed. and trans. F. Barlow (2nd edn., Oxford, 1992).

Liðsmannaflokkr (Song of the Lithsmen), ed. Jónsson AI, 422–23; BI (with Danish translation), 391–93; Kock, i. 194–95; Jónsson and Kock printed some parts of this poem under other headings, see Fidjestøl, *Det norrøne Fyrstediktet*, p.61; with English translation, *END*, pp.140–43 (incomplete); Poole, 'Skaldic Verse and Anglo-Saxon History', 281–83, and Poole, *Viking Poems on War and Peace*, pp.86–90 (complete).

Memorials of St Dunstan, ed.W. Stubbs (RS 63, 1874).

Memorials of St Edmund's Abbey, ed.T. Arnold (RS 96, 1890–96).

Den norsk-isländska Skaldediktningen, ed. E.A. Kock (Lund, 1946–49).

Den norsk-islandske Skjaldedigtning, ed. F. Jónsson (Copenhagen, 1912–15).

Osbern, *Vita S. Elphegi*, ed. H. Wharton, *Anglia Sacra* (London, 1691), ii. 122–42.

Osbern, *Translatio Sancti Ælfegi Cantuariensis archiepiscopi et martiris*, ed. A.R. Rumble, with an English translation by Rosemary Morris and A.R. Rumble, *The Reign of Cnut*, ed. Rumble, pp.294–315.

Ottar the Black, *Höfuðlausn* (Head-Ransom), ed. Jónsson AI, 290–96; BI (with Danish translation), 268–72; Kock, i. 137–39; English translation of verses 7–11, 13–14, *EHD*, pp.333–4.

Ottar the Black, *Knútsdrápa*, ed. Jónsson AI, 296–98; BI (with Danish translation), 272–75; Kock, i. 140–41; English translation, *EHD*, pp. 335–36.

Ottar the Black, *Lausavísur* (Verses), ed. Jónsson AI, 299; BI (with Danish translation), 275; Kock, i. 141; Townend, 'Contextualising the *Knútsdrápur*', 158, with English translation.

Ralph of Diceto, *Abbreviationes Chronicorum*, ed. W. Stubbs, *The Historical Works of Master Ralph de Diceto* (RS 68, 1876).

Ralph Glaber, *Historiarvm Libri Qvinqve*, ed. J. France (Oxford, 1989).

Receuil des actes des ducs de Normandie de 911 à 1066, ed. M. Fauroux (Caen, 1961).

Richard of Cirencester, *Speculum Historiale*, ed. J.E.B. Major (RS 30, 1863–69).

Roger of Wendover, *Flores Historiarum*, ed. H.O. Coxe (London, 1841–44).

Saxo Grammaticus, *Danorum Regum Heroumque Historia Books X-XVI*, ed. and trans. E. Christiansen (*BAR* International Series, vols. 84, 118, 1980–81).

Scriptores Minores Historiæ Danicæ Medii Ævi, ed. M. Cl. Gertz (Copenhagen, 1917–22).

Select English Historical Documents of the Ninth and Tenth Centuries, ed. F.E. Harmer (Cambridge, 1914).

Sighvat the Skald, *Austrfaravísur* (Eastern Travel Verses), ed. Jónsson AI, 233–40; BI (with Danish translation), 220–25; Kock, i. 114–17; verses 2, 4–5, 7, 9, 11–12, 15 (with English translation), Turville-Petre, *Skaldic Poetry*, pp.79–83.

Sighvat the Skald, *Erlingsflokkr* (poem on Erling Skjalgsson), ed. Jónsson AI, 244–47; BI (with Danish translation), 228–31; Kock, i. 118–20.

Sighvat the Skald, *Knútsdrápa*, ed. Jónsson AI, 248–51; BI (with Danish translation), 232–34; Kock, i. 120–21; English translation, omitting verse 5, *EHD*, pp.337–38.

Sighvat the Skald, *Lausavísur* (Verses), ed. Jónsson AI, 265–75; BI (with Danish translation), 246–54; Kock, i. 127–31; English translation of verses 15–19, *EHD*, pp. 339–40.

Sighvat the Skald, *Vestrfaravísur*, (Western Travel Verses), ed. Jónsson AI, 241–43; BI (with Danish translation), 226–28; Kock, i. 117–18; English translation of verses 1–3, 5–7, *EHD*, pp.338–39.

Sightvat the Skald, *Víkingavísur* (Viking Verses, on Olaf Haraldsson, king of Norway), ed. Jónsson AI, 223–28; BI (with Danish translation), 213–16; Kock, i. 111–13; with English translation, Fell, 'Víkingavísur', pp.110–22; English translation of verses 6–9, *EHD*, pp.332–33; of verse 9, Poole, 'Skaldic Verse and Anglo-Saxon History', 268.

Snorri Sturluson, *Heimskringla*, ed. B. Aðalbjarnarson (Íslenzk Fornrit, xxvi-viii, 1941–62).

St Benet of Holme 1020–1210, ed. J.R. West (Norfolk Record Society, 1932).

Stefnir Thorgilsson, *Lausavísur* (Verses), ed. Jónsson AI, 153–54; BI (with Danish translation), 146; Kock, i. 80.

Swegen Aggeson, *Lex Castrensis*, in *Scriptores Minores*, ed. Gertz, i. 64–92; English translation by E. Christiansen, *The Works of Sven Aggesen Twelfth-Century Danish Historian* (London, 1992), pp.31–43.

Symeon of Durham, *Historia Regum*, in *Symeonis Monachi Opera Omnia*, ed. T. Arnold (RS 75, 1882–85).

Symeon of Durham, *Libellvs de exordio atque procvrso istivs, hoc est Dvnelmensis, ecclesie*, ed. D. Rollason (Oxford, 2000).

The Text of the Book of Llan Dâv, ed. J.G. Evans and J. Rhys (Oxford, 1893).

Thietmar of Merseburg, *Chronicon*, ed. R. Holtzmann (2nd edn., Berlin, 1955).

Thorarin Praise-Tongue, *Glælognskviða* (on Norway under Swegen and Ælfgifu), ed. Jónsson AI, 324–27; BI (with Danish translation), 300–1; Kock, i. 152–53.

Thorarin Praise-Tongue, *Höfuðlausn* (Head-Ransom – only the refrain survives), ed. Jónsson AI, 322; BI (with Danish translation), 298; Kock, i. 151.

Thorarin Praise-Tongue, *Tøgdrápa* (on Cnut), ed. Jónsson AI, 322–24; BI (with Danish translation), 203–06; Kock, i. 151–52; English translation, *EHD*, pp.340–41; English translation of verse 7, Townend, 'Contextualising the *Knútsdrápur*', 157, n. 65.

Thord Kolbeinsson, *Eiríksdrápa*, ed. Jónsson AI 213–17; BI (with Danish translation), 203–06; Kock, i. 106–08; English translation of verses 8–14, *EHD*, pp.334–35; of verse 11, Poole, 'Skaldic Verse and Anglo-Saxon History', p. 289.

Thorleif Rauthfeldarson, *Drápa* on Swegen Forkbeard, ed. Jónsson AI, 141; BI (with Danish translation), 133; Kock, i. 73.

Vita Oswaldi archiepiscopi Eboracensis, in *The Historians of the Church of York*, ed. J. Raine (RS 71, 1879–94).

Widukind, *Rerum Gestarum Saxonicarum Libri Tres*, ed. P. Hirsch (5th edn., Hannover, 1935).

William of Jumièges , *Gesta Normannorum Ducum*, ed. and trans. E.M.C. van Houts (Oxford, 1992–95).

William of Malmesbury, *De Antiquitate Glastonie Ecclesie*, ed. J. Scott (Woodbridge, 1981).

William of Malmesbury, *De Gestis Pontificum Anglorum*, ed. N.E.S.A. Hamilton (RS 52, 1870).

William of Malmesbury, *Gesta Regum Anglorum: The History of the English Kings*, ed. and trans. R.A.B. Mynors, R.M. Thomson and M. Winterbottom (Oxford, 1998–99).

William of Malmesbury, *Historia Novella*, ed. K.R. Potter (London, 1962).

William of Malmesbury, *Vita Wulfstani*, ed. R.R. Darlington (Camden Society, Third Series, xl, 1928); trans. M. Swanton, *Three Lives of the Last Englishmen* (London, 1984).

William of Poitiers, *Gesta Guillelmi*, ed. and trans. R.H.C. Davis and M. Chibnall (Oxford, 1998); with French translation, *Histoire de Guillaume le Conquérant*, ed. R. Foreville (Paris, 1952).

Wipo, *Gesta Chuonradi II. Imperatoris*, ed. H. Bresslau (3rd edn., Hannover, 1915).

Wulfstan of York, *Canons of Edgar*, ed. R. Fowler (Early English Text Society 266, 1972).

Wulfstan of York, *The Institutes of Polity*, ed. K. Jost (Berne, 1959); translated *ASP*,
  pp.125–38.
Wulfstan of York, *Sermo Lupi ad Anglos*, ed. D. Whitelock (3rd edn., London, 1963);
  translated *EHD*, pp.928–34.
The York Gospels, ed. N. Barker (Roxburghe Club, 1986).

SECONDARY SOURCES

Abels, R.P., *Lordship and Military Obligation in Anglo-Saxon England* (Berkeley, 1988).
Abrams, L., 'The Anglo-Saxons and the Christianization of Scandinavia', *ASE*, 24
  (1995), 213–49.
Andersen, H.H., *et al.*, *Danevirke* (Copenhagen, 1976).
Andersson, T.M., 'The Viking Policy of Ethelred the Unready', *Scandinavian Studies*,
  59 (1987), 284–95.
Anglo-Saxon Charters: an annotated list and bibliography, ed. P.H. Sawyer (London, 1968).
  See also *Electronic Sawyer*.
Anglo-Saxon Coins: Studies Presented to Sir Frank Stenton, ed. R.H.M. Dolley (London,
  1961).
Anglo-Saxon Monetary History: Essays in memory of Michael Dolley, ed. M.A.S.
  Blackburn (Leicester, 1986).
Archibald, M.M., *et al.*, 'Four early medieval coin dies from the London waterfront',
  Numismatic Chronicle, 155 (1995), 163–200.
Backhouse, J. *et al.*, *The Golden Age of Anglo-Saxon Art 966–1066* (London, 1984).
Bailey, R.N., *Viking Age Sculpture in Northern England* (London, 1980).
Barker, E.E., 'Sussex Anglo-Saxon Charters', *Sussex Archaeological Collections*, lxxxviii
  (1949), 51–113.
Barlow, F., 'Two Notes: Cnut's Second Pilgrimage and Queen Emma's Disgrace in
  1043', *EHR*, lxxiii (1958), 649–56.
Barlow, F., *The English Church 1000-1066* (London, 1963).
Barlow, F., *Edward the Confessor* (London, 1970).
Bates, D., *Normandy before 1066* (London, 1982).
Bates, D., 'Lord Sudeley's Ancestors: The Family of the Counts of Amiens, Valois and
  the Vexin in France and England during the eleventh Century', in *The Sudeleys –
  Lords of Toddington* (The Manorial Society of Great Britain, London, 1987).
The Battle of Maldon AD 991, ed. D. Scragg (Oxford, 1991).
Becker, C.J., 'The Coinages of Harthacnut and Magnus the Good at Lund
  c.1040–c.1046', *Studies in Northern Coinages of the Eleventh Century*, ed. C.J. Becker
  (Copenhagen, 1981), pp.119–74.
Becker, C.J., 'Studies in the Danish coinage at Lund during the period c.1030-c.1046',
  in *Viking Age Coinage*, ed. Blackburn and Metcalf, pp.449–77.
Beech, G., 'England and Aquitaine in the century before the Norman Conquest',
  ASE, 19 (1990), 81–101.
Bendixen, K., 'The currency in Denmark from the beginning of the Viking Age until
  c.1100', in *Viking Age Coinage*, ed. Blackburn and Metcalfe, pp.405–18.
Bethurum Loomis, D., '*Regnum* and *sacerdotium* in the early eleventh century', in
  England before the Conquest, ed. Clemoes and Hughes, pp.129–45.
Biddle, M., 'Excavations at Winchester 1965: fourth interim report', *The Antiquaries
  Journal*, xlvi (1966), 308–32.

Bishop, T.A.M., *English Caroline Minuscule* (Oxford, 1971).

Bishop Æthelwold: His Career and Influence, ed. B. Yorke (Woodbridge, 1988).

Blackburn, M.A.S., 'English Dies used in the Scandinavian Imitative Coinages', *Hikuin*, 11 (1985), 101–24.

Blackburn, M.A.S., 'A variety of Cnut's *Short Cross* coinage depicting a banner', *Numismatiska Meddelanden*, xxxvii (1989), 39–43.

Blackburn, M.A.S., 'Do Cnut the Great's first coins as king of Denmark date from before 1018?', *Sigtuna Papers*, ed. Jonsson and Malmer, pp. 55–68.

Blackburn, M.A.S., 'Hiberno-Norse coins of the *Helmet* type', *Studies in Late Anglo-Saxon Coinage*, ed. Jonsson, pp. 9–24.

Blackburn, M.A.S., 'Æthelred's Coinage and the Payment of Tribute', *The Battle of Maldon*, ed. Scragg, pp. 156–69.

Blackburn, M.A.S. and Lyon, C.S.S., 'Regional die-production in Cnut's *Quatrefoil* issue', *Anglo-Saxon Monetary History*, ed. Blackburn, pp. 223–72.

Blackburn, M.A.S. and Metcalf, D.M., *Viking Age Coinage in the Northern Lands* (*BAR* International Series, 122, 1981).

Boon, G.C., *Welsh Hoards 1979–1981: the Coinage of Cnut in Wales, the Coinage of the Empress Maud, the Earliest Portrait Easterlings* (Cardiff, 1986).

Bresslau, H., 'Ein Beitrag zur Kenntnis von Konrads II Beziehungen zu Byzanz und Dänemark', *Forschungen zur Deutsche Geschichte*, x (1870), 606–13.

Bresslau, H., *Jahrbücher des Deutschen Reichs unter Konrad II* (Leipzig, 1879–84).

Brooks, N.P., *The Early History of the Church of Canterbury* (Leicester, 1984).

Brooks, N.P., 'Arms, Status and Warfare in Late-Saxon England', *Ethelred the Unready*, ed. Hill, pp. 81–103.

Brooks, N.P., 'Weapons and Armour', *The Battle of Maldon*, ed. Scragg, pp. 208–19.

Butler, V.J., 'The Metrology of the Late Anglo-Saxon Penny', *Anglo-Saxon Coins*, ed. Dolley, pp. 195–214.

Cam, H.M., *Liberties & Communities in Medieval England* (Cambridge, 1944).

Cameron, K., 'The Minor Names and Field-Names of the Holland division of Lincolnshire', *The Vikings*, ed. T. Andersson and K.I. Sandred (Uppsala, 1978).

Campbell, A., 'Saxo Grammaticus and Scandinavian Historical Tradition', *SBVS*, 13 (1946–53), 1–22.

Campbell, A., 'Knúts Saga', *SBVS*, 13 (1946–53), 238–48.

Campbell, A., *Skaldic Verse and Anglo-Saxon History* (London, 1971).

Campbell, J., 'Norwich', *The Atlas of Historic Towns*, ii., ed. M.D. Lobel (London, 1975).

Campbell, J., et al., *The Anglo-Saxons* (Oxford, 1982).

Campbell, J., *Essays in Anglo-Saxon History* (London, 1986).

Campbell, J., *The Anglo-Saxon State* (London, 2000).

Campbell, J., 'Anglo-Saxon Courts', *Court Culture in the Early Middle Ages: the Proceedings of the First Alcuin Conference*, ed. C. Cubitt (Leiden, 2003), 155–169

Campbell, M.W., 'Queen Emma and Aelfgifu of Northampton: Canute the Great's Women', *Medieval Scandinavia*, 4 (1971), 66–79.

Campbell, M.W., 'The *Encomium Emmae Reginae*: Personal Panegyric or Political Propaganda?', *Annuale Mediaevale*, 19 (1979), 27–45.

Chaplais, P., 'The Authenticity of the Royal Anglo-Saxon Diplomas of Exeter', *Bulletin of the Institute of Historical Research*, xxxix (1966), 1–34.

Chaplais, P., 'The Origin and Authenticity of the Royal Anglo-Saxon Diploma', *Prisca Munimenta*, ed. Ranger, pp. 28–42.

Chaplais, P., 'The Anglo-Saxon Chancery: from the Diploma to the Writ', *Prisca Munimenta*, ed. Ranger, pp.43–62.

Chaplais, P., 'The Royal Anglo-Saxon "Chancery" of the Tenth Century Revisited', *Studies in Medieval History presented to R.H.C. Davis*, ed. H. Mayr-Harting and R.I. Moore (London, 1985), pp.41–51.

Chaplais, P., 'William of Saint-Calais and the Domesday Survey', *Domesday Studies*, ed. Holt, pp.65–77.

Christiansen, E., 'Canute: model of Christian kingship or brigand Dane made good?', *History Today*, (November, 1986), 34–39.

Christiansen, E., *The Works of Sven Aggesen*, see Primary Sources under Swegen Aggeson.

Clark, C., 'The narrative mode of *The Anglo-Saxon Chronicle* before the Conquest', *England before the Conquest*, ed. Clemoes and Hughes, pp.215–35.

Clayton, M., 'Of Mice and Men: Ælfric's Second Homily for the Feast of a Confessor', *Leeds Studies in English*, New Series 24 (1993), 1–26.

Corbett, W.J., 'The Development of the Duchy of Normandy and the Norman Conquest of England', *Cambridge Medieval History*, v (Cambridge, 1926), 481–520.

Cowdrey, H.E.J., 'The Peace and the Truce of God in the Eleventh Century', *Past & Present*, 46 (1970), 42–67.

Crook, J., '"A worthy antiquity": the movement of King Cnut's bones in Winchester Cathedral', *The Reign of Cnut*, ed. Rumble, pp.165–91.

Cross, J.E., 'The ethic of war in Old English', *England before the Conquest*, ed. Clemoes and Hughes, pp.269–82.

Damgaard-Sorensen, T., 'Danes and Wends: a study of the Danish attitude towards the Wends', *People and Places in Northern Europe*, ed. Wood and Lund, pp.171–86.

Darby, H.C., *Domesday England* (Cambridge, 1977).

Darlington, R.R., 'Ecclesiastical Reform in the Late Old English Period', *EHR*, li (1936), 385–428.

Darlington, R.R., 'Introduction to the Wiltshire Domesday', *VCH Wilts.* ii (London, 1955), 42–112.

Darlington, R.R. and McGurk, P., 'The *Chronicon ex Chronicis* of "John" of Worcester and its Use of Sources for English History before 1066', *Anglo-Norman Studies*, v (1982), 185–96.

Dart, J., *The History and Antiquities of the Cathedral Church of Canterbury* (London, 1727).

Davis, G.R.C., *Medieval Cartularies of Great Britain* (London, 1958).

Dickins, B., 'The day of Byrhtnoth's death and other obits from a twelfth-century Ely kalendar'; 'The day of the battle of Æthelingadene (ASC 1001 A)', *Leeds Studies in English*, vi (1937), 14–27.

Dodwell, C.R., *Anglo-Saxon Art: A new perspective* (Manchester, 1982).

Dolley, R.H.M., 'The Regional Distribution of Dies in the West Country c.1017–1023', *Spink and Son's Numismatic Circular*, lxiv (1956), cols. 321–25, 374–76.

Dolley, R.H.M., 'An Apocryphal Corpse of Canute', *Spink and Son's Numismatic Circular*, lxix (1961), 9–10.

Dolley, R.H.M., 'A Cnut Die-Link between the Mints of Salisbury and Wilton', *BNJ*, xxxi (1962), 53–54.

Dolley, R.H.M., 'The nummular brooch from Sulgrave', *England before the Conquest*, ed. Clemoes and Hughes, pp.333–49.

Dolley, R.H.M., 'An Introduction to the Coinage of Æthelraed II', *Ethelred the Unready*, ed. Hill, pp. 115–33.

Dolley, R.H.M. and Ingold, J., 'Some thoughts on the Engraving of the Dies for the English Coinage *c.*1025', *Commentationes*, 1 (1961), 187–222.

Dolley, R.H.M. and Metcalf, D.M., 'The Reform of the English Coinage under Eadgar', *Anglo-Saxon Coins*, ed. Dolley, pp. 136–68.

Dolley, R.H.M. and Talvio, T., 'The Twelfth of the Agnus Dei pennies of Æthelraed II', *BNJ*, xlvii (1977), 131–33.

Dolley, R.H.M. and Talvio, T., 'A Thirteenth *Agnus Dei* Penny of Æthelraed II', *BNJ*, xlix (1979), 122–25.

Domesday Studies, ed. J.C. Holt (Woodbridge, 1987).

Dugdale, W., *Monasticon Anglicanum*, ed. J. Caley *et al.* (London, 1817–30).

Dumville, D.N., 'Kingship, Genealogies and Regnal Lists', *Early Medieval Kingship*, ed. P.H. Sawyer and I.N. Wood (Leeds, 1977), pp. 72–104.

Dumville, D.N., 'Some aspects of annalistic writing at Canterbury in the eleventh and early twelfth centuries', *Peritia*, 2 (1983), 23–57.

Duncan, A.A.M., 'The battle of Carham, 1018', *Scottish Historical Review*, lv (1976), 20–28.

Eaglen, R.J. and Grayburn, R., 'Gouged Reverse Dies in the Quatrefoil Issue of Cnut', *BNJ*, 70 (2001), 12–37.

Einarsdóttir, Ó., *Studier I Kronologisk Metode i tidlig Islandsk Historieskrivning* (Stockholm, 1964).

Electronic Sawyer. This updated version of P.H. Sawyer's handlist of Anglo-Saxon charters is available on the website of the British Academy-Royal Historical Society Joint Committee on Anglo-Saxon Charters at http://www.trin.cam.ac.uk/chartwww/

England before the Conquest: Studies in primary sources presented to Dorothy Whitelock (Cambridge, 1971).

Ethelred the Unready: Papers from the Millenary Conference, ed. D. Hill (*BAR* British Series, 59, 1978).

Evans, A.C., *The Sutton Hoo Ship Burial* (London, 1986).

Feilitzen, O. von, *The Pre-Conquest Personal Names of Domesday Book* (Uppsala, 1937).

Fell, C., 'Víkingarvísur', *Specvlvm Norroenvm*, ed. U. Dronke *et al.* (Odense, 1981), pp. 106–22.

Fellows-Jensen, G., 'Danish place-names and personal names in England: the influence of Cnut?', *The Reign of Cnut*, ed. Rumble, pp. 125–40.

Fidjestøl, B., *Det norrøne Fyrstediktet* (Øvre Ervik, 1982).

Finberg, H.P.R., *The Early Charters of Devon and Cornwall* (Leicester, 1953).

Finberg, H.P.R., 'Supplement to "The Early Charters of Devon and Cornwall"', in W.G. Hoskins, *The Westward Expansion of Wessex* (Leicester, 1960), pp. 23–35.

Finberg, H.P.R., *The Early Charters of the West Midlands* (Leicester, 1961).

Finberg, H.P.R., *The Early Charters of Wessex* (Leicester, 1964).

Fisher, D.J.V., *The Anglo-Saxon Age c.400–1042* (London, 1973).

Flanagan, M.T., *Irish Society, Anglo-Norman Settlers, Angevin Kingship* (Oxford, 1989).

Fleming, R., 'Domesday Estates of the King and the Godwines: A Study in Late Saxon Politics', *Speculum*, 58 (1983), 987–1007.

Fleming, R., *Kings and Lords in Conquest England* (Cambridge, 1991).

Fletcher, R., *Bloodfeud: Murder and Revenge in Anglo-Saxon England* (London, 2002).

Flete, J., *The History of Westminster Abbey*, ed. J.A. Robinson (Cambridge, 1909).

Foote, P.G., *Aurvandilstá: Norse Studies* (Odense, 1984).

Foote, P.G. and Wilson, D.M., *The Viking Achievement* (London, 1970).

Frank, R., *Old Norse Court Poetry: The Dróttkvætt Stanza* (Islandica, xlii, 1978).

Frank, R., 'Viking atrocity and Skaldic verse: The Rite of the Blood-Eagle', *EHR*, xcix (1984), 332–43.

Frank, R., 'Did Anglo-Saxon Audiences Have a Skaldic Tooth?', *Scandinavian Studies*, 59 (1987), 338–55.

Frank, R., 'The Blood-Eagle again', *SBVS*, 22 (1988), 287–89.

Frank, R., 'King Cnut in the verse of his skalds', *The Reign of Cnut*, ed. Rumble, pp. 106–24.

Freeman, E.A., *The History of the Norman Conquest of England* (2nd edn., 6 vols., Oxford, 1870–79).

Galster, G., 'Cnvt Rex = Gorm den Gamle's fader', *Nordisk Numismatisk Unions Medlemsblad*, (1975), 181–84.

Garmonsway, G.N., *Canute and his Empire* (London, 1964).

Gelling, M., *The Early Charters of the Thames Valley* (Leicester, 1979).

Gem, R., 'A Recession in English Architecture during the early eleventh century and its effect on the development of the Romanesque style', *Journal of the British Archaeological Association*, Third Series, xxxviii (1975), 28–49.

Gerchow, J., *Die Gedenküberlieferung der Angelsachsen* (Berlin, 1988).

Gerchow, J., 'Prayers for King Cnut: the Liturgical Commemoration of a Conqueror', *England in the Eleventh Century*, ed. C. Hicks, Harlaxton Medieval Studies 2 (Stamford, 1992), 219–38.

Gillingham, J., '"The Most Precious Jewel in the English Crown": levels of Danegeld and heregeld in the early eleventh century', *EHR*, civ (1989), 373–84.

Gillingham, J., 'Chronicles and Coins as Evidence for Levels of Tribute and Taxation in Late Tenth- and Early Eleventh-Century England', *EHR*, cv (1990), 939–50.

Godden, M.R., 'Ælfric's Saints' Lives and the Problem of Miracles', *Leeds Studies in English*, xvi (1985), 83–100.

Godden, M.R., 'Ælfric and Anglo-Saxon Kingship', *EHR*, cii (1987), 911–15.

Godden, M.R., 'Money, power and morality in late Anglo-Saxon England', *ASE*, 19 (1990), 41–65.

Godden, M. (R.), 'Apocalypse and Invasion in Late Anglo-Saxon England', *From Anglo-Saxon to Early Middle English: Studies presented to E.G. Stanley*, ed. M. Godden et al. (Oxford, 1994), 130–62.

Graham-Campbell, J., *The Viking World* (London, 1989).

Gransden, A., *Historical Writing in England c.550 to c.1307* (London, 1974).

Gransden, A., 'The legends and traditions concerning the origins of the Abbey of Bury St Edmunds', *EHR*, c (1985), 1–24.

Gräslund, B., 'Knut den store och sveariket: Slaget vid Helgeå i ny belysning', *Scandia*, 52 (1986), 211–38.

Gwynn, A., 'The origins of the see of Dublin', *Irish Ecclesiastical Record*, lvii (1941), 40–55, 97–112.

Gwynn, A., 'The First Bishops of Dublin', *Reportorium Novum*, 1 (1955), 1–26.

Hall, R., *The Viking Dig: the Excavations at York* (London, 1984).

Hart, C.R., *The Early Charters of Eastern England* (Leicester, 1966).

Hart, C.R., *The Early Charters of Northern England and the North Midlands* (Leicester, 1975).

Harvey, S.P.J., 'Domesday Book and its predecessors', *EHR*, lxxxvi (1971), 753–73.

Harvey, S.P.J., 'Recent Domesday Studies', xcv (1980), 121–33.

Haskins, C.H., 'A Charter of Canute for Fécamp', *EHR*, xxxiii (1918), 342–44.

Heslop, T.A., 'The production of *de luxe* manuscripts and the patronage of King Cnut and Queen Emma', *ASE*, 19 (1990), 151–95.

Hill, D., *An Atlas of Anglo-Saxon England* (Oxford, 1981).

Hill, D., 'An urban policy for Cnut?', *The Reign of Cnut*, ed. Rumble, pp.101–05.

Hollis, S., 'The thematic structure of the *Sermo Lupi*', *ASE*, 6 (1977), 175–95.

Hollister, C.W., *Anglo-Saxon Military Institutions* (Oxford, 1962).

Hooper, N.A., 'The Housecarls in England in the eleventh century', *Anglo-Norman Studies*, vii (1984), 161–76.

Hooper, N.A., 'An Introduction to the Berkshire Domesday', *The Berkshire Domesday* (London, 1988).

Hooper, N.A., 'An Introduction to the Wiltshire Domesday', *The Wiltshire Domesday* (London, 1989).

Hooper, N.A., 'Some Observations on the Navy in Late Anglo-Saxon England', *Studies in Medieval History presented to R. Allen Brown*, ed. C. Harper-Bill *et al.* (Woodbridge, 1989).

Hooper, N.A., 'Military developments in the reign of Cnut', *The Reign of Cnut*, ed. Rumble, pp.89–100.

Hudson, B.T., 'Cnut and the Scottish Kings', *EHR*, cvii (1992), 350–60.

Hudson, J., 'Administration, Family and Perceptions of the Past in Late Twelfth-Century England: Richard FitzNigel and the Dialogue of the Exchequer', *The Perception of the Past in Twelfth-Century Europe*, ed. P. Magdalino (London, 1992), pp.75–98.

Hvass, S., 'Jelling from Iron Age to Viking Age', *People and Places*, ed. Wood and Lund, pp.149–60.

Jansson, S.B.F., *Swedish Vikings in England: the evidence of the rune stones* (London, 1966).

Jespersen, O., *Growth and Structure of the English Language* (Oxford, 1972).

John, E., *Orbis Britanniae* (Leicester, 1966).

John, E., 'The *Encomium Emmae Reginae*: a riddle and a solution', *Bulletin of the John Rylands University Library*, 63 (1980–81), 58–94.

John, E., 'The World of Abbot Aelfric', *Ideal and Reality in Frankish and Anglo-Saxon Society*, ed. P. Wormald *et al.* (Oxford 1983), pp.300–16.

Jónsson, F., *Den oldnorske og oldislandske Litteraturs Historie* (2nd edn., Copenhagen, 1920–24).

Jonsson, K., 'The coinage of Cnut', *The Reign of Cnut*, ed. Rumble, pp.193–230.

Kapelle, W.E., *The Norman Conquest of the North: The Region and its Transformation, 1000–1135* (London, 1979).

Ker, N.R., 'Hemming's Cartulary: a description of the two Worcester cartularies in Cotton Tiberius A xiii', *Studies in Medieval History presented to Frederick Maurice Powicke*, ed. R.W. Hunt (Oxford, 1948), pp.49–75.

Ker, N.R., *Catalogue of Manuscripts containing Anglo-Saxon* (Oxford, 1957).

Ker, N.R., 'The handwriting of Archbishop Wulfstan', *England before the Conquest*, ed. Clemoes and Hughes, pp.315–31.

Keynes, S.D., 'The declining reputation of King Æthelred the Unready', *Ethelred the Unready*, ed. Hill, pp.227–53.

Keynes, S.D., *The Diplomas of King Æthelred 'The Unready' 978–1016* (Cambridge, 1980).

Keynes, S.D., 'The Crowland Psalter and the sons of King Edmund Ironside', *Bodleian Library Record*, xi (1985), 359–70.

Keynes, S.D., 'The Additions in Old English', *The York Gospels*, pp.81–99.

Keynes, S.D., 'A Tale of Two Kings: Alfred the Great and Æthelred the Unready', *TRHS*, 36 (1986), 195–217.

Keynes, S.D., 'Royal government and the written word in late Anglo-Saxon England', *The Uses of Literacy in Early Medieval Europe*, ed. R. McKitterick (Cambridge, 1990), pp.226–57.

Keynes, S.D., 'Crime and Punishment in the Reign of King Æthelred the Unready', *People and Places*, ed. Wood and Lund, pp.67–81.

Keynes, S.D., 'The Historical Context of the Battle of Maldon', *The Battle of Maldon*, ed. Scragg, pp.81–113.

Keynes, S.D., 'The Æthelings in Normandy', *Anglo-Norman Studies*, xiii (1991), 173–205.

Keynes, S.D., 'Cnut's earls', *The Reign of Cnut*, ed. Rumble, pp.43–88.

Kiernan, K.S., *Beowulf and the Beowulf Manuscript* (New Brunswick, 1981).

Kinsey, R.S., 'Anglo-Saxon Law and Practice relating to Mints and Moneyers', *BNJ*, xxix (1958–9), 12–50.

Kirby, D.P., 'Notes on the Saxon Bishops of Sherborne', *Proceedings of the Dorset Natural History & Archaeological Society*, 87 (1965), 213–22.

Kirby, D.P., *The Making of Early England* (London, 1967).

Knowles, D., *The Monastic Order in England* (Cambridge, 1950).

Knowles, D. et al., *The Heads of Religious Houses England and Wales 940–1216* (Cambridge, 1972).

Körner, S., *The Battle of Hastings, England and Europe 1035–1066* (Lund, 1964).

Kristensen, A.G., 'Danelaw institutions and Danish society in the Viking Age', *Medieval Scandinavia*, viii (1975), 27–85.

Krogh, K.J., 'The Royal Viking Age Monuments at Jelling in the Light of Recent Archaeological Excavations', *Acta Archaeologica*, 53 (1982), 183–216.

Kulturhistorisk Leksikon for nordisk middelalder (Copenhagen, 1956–78).

Lagerqvist, L.O., 'The Coinage at Sigtuna in the names of Anund Jacob, Cnut the Great and Harthacnut', *Commentationes*, 2 (1968), 385–413.

Lagerqvist, L.O. and Dolley, R.H.M., 'The Problem of the "Fleur-de-lis" sceptre on the Sigtuna coins of Cnut', *BNJ*, xxx (1960–61), 252–61.

Lapidge, M., 'The *Life of St Oswald*', *The Battle of Maldon*, ed. Scragg, pp.51–58.

Larson, L.M., *The King's Household in England before the Norman Conquest* (Madison, 1904).

Larson, L.M., 'The Political Policies of Cnut as king of England', *American Historical Review*, xv (1910), 720–43.

Larson, L.M., *Canute the Great* (London, 1912).

Lawson, M.K., 'Aspects of the reign of Cnut' (Unpublished Oxford D. Phil. thesis, 1980).

Lawson, M.K., 'The collection of Danegeld and Heregeld in the reigns of Aethelred II and Cnut', *EHR*, xcix (1984), 721–38.

Lawson, M.K., '"Those stories look true": levels of taxation in the reigns of Æthelred II and Cnut', *EHR*, civ (1989), 385–406.

Lawson, M.K., 'Danegeld and Heregeld Once More', *EHR*, cv (1990), 951–61.

Lawson, M.K., 'Archbishop Wulfstan and the homiletic element in the Laws of Æthelred II and Cnut', *EHR*, civ (1992), 385–406; reprinted *The Reign of Cnut*, ed. Rumble, pp.141–64.

Lawson, M.K., *Cnut: the Danes in England in the Early Eleventh Century* (London, 1993).

Lawson, M.K., *The Battle of Hastings 1066* (rev. edn., Stroud, 2003).

Leimus, I., 'A fourteenth *Agnus Dei* penny of Æthelred II', *Studies in Late Anglo-Saxon Coinage*, ed. Jonsson, pp. 157–63.

Leland, J., *De Rebus Britannicis Collectanea*, ed. T. Hearne (Oxford, 1715).

Loyn, H.R., *The Vikings in Britain* (London, 1977).

Loyn, H.R., *The Governance of Anglo-Saxon England* (London, 1984).

Lund, N., 'The armies of Swein Forkbeard and Cnut: *leding* or *lið*?', *ASE*, 15 (1986), 105–18.

Lund, N., '"Denemearc", "tanmarkar but" and "tanmaurk ala"', *People and Places*, ed. Wood and Lund, pp. 161–69.

Lund, N., 'The Danish Perspective', *The Battle of Maldon*, ed. Scragg, pp. 114–42.

Lund, N., 'Cnut's Danish kingdom', *The Reign of Cnut*, ed. Rumble, pp. 27–42.

Lyon, C.S.S., 'Historical Problems of Anglo-Saxon Coinage – (3): Denominations and Weights', *BNJ*, xxxviii (1969), 204–22.

Lyon, C.S.S., 'Variations in Currency in Late Anglo-Saxon England', *Mints, Dies and Currency*, ed. R.A.G. Carson (London, 1971), pp. 101–20.

Lyon, C.S.S., 'Some problems in interpreting Anglo-Saxon Coinage', *ASE*, 5(1976), 173–224.

Lyon, C.S.S., 'Die Estimation: Some Experiments with Simulated Samples of a Coinage', *BNJ*, 59 (1989), 1–12.

Lyon, C.S.S., 'Die-Cutting in the *Last Small Cross* Type of Æthelred II and some Problematic Lincoln and East Anglian Dies and Die-Links', *BNJ*, 68 (1998), 21–41.

Lyon, C.S.S., 'Anglo-Saxon Numismatics', *BNJ*, 73 (2003), 58–75.

Mack, K., 'Changing Thegns: Cnut's Conquest and the English Aristocracy', *Albion*, 16 (1984), 375–87.

McNulty, J.B., 'The Lady Aelfgyva in the Bayeux Tapestry', *Speculum*, 55 (1980), 659–68.

Maddicott, J.R., 'Trade, industry and the wealth of King Alfred', *Past & Present*, 123 (1989), 1–51.

Mahany, C. and Roffe, D., 'Stamford: the Development of an Anglo-Scandinavian Borough', *Anglo-Norman Studies*, v (1982), 197–219.

Maitland, F.W., *Domesday Book and Beyond* (Cambridge, 1987).

Major, K., 'Blyborough Charters', *A Medieval Miscellany for Doris Mary Stenton* (Pipe Roll Society, New Series 36, 1960).

Malmer, B., *King Canute's Coinage in the Northern Lands* (London, 1974).

Malmer, B., 'A note on the Coinage of Sigtuna, at the time of Anund Jacob', *Numismatiska Meddelanden*, xxxvii (1989), 259–62.

Marwood, G.W., *The Stone Coffins of Bosham Church* (Chichester, 1974).

Maund, K.L., *Ireland, Wales and England in the Eleventh Century* (Woodbridge, 1991).

Mayr-Harting, H.M., *Ottonian Book Illumination* (London, 1991).

Medieval Trade in the Mediterranean World, ed. R.S. Lopez and I.W. Raymond (New York, 1955).

Meehan, B., 'The siege of Durham, the battle of Carham and the cession of Lothian', *Scottish Historical Review*, lv (1976), 1–19.

Metcalf, D.M., 'The Ranking of the Boroughs: Numismatic Evidence from the Reign of Æthelred II', *Ethelred the Unready*, ed. Hill, pp. 159–212.

Metcalf, D.M., 'Continuity and Change in English Monetary History *c*.973–1086. Part I.', *BNJ*, l (1980), 20–49.

Metcalf, D.M., 'Continuity and Change in English Monetary History c.973–1086. Part 2.', *BNJ*, li (1981), 52–90.

Metcalf, D.M., 'Large Danegelds in relation to War and Kingship. Their Implications for Monetary History, and Some Numismatic Evidence', *Weapons and Warfare in Anglo-Saxon England*, ed. S.C. Hawkes (Oxford, 1989), pp.179–89.

Metcalf, D.M., 'Can we believe the very large figure of £72,000 for the geld levied by Cnut in 1018?', *Studies in Late Anglo-Saxon Coinage*, ed. Jonsson, pp.165–76.

Metcalf, D.M. and Northover, J.P., 'Sporadic debasement in the English coinage c.1009–1052', *Numismatic Chronicle*, 162 (2002), 217–36.

Miller, E., *The Abbey & Bishopric of Ely* (Cambridge, 1951).

Moberg, O., *Olav Haraldsson, Knut den store och Sverige* (Lund, 1941).

Moberg, O., 'Knut den store's motståndare i slaget vid Helgeå', *Scandia*, 51 (1985), 7–17.

Moesgaard, J.C. and Tornbjerg, S.A., 'A Sixteenth *Agnus Dei* Penny of Æthelred II', *Numismatic Chronicle*, 159 (1999), 327–32.

Morris, C.J., *Marriage and Murder in eleventh-century Northumbria: a study of 'De Obsessione Dunelmi'*, University of York Borthwick Papers No. 82 (1992).

Mossop, H.R., *The Lincoln Mint c.890-1279* (Newcastle, 1970).

Myres, J.N.L., *A Corpus of Anglo-Saxon Pottery of the Pagan Period* (Cambridge, 1977).

Myres, J.N.L., *The English Settlements* (Oxford, 1986).

Nelson, J.L., *Politics and Ritual in Early Medieval Europe* (London, 1986).

Nielsen, K.M., ed., 'Jelling Problems: a discussion', *Medieval Scandinavia*, vii (1974).

Nightingale, P., 'The Ora, the Mark, and the Mancus: Weight Standards and the Coinage in Eleventh-century England. Part 1', *Numismatic Chronicle*, 143 (1983), 248–57.

Nightingale, P., 'The Ora, the Mark, and the Mancus: Weight Standards and the Coinage in Eleventh-century England. Part 2', *Numismatic Chronicle*, 144 (1984), 234–48.

Nightingale, P., 'The Evolution of Weight-Standards and the Creation of New Monetary and Commercial Links in Northern Europe from the Tenth Century to the Twelfth Century', *Economic History Review*, Second Series, xxxviii (1985), 192–209.

Nightingale, P., 'The Origin of the Court of Husting and Danish Influence on London's Development into a Capital City', *EHR*, cii (1987), 559–78.

Niles, J.D., 'Skaldic Technique in *Brunanburh*', *Scandinavian Studies*, 59 (1987), 356–66.

O'Hara, M.D., 'An iron reverse die of the reign of Cnut', *The Reign of Cnut*, ed. Rumble, pp.231–71.

Olsen, O., 'St Jørgensbjærg kirke', *Aarbøger for nordisk Oldkyndighed og Historie 1960* (Copenhagen, 1961), 1–71.

Pagan, H.E., 'A Cnut hoard from Cornwall', *Numismatic Circular*, xcv (1987), 39.

Partner, N.F., *Serious entertainments: the writing of history in twelfth-century England* (Chicago, 1977).

Peckham, W.D., 'The Bosham Myth of Canute's daughter', *Sussex Notes and Queries*, xvii (1970), 179–84.

People and Places in Northern Europe 500–1600: Essays in Honour of Peter Hayes Sawyer, ed. I.N. Wood and N. Lund (Woodbridge, 1991).

Petersson, H.B.A., *Anglo-Saxon Currency: King Edgar's Reform to the Norman Conquest* (Lund, 1969).

Petersson, H.B.A., 'Coins and weights. Late Anglo-Saxon pennies and mints
c.973–1066', *Studies in Late Anglo-Saxon Coinage*, ed. Jonsson, pp.208–433.

Poole, R.G., 'Skaldic Verse and Anglo-Saxon History: Some Aspects of the Period
1009–1016', *Speculum*, 62 (1987), 265–98.

Poole, R.G., *Viking Poems on War and Peace: A Study in Skaldic Narrative* (Toronto,
1991).

Prisca Munimenta, ed. F. Ranger (London, 1973).

Ramsay, J.H., *The Foundations of England or Twelve Centuries of British History
(B.C.55–A.D.1154)* (Oxford, 1898).

Ramskou, T., 'Vikingebroen', *Skalk*, No. 1 (1977), 3–9.

Raraty, D.C.J., 'Earl Godwine of Wessex: The Origins of his Power and his Political
Loyalties', *History*, 74 (1989), 3–19.

The Reign of Cnut: King of England, Denmark and Norway, ed. A.R. Rumble (Leicester,
1994).

Richardson, H.G. and Sayles, G.O., *Law and Legislation from Æthelberht to Magna Carta*
(Edinburgh, 1966).

Ridyard, S.J., *The Royal Saints of Anglo-Saxon England: a study of West Saxon and East
Anglian cults* (Cambridge, 1988).

Robinson, J.A., *The Saxon Bishops of Wells* (London, 1918).

Rodger, N.A.M., 'Cnut's Geld and the Size of Danish Ships', *EHR*, cx (1995),
392–403.

Rodger, N.A.M., *The Safeguard of the Sea: A Naval History of Britain. Volume One 660-
1649* (London, 1997).

Roesdahl, E., *Viking Age Denmark* (London, 1982).

Roesdahl, E., 'The Danish Geometrical Viking Fortresses and Their Context', *Anglo-
Norman Studies*, ix (1986), 209–26.

Roesdahl, E. *et al.*, *The Vikings in England* (London, 1981).

Rollason, D.W., 'List of saints' resting places in Anglo-Saxon England', *ASE*, 7 (1978),
61–93.

Rollason, D.W., 'The cults of murdered royal saints in Anglo-Saxon England', *ASE*,
11 (1983), 1–22.

Rollason, D.W., *Saints and Relics in Anglo-Saxon England* (Oxford, 1989).

Ross, M.C., 'Concubinage in Anglo-Saxon England', *Past & Present*, 108 (1985), 3–34.

Round, J.H., 'Introduction to the Worcestershire Domesday', *VCH Worcs.* i. (London,
1901), 235–80.

Sawyer, P.H., '1066–1086: A Tenurial Revolution?', *Domesday Book: A Reassessment*, ed.
P.H. Sawyer (London, 1985).

Sawyer, P.H., 'Anglo-Scandinavian trade in the Viking Age and after', *Anglo-Saxon
Monetary History*, ed. Blackburn, pp.185–99.

Sawyer, P.H., 'Ethelred II, Olaf Tryggvason, and the conversion of Norway',
Scandinavian Studies, 59 (1987), 299–307.

Sawyer, P.H., 'Knut, Sweden and Sigtuna', *Avstamp – för en ny Sigtunaforskning*, ed. S.
Tesch (Sigtuna, 1989), 88–93.

Sawyer, P.H., *När Sverige blev Sverige* (Alingsås, 1991).

Sawyer, P.H., 'Cnut's Scandinavian empire', *The Reign of Cnut*, ed. Rumble, pp. 10–22;
with an Appendix on 'The evidence of Scandinavian runic inscriptions', by Birgit
Sawyer, pp.23–26.

Schramm, P.E., *Herrschaftszeichen und Staatssymbolik* (Stuttgart, 1954–56).

Schramm, P.E. and Mütherich, F., *Denkmale der deutschen Könige* (Munich, 1962–78).

Searle, W.G., *Anglo-Saxon Bishops, Kings and Nobles* (Cambridge, 1899).

Seebohm, F., *Tribal Custom in Anglo-Saxon Law* (London, 1902).

Sigtuna Papers: Proceedings of the Sigtuna Symposium on Viking Age Coinage 1–4 June 1989, ed. K. Jonsson and B. Malmer, *Commentationes*, New Series 6 (1990).

Skovgaard-Petersen, I. *et al.*, *Danmarks Historie i. Tiden indtil 1340* (Copenhagen, 1977).

Smart, V.J., 'Moneyers of the late Anglo-Saxon coinage: the Danish dynasty 1017–42', *ASE*, 16 (1987), 233–308.

Smyth, A.P., *Scandinavian Kings in the British Isles 850–880* (Oxford, 1977).

Stafford, P.A., 'Historical Implications of the Regional Production of Dies under Æthelred II', *BNJ*, xlviii (1978), 35–51.

Stafford, P.A., 'The Reign of Æthelred II, a study in the limitations on Royal Policy and Action', *Ethelred the Unready*, ed. Hill, pp.15–46.

Stafford, P.A., 'The King's Wife in Wessex 800-1066', *Past & Present*, 91 (1981), 3–27.

Stafford, P.A., 'The laws of Cnut and the history of Anglo-Saxon royal promises', *ASE*, 10 (1982), 173–90.

Stafford, P.A., *Unification and Conquest: A Political and Social History of England in the Tenth and Eleventh Centuries* (London, 1989).

Steenstrup, J.C.H.R., *Normannerne* (Copenhagen, 1876–82).

Stenton, Sir F.M., *Anglo-Saxon England* (3rd edn., Oxford, 1971).

Stevenson, W.H., 'An Alleged Son of King Harold Harefoot', *EHR*, xxviii (1913), 112–17.

Stewart, I., 'Coinage and recoinage after Edgar's reform', *Studies in Late Anglo-Saxon Coinage*, ed. Jonsson, pp.455–85.

Studies in Late Anglo-Saxon Coinage, ed. K. Jonsson (*Numismatiska Meddelanden*, xxxv, Stockholm).

Temple, E., *Anglo-Saxon Manuscripts 900-1066* (London, 1976).

Thomson, R., *William of Malmesbury* (Woodbridge, 1987).

Townend, M., 'Contextualising the *Knútsdrápur*: skaldic praise-poetry at the court of Cnut', *ASE*, 30 (2001), 145–79.

Turville-Petre, E.O.G., *Origins of Icelandic Literature* (Oxford, 1953).

Turville-Petre, E.O.G., *Skaldic Poetry* (Oxford, 1976).

Van Houts, E.M.C., 'The Political Relations between Normandy and England before 1066 according to the "Gesta Normannorum Ducum"', *Les Mutations socioculturelles au tournant des XIe-XIIe siècles*, ed. R. Foreville, *Actes du IVe colloque internationale Anselmien* (Paris, 1984), pp.85–97.

Van Houts, E.M.C., 'Historiography and Hagiography at Saint-Wandrille: the "Inventio et Miracula Sancti Vulfranni"', *Anglo-Norman Studies*, xii (1989), 233–51.

Van Houts, E.M.C., 'A note on Jezebel and Semiramis, two Latin poems from the early eleventh century', *Journal of Medieval Latin*, 2 (1992), 18–24.

Weibull, L., *Nordisk historia: forskningar och undersökningar* (Lund, 1948).

Wessen, E., *Historiska Runinskrifter* (Stockholm, 1960).

Whitelock, D., 'Wulfstan and the Laws of Cnut', *EHR*, lxiii (1948), 433–52.

Whitelock, D., 'Wulfstan's Authorship of Cnut's Laws', *EHR*, lxx (1955), 72–85.

Williams, A., 'Some Notes and Considerations on Problems Connected with the English Royal Succession, 860–1066', *Anglo-Norman Studies*, i (1978), 144–67.

Williams, A., '"Cockles amongst the wheat": Danes and English in the western midlands in the first half of the eleventh century', *Midland History*, xi (1986), 1–22.

Williams, A., *Æthelred the Unready: the Ill-Counselled King* (London, 2003).

Wilson, D.M., 'Danish kings and England in the late tenth and early eleventh centuries – economic implications', *Anglo-Norman Studies*, iii (1981), 188–96.

Wormald, F., 'The English Saints in the Litany in Arundel MS. 60', *Analecta Bollandiana*, lxiv (1946), 74–86.

Wormald, F., *English Drawings of the Tenth and Eleventh Centuries* (London, 1952).

Wormald, F., 'The Sherborne "Chartulary"', *Fritz Saxl Memorial Essays*, ed. D.J. Gordon (London, 1957), pp.101–19.

Wormald, P., 'Æthelred the Lawmaker', *Ethelred the Unready*, ed. Hill, pp.47–80.

Wormald, P., 'A handlist of Anglo-Saxon lawsuits', *ASE*, 17 (1988), 247–81.

Wormald, P., *The Making of English Law: King Alfred to the Twelfth Century. Volume 1: Legislation and its Limits* (Oxford, 1999).

Yorke, B., *Wessex in the Early Middle Ages* (Leicester, 1995).

GENEALOGICAL TABLES

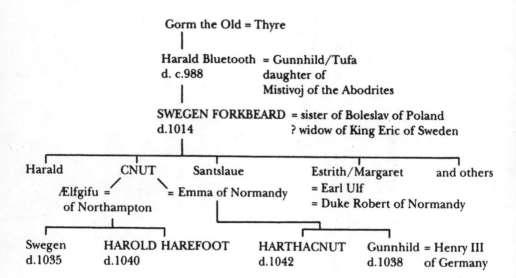

The English royal and Norman ducal families (kings of England in capitals)

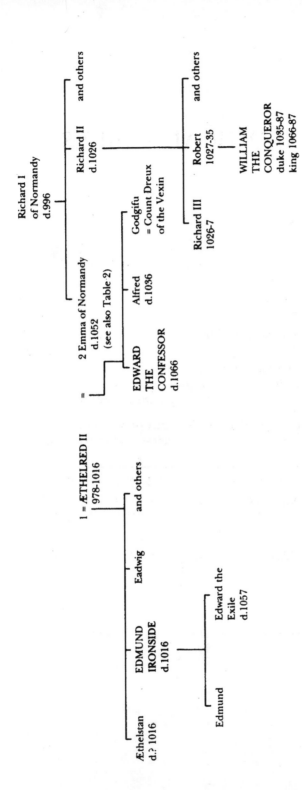

The Danish royal family (kings of England in capitals)

INDEX

The following abbreviations have been employed: abb = abbot; abp = archbishop; bp = bishop; bpric = bishopric; br = brother; ct = count; dk = duke; dr = daughter; emp = emperor; k = king; s = son. The characters Æ and æ have been indexed as if they were 'AE' and 'ae'; similarly, other special characters as if they were their English equivalents - å and á as 'a', for example, and ó and ö as 'o'.

Hemming, monk, 71-72, 76, 152-53, 167
Henry of Huntingdon, 72
Henry I, k of England, 193
Henry I, k of France, 106
Henry II, German emp, 59, 61, 104, 118,
  127-28
Henry III, German emp, 104-05, 128
Heraclius, Byzantine emp, 125-26
Hereford, 77
Hereford, bpric of, 70-71,
Herefordshire, 153, 155, 169, 175, 177
heregeld, see taxation,
Hermann, bp of Ramsbury and Sherborne,
  72, 117
herred, 23
Hertfordshire, 151, 170, 199
hidage system, 35
Hiring, s of Harald Bluetooth, 29-30
Holstein, 11 n. 1, 105 n. 96
Holy River, battle of, 56-57, 94-96, 161,
  172, 178
housecarls, 131, 164-68, 184, 191
Hrani, earl, 153, 155, 169, 171, 175, 177
Hrothgar, Danish k, 12
Hrothwulf, Danish k, 12
Hugh Candidus, 76
Hugh Capet, k of France, 48
Humber, river, 26, 194
Hungary, 84
Huntingdon, 181, 182 n. 144
Huntingdonshire, 152, 157
husting, London court, 187-88

Iehmarc, k, 100-02
Ilchester, 181
Ine, k of Wessex, 199
Ipswich, 180
Ireland, 16, 25, 31, 33, 42, 80, 102-03, 110,
  222
Ivar the Boneless, 16

Jelling, 16, 19-22, 188
Jersey, 105
Jerusalem, 105-06, 112
John XIX, pope, 97 n. 65, 99, 185, 198
Jomsvikings, 161 n. 57
Joseph, bp of Llandaff, 102
Julian the Apostate, Roman emp, 133
Jumièges Abbey, 74

Jurminus, St, 136
Justin, Scandinavian leader, 24
Jutes, 11
Jutland, 11, 23

Karl, 156
Karl, 1066 landholder, 158
Kartoca, 156, 158
Kenneth, k, 103
Kent, 11-12, 27-28, 30, 41, 43, 112, 156,
  159, 178, 184
Kingston, 71
Kunigund, wife of Emp Henry II, 128

Lacman, Swedish k, 94 n. 49
Lambert, baptismal name of Cnut, 121
Lambeth, 151
law codes,
  I Æthelstan, 60
  II Æthelstan, 186
  I Edmund, 60-61
  I Æthelred, 65
  III Æthelred, 186
  IV Æthelred, 186-87
  V,VI Æthelred, 61-62, 64-65
  VIII Æthelred,
  I, II Cnut, 64-65, 186-191
leding, 23
Leicestershire, 38
Leofflæd, 70, 155
Leofgar, bp of Lichfield, 136
Leofnoth, 159
Leofric, abb of Ely, 137
Leofric, earl, 37, 103, 140, 154, 162, 171,
  175, 177, 197-98, 216
Leofric, shire-reeve, 169
Leofrune, ? abbess of Minster-in-Thanet,
  118 n. 38
Leofsige, abb of Ely, 116, 137
Leofsige, bp of Worcester, 56, 169
Leofsine, abb of Thorney, 137
Leofwine, abb of Ely, 133
Leofwine, ealdorman, 162, 169, 171
Letter of 1019-20, 56, 65-66, 87, 89
Letter of 1027, 66, 73
Lewes, 180-81
Liðsmannaflokkr, poem, 77-78
Limerick, 81
Limfjord, 97

English Monarchs

A series of biographies of the kings and queens of England by
acknowledged experts in the field.

Published

David Bates, *William the Conqueror*
'As expertly woven as the Bayeux Tapestry' *BBC History Magazine*

Keith Dockray, *Henry V*
'Offers a warts-and-all depiction of the Lancastrian monarch'
History Today

Michael Hicks, *Edward V: The Prince in the Tower*
'The first time in ages that a publisher has sent me a book that I actually
want to read! Congratulations' *David Starkey*

Michael Hicks, *Richard III*
'A most important book by the greatest living expert on Richard...
makes for compulsive reading' *BBC History Magazine*

Ryan Lavelle, *Aethelred II*

M.K. Lawson, *Cnut: England's Viking King*
'An exhaustive review of the original sources... excellent'
English Historical Review

Richard Rex, *Elizabeth I: Fortune's Bastard?*
'Polished' *History Today*

Forthcoming

Douglas Biggs, *Henry IV*
Emma Mason, *William II: Rufus, the Red King*
W.M. Ormrod, *Edward III*
A.J. Pollard, *Henry VI*
Ralph V. Turner, *King John: England's Evil King?*
Peter Rex, *Harold II: The Last Saxon King*

Further titles are in preparation

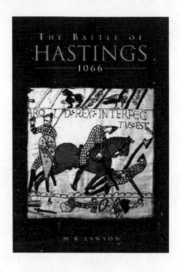

Also available from Tempus:

The Battle of Hastings 1066
M.K. Lawson
£25
07524 2689 3

If you are interested in purchasing other books published by Tempus,
or in case you have difficulty finding any Tempus books in your local bookshop,
you can also place orders directly through our website

www.tempus-publishing.com